CROSSING
DENALI

CROSSING DENALI

AN ORDINARY MAN'S ADVENTURE
ATOP NORTH AMERICA

MICHAEL FENNER

MOUNTAINEERS
BOOKS

Mountaineers Books is the publishing division of The Mountaineers, an organization founded in 1906 and dedicated to the exploration, preservation, and enjoyment of outdoor and wilderness areas.

MOUNTAINEERS BOOKS

1001 SW Klickitat Way, Suite 201 • Seattle, WA 98134
800.553.4453 • www.mountaineersbooks.org

Printed in the United States of America
Distributed in the United Kingdom by Cordee, www.cordee.co.uk
19 18 17 16   1 2 3 4 5

Copy editor: Kirsten Colton, The Friendly Red Pen
Design and layout: Heidi Smets Graphic Design
Cartographer: Marge Mueller, Gray Mouse Graphics

Cover photograph: *West Buttress, Denali*, ©Bill Hatcher, Getty Images
Frontispiece: *Top of fractured wall at Camp III, Denali*, ©Michael Fenner

Library of Congress Cataloging-in-Publication Data
Names: Fenner, Michael N.
Title: Crossing Denali: an ordinary man's adventure atop North America /
    Michael N. Fenner.
Description: Seattle, WA : Mountaineers Books, [2016]
Identifiers: LCCN 2015031693| ISBN 9781594859915 (paperback) | ISBN
    9781594859922 (ebook)
Subjects: LCSH: Fenner, Michael N. | Mountaineers—United States. |
    Mountaineering—Alaska—Denali, Mount. | Denali, Mount
    (Alaska)—Description and travel.
Classification: LCC GV199.92.F44 A3 2016 | DDC 796.522092—dc23
LC record available at http://lccn.loc.gov/2015031693

Mountaineers Books titles may be purchased for corporate, educational, or other promotional sales, and our authors are available for a wide range of events. For information on special discounts or booking an author, contact our customer service at 800-553-4453 or mbooks@mountaineersbooks.org.

♻ Printed on recycled paper

ISBN (paperback): 978-1-59485-991-5
ISBN (ebook): 978-1-59485-992-2

TO AGNES

That which defines me and binds me—body, personality, and soul—is the result of all that I have been in my yesterdays. For tomorrow's sake, I will make today the most important day of my life.

—*A personal creed*

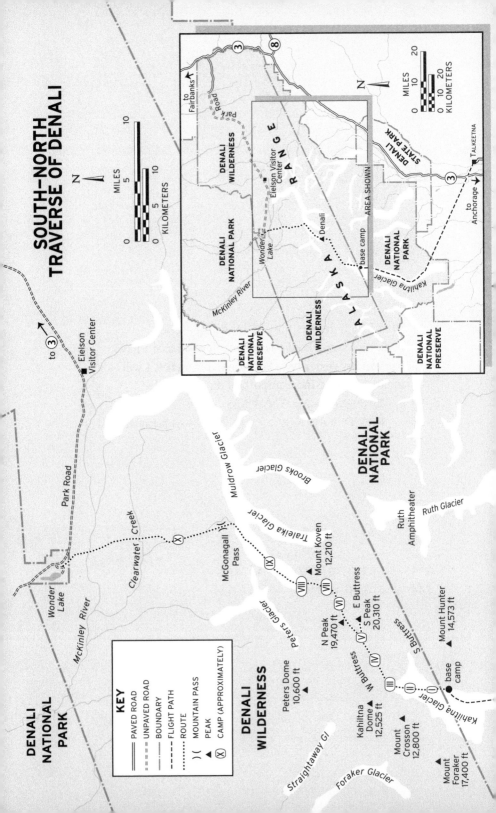

SOUTH–NORTH
TRAVERSE OF DENALI

N

MILES
0   5   10

KILOMETERS
0   5   10

Eielson
Visitor Center

to (3) →

Park Road

Wonder
Lake

McKinley River

Clearwater Creek

Muldrow Glacier

Brooks Glacier

Traleika Glacier

McGonagall
Pass

Peters Glacier

Mount Koven
12,210 ft

N Peak
19,470 ft

E Buttress

S Peak
20,310 ft

W Buttress

Kahiltna
Dome
12,525 ft

Peters Dome
10,600 ft

S Buttress

Mount Hunter
14,573 ft

base
camp

Kahiltna Glacier

Mount
Crosson
12,800 ft

Mount
Foraker
17,400 ft

Straightaway Gl

Foraker Glacier

Ruth
Amphitheater

Ruth Glacier

**DENALI
NATIONAL
PARK**

**DENALI
NATIONAL
PARK**

**DENALI
WILDERNESS**

KEY

— PAVED ROAD
═ ═ UNPAVED ROAD
— · — BOUNDARY
- - - FLIGHT PATH
· · · ROUTE
)(MOUNTAIN PASS
▲ PEAK
Ⓧ CAMP (APPROXIMATELY)

Inset map

N

MILES
0   5   10   20

KILOMETERS
0   10   20

to
Fairbanks →

(3) (8)

Park Road

**DENALI
WILDERNESS**

Eielson Visitor
Center

**DENALI
NATIONAL PARK**

Wonder
Lake

McKinley River

A L A S K A   R A N G E

Denali ▲

base camp

Kahiltna Glacier

**DENALI
NATIONAL
PARK**

**DENALI
STATE PARK**

TALKEETNA •

(3)

to Anchorage →

**DENALI
NATIONAL
PRESERVE**

**DENALI
WILDERNESS**

**DENALI
NATIONAL
PRESERVE**

AREA SHOWN

CONTENTS

11   AUTHOR'S NOTE

13   INTRODUCTION

22   **THE LAST FRONTIER**

38   **FINAL PREPARATIONS**

51   **MEETING THE MOUNTAIN**

67   **THE LOWER KAHILTNA GLACIER**

75   **THE MIDDLE MOUNTAIN**

81   **DIGGER MAN**

93   **TUMULTS AND TWEAKS**

108 **GENET BASIN**

122 **LOSING IT**

136 **MINUS ONE**

145 **GETTING INTO POSITION**

155 **SURREALISM AT 20,310 FEET**

163 **THE HARPER GLACIER**

178 **KARSTENS RIDGE**

196 **FALL AND REDEMPTION**

231 **GREEN GROWING THINGS**

244 **GOING HOME**

251 EPILOGUE

253 ACKNOWLEDGMENTS

AUTHOR'S NOTE

Denali means "the high one" in the language of the Athabascan people, who are native to southcentral Alaska, and this was what the mountain was called for generations. In the 1890s, it was renamed for Republican presidential candidate William McKinley. Recently, efforts have been made to restore the original name to the tallest point on the North American continent, efforts that were thwarted by congressional representatives from McKinley's home state of Ohio. In 1980, in an act of partial compromise, the wildlife resources area around Mount McKinley was renamed Denali National Park and Preserve. Then in August 2015 the mountain's name was officially changed back to Denali. I have chosen to use the names Denali and McKinley interchangeably throughout this book, although—out of respect for local tradition—Denali is the one I prefer.

In telling the story of my climb of Denali, I have endeavored to be as fair and accurate as possible in regard to my teammates and the events that we shared. To provide an accurate account, I have relied on my journal notes, personal memories, and personal communications, as well as the considerable number of photographs taken by me and other members of the team. Of course, others may remember certain events differently, and my perspective will not match everyone else's in every instance. I have changed the names and physical descriptions of a few characters to better preserve their privacy.

INTRODUCTION

Jack was operating in the icefall with the precision of a surgeon. As lead guide, he was responsible for cutting a path for the six of us behind him, a path that would take us safely through the treacherous maze of ice blocks. And he was doing a masterful job of it—his line threaded us around one seemingly impassable obstacle after another.

I planted my left crampon just inches from the edge of a crevasse, and from that vantage I could see the fissure was deep enough to consume anything that had the misfortune to slip into it. Above my right shoulder was a dangerous serac—a house-sized hunk of glacial ice—balanced precariously on edge, surely capable of crashing down and crushing us at any moment.

It was late in the evening of our twenty-first day on Denali. We had made good progress since leaving Camp Seven almost ten hours ago, but I was close to the limits of my patience and endurance. It had been a long and difficult day, the latest in a string of long and difficult days. I hoped that our next stop, Camp Eight, would lie on the patch of level terrain just ahead, just beyond this most dangerous section of the Muldrow Glacier.

My confidence in Jack had never been greater than it was right now. But truth be told, I had more often seen him act like a jerk than a saint during our expedition. Even now, while I admired him, I couldn't fully dismiss the past three weeks of caustic arrogance.

Of course, it really didn't matter if we liked Jack or hated him—we *needed* him. This icefall was only the latest reminder. The conditions here on the deserted north side of Denali had turned out to be so unpredictable and dangerous that any chance of our getting home alive depended on his continued superb performance.

As Jack moved out and onto the first safe-looking ground any of us had seen in two hours, I sighed in relief. His pace picked up, displaying fresh confidence—still cautious and measured but quicker by half than his pace in the icefall.

A few minutes later, I followed Mike Hamill, our other guide, onto level ground on the second rope. The tension that had been building in my chest all afternoon dissipated over the next dozen breaths. A tiny, cautious smile came to my lips. Camp Eight was surely no more than a short walk away. Once there I could finally enjoy some real relief, in no small part related to getting this ninety-pound pack off of my back.

Now, with the claustrophobic path through the cliffs behind us, I could better appreciate the beauty of my surroundings. I faced an enormous open space, vaster than the largest concert hall. In the evening's soft light, the glacier had a magical quality—almost angelic—sublime in its various shades of white and blue. Deep shadows had taken over; looking out beyond Jack, I saw only the subtlest undulations in what looked like a completely unthreatening and monotonous surface.

A deadly quiet enveloped us. The near absence of sound, besides the rhythmic vibrations of my breath and the creaking of my walking sticks, only added to the otherworldliness of this icy amphitheater.

I paused and breathed deeper. The air tasted of unspoiled wilderness. The purity of this Arctic environment had, from the moment I first stepped onto Denali's glaciers, been refreshing my soul. And here, on the north side of Denali, that purity was exquisitely fierce. For the past five days, since we had crossed over, this wild, desolate place had been ours alone. Nothing and no one distracted us from the mountain itself.

But still, the absence of all outside human contact was somewhat disconcerting. The several hundred other climbers on Denali were all on the south side, at least a three-day walk from here. To reach them, we would have to retreat five miles back to the origin of the Muldrow Glacier, climb back up the four-thousand-foot length of razor-sharp Karstens Ridge, and ascend an additional two thousand feet on the Harper Glacier, past its many huge, open crevasses. Once we reached Denali Pass (the saddle that separates the north and south summits), we would need to drop down again a thousand feet along a treacherous, icy trail—where deadly falls have happened with unfortunate regularity. All that effort would only put us back at austere High Camp—Camp Five—at 17,200 feet, where there would be little hope of finding much help. Our only realistic hope of assistance would be another three thousand feet below, at the makeshift ranger station at the camp at Genet Basin.

Here on the north side, if something happened, we were on our own. We had no satellite phone. No planes had flown overhead. We were utterly and completely alone.

At that moment, the unthinkable happened.

"Jack fell in! Jack fell into a crevasse!" Rick shouted. Rick Barr, one of my tent mates, was supposed to be the second man on Jack's rope. Only now there was nothing in front of him except a broad black hole—a hole that hadn't been there seconds before. Rick was lying on the ground, one end of his ice ax plunged deeply into the snow. The other end he clenched in a death grip, pushing down with all his weight to prevent Jack from pulling him into the crevasse as well.

I stared with an open mouth at the back of Rick's orange wind jacket. My heart sank. How could this be happening? Was Jack dead or had he been seriously injured in what must have been a thirty-foot fall? If so, weren't the rest of us lost as well?

As the intense pressure returned to my chest, I understood that it had been foolish of me to think I could relax. The dangers of Denali had never left. Jack's fall had demonstrated again this mountain's terrifying secret: that I couldn't trust a single footstep, no matter how safe the ground beneath my feet appeared.

On an ordinary Saturday morning and for no particular reason, I stood looking at myself in the mirror. It was springtime, and no one else in the house was up. The crocuses were blooming out in the garden, but not much else. Staring back at me was an overworked, overweight doctor with a pack-a-day smoking habit. The moment was significant: for the first time, I saw myself as a middle-aged man. Out loud, I said, "What have you really accomplished in nearly forty years of living, and what are you planning to do during the second half?"

I would have thought I'd have looked happier. After four years of college, four years of medical school, and five years of surgical residency, I was a practicing surgeon, well respected, enjoying a successful career. I had a lovely growing family: my wife Angie—the woman of my dreams—and two young children were asleep in the house (two more would arrive over the next three years). These should have been the best years of my life. But I'd spent so much time training and so many hours working at the hospital that I had little energy left for anything else. Instead I'd become increasingly grumpy and seriously unhealthy. I smoked, ate poorly, and exercised little. The doctor wasn't turning out to be very good at taking care of himself.

Maybe it wasn't a smile that I expected to see on my face as much as a look of satisfaction. It wasn't there. What was missing? For one, I wondered if this man in the mirror was the finished product. Was there anything else? Would there be any more surprises? Would the rest of my life follow the same script?

I had more questions than answers, but I knew two things: I wasn't going to quit until I figured out what I was looking for, and to find those answers, I was going to have to go back to the beginning. Funny, I had spent twenty years trying to prove to myself and everyone else that I was no longer a child, and now I was deciding to work as hard as I could to put myself back into that youngster's shoes.

Over the next several months, I fought to remember everything I could about my formative years and early desires. One theme kept resurfacing: I'd been a dreamer; I had dreamed I would do great things someday.

As far back as I can remember, mountaineering and other similarly exotic adventures had captivated me. As a boy, I'd curl up in bed with books about rockets flying into space, Admiral Byrd flying to the South Pole, or Edmund Hillary and Tenzing Norgay climbing to the top of Everest. I loved to study pictures and maps of foreign places. The people who explored these places were true-life heroes to me—they were willing to risk everything to see their dreams become reality. Becoming an astronaut was so competitive; I doubted I would ever travel to outer space. But climbing a mountain . . . that sounded possible.

I saw my first mountain when my parents took my brothers and me to Rocky Mountain National Park in Colorado. It was July 1969 and I was eight. While we drove from Indiana, Neil Armstrong and Buzz Aldrin took mankind's first steps on another world. The television pictures we stopped to see along the way set my heart pounding. The footprints those astronauts left in the lunar dust forever altered my place on Earth. And the man who took that giant leap and spoke those immortal words touched me in a personal way: Neil's roots were not that different from mine; we were both born in western Ohio.

Two days later I was staring at a line of purple spires through the windshield of my father's white Plymouth Fury. My heart started racing again. A thousand miles had passed by the window since we left home, and for every one of them I was crammed between my brothers in the back, my sweaty legs glued to the blue vinyl seat. But finally, I spotted what I had been watching for—the peaks of the Front Range rising up out of the flat, parched grasslands. At least I thought that's what I saw. As we'd traveled through eastern Colorado, there had been several false alarms.

"No, Michael," my mother would say, "those are only more purple clouds."

But now she confirmed that this was no mirage. I sat in wonder as we drove closer, my forearms and chin resting on the back of her front seat. I thought to myself, "Wow! Mountains are in the same league as outer space!"

Could that boy who'd yearned for an adventurous life reemerge, I wondered? Later in the year of my midlife soul searching, Angie and I took a vacation—an active vacation—to the English countryside. Before we boarded the plane, we stood outside the air-conditioned terminal in St. Louis, which was off-limits to smokers. The August air was sticky, saturated with humidity and jet-exhaust fumes. We each inhaled deeply, taking the final drag from our cigarettes, and then slowly breathed out a fine trail of smoke. That was it. We were done.

Smoking had helped me through the stress of training. But I'd come to hate that it was taking a toll on my health, and that putting a cigarette in my mouth was the first thing I did in the morning and the last thing I did at night. Although I wasn't quite forty, pushing the lawn mower for an hour was about as much exercise as I could tolerate. Even if I didn't die prematurely from lung cancer, I was destined for a sedentary lifestyle for the second half of my life unless something changed. A long plane trip to London provided the perfect opportunity for the two of us to quit the habit. And on our trip we would be hiking each day, not the kind of thing you do while puffing on a fag.

As it turned out, our trekking in Britain—particularly a hike up the crags of Mount Snowdon—was life changing. The mountain, at 3,560 feet, is the highest peak in the United Kingdom outside of Scotland. It is not particularly tall, and our route up was not technically difficult. Still, the day was a mighty challenge, in large part because Angie was three months pregnant with our third child. A hard sideways rain and constantly buffeting winds forced us to stop short of the summit. But the experience whet my appetite for new ways to challenge myself.

My physical transformation continued after we returned home, but although my lungs were becoming healthier, the rest of me was not. The next phase in my metamorphosis left me looking more like a pudgier version of the original caterpillar than a delicate butterfly. I was no longer putting filtered Marlboros into my mouth, but I *was* still stuffing it—with high-calorie foods, that is—to the tune of fifty additional pounds.

Two years later, another opportunity for change presented itself. In preparation for a family reunion in Gulf Shores, Alabama, I bought a pair of running shoes, figuring I would knock off a few miles each morning before breakfast. Clearly, my thinking was misguided. On the first morning out, I nearly collapsed from exhaustion after "running" only two hundred yards. But as I'd done during my long years of medical training, I broke down what at first seemed an impossible task into manageable segments. I joined a running group and started working out four times a week. My rattling cough disappeared; the roll of fat around my middle melted away. Running had other benefits as well. I found it cleared my head and gave me the energy I needed to get through each day. It even curbed my chronic crabbiness. My patience and tenacity were paying off.

Soon I was setting new long-range goals for myself—physical ones. First, I endeavored to improve my 5K time, and then I started adding in longer races. Two years after Gulf Shores, I signed up to run the "big one," my first marathon—the Chicago. Training for it was the most difficult physical task I'd ever attempted. I imagined that finishing the race would feel like reaching a mountaintop, the pinnacle of my new success.

In most ways, the race did not disappoint. Running for three and three-quarters of an hour was unbelievably challenging, although not as hard as the training had been. But as I looked for Angie and our daughter Grace at the finish line, I did not feel like a conquering hero. I hadn't come any closer to satisfying my ambition. *This is it? After all the months and miles of training?* I had expected more at the end of my quest than a paper cup filled with Michelob Ultra and a colorful ribbon wrapped around my neck.

I continued to run. I liked the little highs it gave me. I was in better shape than I had been in since high school track, and my renewed fitness opened up the possibilities of other activities. Most enjoyable were family trips to hike in Colorado, where Angie and I led Grace, Will, Emma, and Calvin on many of the same trails my parents had shown my brothers and me thirty-two years earlier.

But I still felt something was missing. Then, in a chance encounter at my neighbor and colleague Michael Snyder's house, I spotted a photograph of him standing beside the unmistakable summit pyramid of Mount Everest. Michael was not a young man, nor had he ever been a mountain climber, and yet there he was next to the most magical mountain in the world. If he had gone there, maybe I could, too! This was the "something" that was missing—I knew it.

I awoke the next morning with fresh resolve. It was another Saturday morning in early March, and the crocuses were popping up in the garden. I had just gotten back from my run and was getting dressed. This time the person in the mirror appeared more content than the one I'd seen four years earlier. All of those miles had paid off. I felt more well rounded from finding satisfaction outside of work. My newest friends—my running buddies—weren't doctors. Work was no less busy, and five to ten hours of exercise per week only added to a schedule that was already hectic. But I now valued my family and my health more. My "second half" was off to a good start.

And I was feeling content that morning for another reason— the photograph of Everest. It pointed to exactly the sort of exotic adventure I had been yearning for. It was time to stop spending all of my energy preparing for life and instead start living it.

As I researched trekking options later that day, I felt the spirit I'd had as a young boy rekindle. But this was not just another trip to Colorado. Kathmandu was on the exact opposite side of the planet from where I sat—could a person even fly from Illinois to Nepal? To travel any farther away from home to go for a hike, I'd have to put on a space suit and go to the moon.

My adventurous life was beginning. But I didn't yet know how far this journey would take me—all the way to the summit of North America—and how close it would come to taking everything away.

THE LAST FRONTIER

—

SATURDAY, MAY 17

The long months of anticipation and preparation were behind me. I was finally standing on Alaskan soil. I had come to the Last Frontier to scale the biggest mountain on the North American continent.

The seven-hour flight that brought me here from Chicago had crossed three time zones and ascended twenty degrees of latitude, a disorienting shift. I looked around the terminal from my seat on a bench. There wasn't a familiar face in sight. My wife, four children, and everyone else I knew were 2,900 miles away. For the next month, I was to live with eight other men, only one of whom I had met before.

I was the first of my team to arrive in Anchorage, and I still had several hours to kill before the rest of the climbers would arrive. I got up and stretched my legs, and then sat down again. I couldn't help but ponder our tearful goodbye in Springfield yesterday. The afternoon had been tough on Angie. Grace and

Will were in school, so she and our two youngest children, Emma and Calvin, had taken me to the airport to see me off on my puddle-jumper flight to Chicago. She cried but I couldn't. I didn't think that I could afford the luxury. I had to minimize distractions, to remain in control. But afterward, I wished that I'd said more, that I could have found a way to make up for leaving her for a month to manage on her own with four little ones. I wished that I'd known how to reassure her that I—we—would be OK. It would be a very long time before I would have a chance to hold her again and tell her that.

Now my hand instinctively reached up to fondle the ring that was hanging around my neck. There had been a million things to do before leaving, but none felt as significant as removing the plain gold wedding band from my left ring finger and tying it onto a piece of purple cord. At altitude, my body would retain excess water, and because my hands would be hanging down at my sides all day long, gravity would draw some of that fluid into my fingers, causing them to swell. That normally loose-fitting ring could become a tissue-strangling tourniquet. In addition, the metal band was an efficient conductor—drawing precious heat out of my skin and increasing my risk of frostbite. But I didn't want to be without it entirely. I'd felt a sense of ritual as I tied the cord into a loop using a double fisherman's knot, the type of knot a *real mountaineer* would use. For the next month, the ring would be my primary link to Angie.

I shifted on the bench and thought about the wisdom of my decision to leave home for a month—on what could very well be a dangerous climb. Just one unlucky break, perhaps a misstep on a ridge or a tumble into a crevasse, could turn this adventure into a nightmare. But honestly, I didn't fear the exposure to danger. I was terrified of the risk of failure—that I wouldn't get the job done because I didn't measure up. What if I committed a critical error or was not strong or prepared enough?

At the airport hotel in Chicago, as I'd prepared for bed, I had taken a long, hard look into my pupils and asked myself, *Am*

I really ready for this? Can this face pass itself off as a legitimate mountaineer's?

Uncertainty continued to nag me, but for the moment I ignored it. I put aside the effects of altered geography, jetlag, and fatigue, and emptied my mind of all anxious thoughts. I simply allowed myself to be excited.

A pair of inquisitive eyes drew me out of my Anchorage terminal reverie. Their owner had just parked himself on a nearby bench beside an enormous pair of duffels, ones that looked remarkably like my own.

After a few minutes, I said, "Are you Jack?" thinking he was our lead guide, Jack Williams, from RMI—Rainier Mountaineering, Incorporated.

"Nope, Al Hancock's the name, from Fort McMurray, Canada." I recognized the name from the group roster. "Alligator" Al was another client, like me. I immediately envied his looks. With handsome, tanned features and a magnetic smile, Al was forty-three, just a year older than me. He was very fit, an obvious outdoorsman—talkative and sincere, self-confident and opinionated. He worked in the Alberta oil sands industry and had managed to finagle a month off of work by pulling double shifts and cashing in on favors. I was not surprised to learn that he was also very popular with the ladies. Women—apparently several at a time—loved Al.

He made all the people he came in contact with feel good about themselves, and as a result they felt good about him. "How are you doin'?" was his signature line (with a sharp emphasis on *you*). His magic spell worked on me as well. The more he talked, the more I liked being around Al.

His passions, other than women, included riding Harleys and working to become more involved in his thirteen-year-old daughter's life. I soon learned that he had not participated in the RMI Rainier Mountaineering Expedition Course or even climbed Rainier (these were essentially prerequisites for a Denali climb). But Al hadn't needed to. His climbing résumé bested all the rest of ours combined. With clockwork regularity, he headed into the nearby Canadian Rockies with one of his pals on the weekends to tackle various difficult ice-climbing routes.

At four o'clock, a rush of nearby activity interrupted our conversation. The seven remaining members of our team (Al and I made it nine total) had just arrived on the flight from Seattle. A whirlwind immediately descended on the two of us.

Rick Barr introduced himself first. I felt comfortable around Rick immediately. It was easy to forget that we'd been complete strangers only a few minutes before. In sharp contrast to free-spirited Al, Rick was the epitome of structure and order. Of the eight other personalities on the team, his was the most like my own. He had spent his formative years in rural Missouri and then Kansas City, places where his father practiced as an ophthalmologist. Rick was taller by several inches than the rest of us clients. Forty-five and a resident of Denver, he had thick and wavy hair, jet-black with a smattering of gray. He wore glasses, as did I. While Rick was a software engineer, he dreamed of teaching high school biology in some far-off place, somewhere "off the grid."

Rick would be one of my two tent mates, and we would spend many hours over the next several weeks engaged in long talks, often about women or religion at first but always concluding with one of us restating the obvious: that we were climbing one helluva big mountain! While we could have become friends anywhere, here in Alaska, thrown together and forced to smell each other's sweaty socks day after day, we became closer than brothers.

Armando Valencia, who was from San Diego, was the oldest client. He was a happy-go-lucky fellow who displayed absolutely no outward signs of trepidation regarding the upcoming climb. This fifty-five-year-old jokester was the most amiable of us all. He liked to call one of our guides, Ryan Sorsdahl, with whom he'd climbed Mount Rainier, his guardian angel.

Bruce Penn and Keith Hinson were the final two clients on the team. Bruce was 160 pounds, lean and solid. He was tough as nails and strikingly handsome, a forty-two-year-old with more than just a hint of gray coursing through his wiry blond hair. I was not surprised to hear that he was a retired Marine; he looked like one. Bruce was a superbly capable outdoorsman who had climbed Rainier, but not with RMI. He was always eager to involve himself in whatever Jack needed. I especially admired how all of his confidence was tempered by equally generous amounts of common sense and humility.

Bruce lived in Connecticut, where he now worked as vice president of a company that manufactured tiny screws. Like Al, he enjoyed the physical side of work. Their similar backgrounds and shared passion for the outdoors and beautiful women meant that they quickly developed a special bond.

Keith was not cast in the same mold as the rest of us. A Southerner from Tennessee, he was, at thirty-one, the youngest of the clients. He had climbed Rainier with Armando and Ryan. An insurance salesman, Keith was pleasant, quiet, and unassuming. At the same time, he was no weakling. He was every bit as strong as the other clients—plus, he had the advantage of being young.

—

When I had called the RMI office several months earlier to ask about the qualifications of our trio of mountain guides, the woman who'd answered the phone was reassuring. "We are sending you up with three strong guys, all over six feet tall, each of them capable of carrying you off of McKinley should you find yourself in trouble." Now, as the three of them made their way over to the luggage carousel and started tossing their six enormous, well-worn duffels around, there was no mistaking them. They *looked* like mountain guides.

I recognized the only person I knew on the team, twenty-four-year-old Mike Hamill—a junior guide—instantly. Nine months earlier, Angie and I had bid him farewell on Mount Rainier. He had shed a noticeable amount of weight from his already trim frame, no doubt because he had been climbing full time since then. I was excited to see him; he was the primary reason I'd come to Alaska in general, and on this expedition in particular.

But I was taken aback that he didn't seem to remember me. I had assumed that he would recognize my face or remember seeing my name on the client roster. Finally, a few searching moments later, he said, "Your wife is Angie, right?" At least he had found my studly *wife* worth remembering!

Ryan Sorsdahl was the second of our junior guides. He was also twenty-four years old and engaged to be married later that fall. Ryan was tall and powerful looking with a mop of thick, black hair. His face, much like Rick's, had a bold bone structure, but his was softer and made him look significantly younger than Mike. His admirable climbing background included difficult rock ascents on Yosemite's big walls and glacier experience on Rainier and McKinley.

"Where did you go to college?" I asked him, thinking he was another incarnation of RMI's group of overachievers, like the three science majors who'd led Angie and me up Rainier.

"School wasn't for me," he retorted. Discussion over. This, I would learn, wasn't unusual. Serious and no-nonsense, he never adorned his responses to questions—if he responded at all. He cared little about coming across as polished. I had no doubts about his qualifications; I just wasn't sure how I was supposed to interact with him as a person.

This was to be his second bid for McKinley's summit. The previous year, he had been forced down prematurely, having to lead a weakened client back to base camp. That experience, he implied, would only cause him to redouble his efforts this year.

Jack Williams was our lead guide. Although he was younger than all of the clients except Keith, at thirty-nine he was something of an elder statesman among his coworkers. Tall, lanky, and talkative, he was so energetic that he seemed to be in perpetual motion. This energy, when used positively, made him an exceptionally skilled organizer of equipment and people. Jack had twice guided Rick in the past, first on the Rainier Mountaineering Expedition Course and then again in South America. As I got to know Rick, he confided that many clients on Jack's expeditions ended up hating him by the end, having grown tired of his overbearing, demeaning nature. Rick paid no attention to the criticisms. "As far as I was concerned," he countered, "the only thing that mattered was that he got me off the mountain alive and in one piece." At this point I was willing to give Jack the benefit of a doubt. A leader's quality was best determined in the field, was it not?

I tuned out the noisy conversations for a moment as we stood there in the terminal and looked around at my fellow teammates. They were a powerful bunch! There weren't any sheepish, cowering figures here. Each man's stance reflected an inner strength. Each chin stuck straight out. Every pair of eyes appeared eager for what lay ahead.

Their self-assuredness never came across as cockiness, though. I didn't get the idea that anyone here felt it necessary to try to impress anyone else. The process that brought us all together—RMI's application and screening process—assured Jack that his squad would be made up of team players.

For all our sakes, it was imperative that we *did* function as a team. Our expedition was to be a more lengthy and difficult traverse of the mountain. While some of the standard up-and-down route climbers finish their expeditions in less than three weeks, we would be together for the better part of a month. Very soon, Jack would need to forge this diverse collection of strangers into a single, cohesive unit.

▬

A fifteen-passenger van was waiting for us outside the terminal. It would take us to Talkeetna, the small frontier town that was the base for air services to McKinley. The guides showed their stuff by easily tossing our eighteen fifty-pound duffels around, dividing them between the roof's rack and the trailer in tow.

Before we got on the highway, Jack diverted the driver to the local REI so we could pick up some items that were hard to find elsewhere, like mosquito head nets and bear spray. On his recommendation, I bought a new, shorter pair of snowshoes and a lightweight nylon duffel to replace my heavier one.

While a group of us waited for the others to finish shopping, Jack spent a few minutes clarifying some details about our traverse. "The great majority of the 1,200 climbers who attempt McKinley each year come down the same route they go up, the West Buttress, or Washburn route," he started. "Our team has a different agenda. We will ascend the standard route, following the easiest path to the summit, but then we will cross over to McKinley's north side and go down all alone. What's more, we will not be flying off the mountain at the end. We'll have to walk another eighteen miles across bear-infested tundra to reach the Park Road at Wonder Lake. There, a park shuttle bus will take us the rest of the way out. By the time we board that bus, we will have walked fifty miles from our original drop-off point."

We listened to him intently, but we knew all of this already. He was going over it again now to make sure we were all appropriately equipped. Jack continued, "As we ascend the mountain to our higher camps, we'll carry everything up with us, including the food and supplies for our walk out. This is also different from standard climbers. They can cache some of their supplies at intermediate camps to retrieve on the return trip. But there will be a few things we won't need after the summit—some sleds and some clothing items—those we'll leave at the highest camp. Another RMI group following a week behind us will haul them out." He pointed down to my REI purchases. "That's one of the reasons you'll need that new lightweight duffel, Fenner."

After REI, we still had one final stop, the Safeway in Wasilla. (Yes, that Wasilla, of Sarah Palin fame.) Bill, the driver, rolled his eyes. He hadn't planned on these lengthy side trips. Before we left the van, Jack gave us strict instructions to be back in one hour. Anyone arriving late risked being left behind—and we had no reason to doubt his sincerity. None of us wanted to be known as the guy who missed his summit chance because of the grocery store!

While RMI supplied breakfast and dinner, lunches and snacks were up to us. At Safeway, we gathered enough rations for a month of these. Since I had brought the majority of my dry goods with me, I only needed to add a few semiperishable items: a half-dozen bagels, two bricks of cheese, some packaged salami, some extra candies, and a few baby carrots and apples. I remembered craving fresh fruit and vegetables after only six days on Rainier. One advantage of living on a glacier for a month is that it functions as an icebox for perishable food. If I didn't feel like eating all of it the first week, I could save some of it for later.

The dried figs and dates that I brought from Illinois ended up being ideal. Their high-sugar content acted as a natural anti-freeze, so they stayed edible no matter how cold it got. The fresh produce turned out to be a worse choice. Alas, soon after we arrived on the glacier, the daily freeze/thaw cycles turned my apples and carrots to mush. I tossed them into a crevasse while we were still low on the mountain.

Ryan had a unique nutrition philosophy. He planned to gorge himself with high-calorie items—including a family pack of king-sized Snickers bars—on the way up and then live off of the stored fat for the duration. The rest of us planned to ration more traditionally, expecting to have our supplies run out just as we hit the Park Road in three weeks' time.

Within the prescribed hour, everyone had fulfilled his mission and returned to the van. Everyone, that is, except our trio of guides. After we finished the sandwiches we'd bought for dinner, there was nothing left to do but sit and wait. It had already been a very long day, and we clients were anxious to be under way.

The driver's mood was several steps beyond anxious. He was steaming mad and stewing behind the wheel. Occasionally, he mumbled something to himself, but mostly, he just stared straight ahead. Thirty more minutes passed, then forty-five. Still, there was no sign of them. One full hour past Jack's strict deadline, the three of them came sauntering out from behind the store, joking with each other, their hands stuffed into their jeans pockets. As he got in the van, Jack offered no apology or explanation. Bill, however, had no intention of simply letting the matter drop. The two left the van and started arguing heatedly.

"Just where the hell have you been? Don't you know—" I heard Bill say just before they moved out of our hearing range. When it was over, the driver returned sullenly to his seat. Jack followed in time, confident and smirking. His message to Bill was clear. His message to the rest of us was only slightly less direct: don't *ever* forget who is in charge.

It was nine o'clock by the time we resumed our progress up Alaska Route 3, though outside it still appeared to be midday. From the seat in front of me, Al was telling Rick about his former days as a competitive bodybuilder. The idea, he explained with enthusiasm, was to consume huge quantities of protein while, at the same time, limiting fats and carbohydrates. "Looking at my arm was like looking at a lean piece of steak covered by a film of cellophane," I heard Al say.

I listened with one ear to Al's anecdotes while focusing both eyes on Alaska as it whisked by outside my window. The two-lane highway cut a path through woodlands, roughly paralleling the milky-gray turbulence of the Susitna River. The scenery ranged from merely gorgeous to absolutely stunning. I loved the feeling of knowing that another great adventure was about to unfold. Over the previous two years, I'd twice before felt this thrill of anticipation.

The first time was on my flight to Nepal, as I followed through on my childhood dream to see the Himalayas. On my monthlong guided trek through the Everest region, I found a life stripped of all things superfluous. All that remained at the end of each day were the sweat from a hard day's work, dozens of vivid memories, and a set of emotions so basic that they couldn't be reduced into simpler terms. While I drank in postcard views of Everest's southwest face and walked beneath the icy domes of other Himalayan gems, I learned what it meant to live the words of my tent mate and fellow trekker on the trip, Marv: "Mike, all we really have is *this* moment."

After that, I realized there was only one thing left for me to do—learn how to climb the peaks that attracted me so undeniably. I never considered that I would be able to scale Everest itself, but maybe, just maybe, I could start with some smaller ones. Then I could return to the Himalayas someday to climb one of the "easier" eight-thousand-meter giants, like Cho Oyu.

The year after my Nepal trip, Angie and I flew together on a shorter but equally life-changing plane trip to Washington State. During our six-day expedition course with RMI, we learned to establish a series of progressively higher camps and practiced glacier climbing techniques. And it was there that I met Mike Hamill, who was our rope leader. His competence and spirit—along with his confidence in my ability—were inspiring.

In the Cascades, as in the Himalayas, I experienced the thrills and fears that only mountainous places can produce. The spirituality that had been my constant companion in Nepal worked again to satisfy my ceaseless cravings for things missing from my life in Illinois. During one rest break on Rainier, in a spot called Cathedral Rocks, I felt the same sense of isolation, a taste of what it means to be deep in the wilderness that I'd felt on the Nepalese highpoints of Chukhung Ri and Kala Pattar. The moment was so transcendent that even now when I meditate, I travel back to Cathedral Rocks. I'm sitting on one of the many angular boulders, feeling the bite of a crisp cold wind strike against my sunburned cheeks, letting the high-altitude sun warm the sleeves of my fleece jacket.

As the van whizzed on through the bright Alaskan night, I let my mind wander back to our summit day on Rainier. In the predawn blackness, Mike Hamill, Angie, and I tethered ourselves together at the waist, just as we had every other day. An eerie trail of headlamps extended far up ahead, to Disappointment Cleaver and beyond. A second grouping of headlamps slowly moved up toward our position from below, down by Camp Muir. Seattle city lights glowed faintly on the horizon, seventy-five miles to the north. Above us, a star-filled sky shone with heavenly radiance, the Milky Way band stretching from one horizon to the other. Only in the upper Khumbu had I seen a sky of comparable brilliance.

As we set off on a well-packed trail at a steady pace, I concerned myself with only the few illuminated yards of snow directly in front of me. *Left foot, right foot, step up, adjust the pack, remember to breathe. Watch the rope in front so I don't step on it. Left foot, right foot, breathe again* . . . The marching routine quickly became automatic. Each step brought me closer to the top; each footprint I left behind in the snow was a celebration of life.

In the next instant, I understood why I was here. This was why I climbed. I *could* do this. I *did* have the desire. Climbing was more than just another competition like the marathon. Being on the mountain filled me with satisfaction. Climbing made me feel special, unique among my peers. I knew only a handful of people who would even dream of doing something like this. And as for all of the play-it-safe naysayers that I knew and worked with, I didn't give a damn if any of them thought it was important that I was climbing this mountain right now. It was enough that it mattered to me.

By the time the sun began to rise, we were approaching the mountain's upper reaches. I marveled at its splendor. It had taken a hell of a lot of effort to get to where I was. Now it all felt worthwhile. What a great day to be alive!

We were climbing on a snowy forty-five-degree incline, stepping across minor crevasses that allowed me to peer down into the glacier's turquoise innards. I passed by jumbled heaps of seracs that, through the course of hundreds of freeze/thaw cycles, had morphed into abstract sculptures. But mostly I just looked at the path ahead, at the pure whiteness, uniform in tone and texture, trying to keep my tired body moving.

Thirty minutes later, and without warning, we were standing on the edge of the volcano's crater, staring down into a broad, snow-filled bowl. The surface was featureless save for a well-traveled path that crossed over to the other side. Then it struck me. We were almost there! We were within arm's reach of the summit!

Mike Hamill was waiting for Angie and me on top. He gave me a big thumbs-up, but he saved his grandest congratulations—a bear hug—for her. "That first day I really didn't think that you would make it, but you were just amazing!" he shouted over the roar of the wind. "You got stronger every day. Amazing!" Mike always had the knack of saying just the right thing at just the right moment.

When it was my turn to embrace my wife, tears welled up in my eyes. One long hug squeezed many days of tension out of my chest. Now the wind carried all of it away into the upper atmosphere. I was tremendously satisfied with what we had done, and I adored Angie for it. She had worked so hard for so long so that we both could be standing here together.

During the last two days on Rainier, Mike and I talked about my idea of climbing other mountains, including Denali.

"How does it compare to what we just did?" I asked.

"On Denali," Mike replied, "the real climbing begins at a height level with Rainier's summit. Then it continues up for another vertical mile. It's longer and harder and there's a lot more equipment to manage."

"So what do you think? Do you think I could do it?"

"Yeah, probably. I think you could."

By the time we were down the mountain, drinking beers and eating pizza, my mind was already in Alaska, climbing that last mile up to Denali's 20,310-foot-tall summit.

By the time we and our nine hundred pounds of gear pulled into Talkeetna, the driver and Jack were back at it. By the driver's figuring, we should have arrived three hours ago. Now his entire evening was shot. Plus, he had to be back on the road again first thing in the morning. Jack refused to apologize. In fact, he offered him nothing at all.

The rest of us were happy to put this episode behind us and go check out the town that would serve as our home base for the next few days. How long exactly, we couldn't be sure. It would be two days at a minimum—longer if the weather was uncooperative.

Talkeetna was both rustic and comfortably charming. Back when the main highway from Anchorage to Fairbanks was constructed, its designers intentionally chose to bypass Talkeetna. A separate fifteen-mile spur road was built to take the traveler the final distance. In other words, you had to want to go to Talkeetna to end up here. Unlike urban Anchorage and suburban Wasilla, it was closer to what I imagined the "real" Alaska would look like—simple and far off of the beaten path. Main Street was the only paved street in town, and the businesses that bordered it were colorfully painted and wooden. At its terminus was the unspanned breadth of the wild Susitna River. This most recent brand of Alaskan tonic took hold of me immediately.

The modern airstrip at the entrance to town was its raison d'être. It serviced two important but highly disparate populations: the mountain climbers and the cruise ship passengers. Several competing air charters provided glacier landings for climbers and so-called "flight-seeing" runs for tourists. When favorable weather moved in, the planes would empty out the town. Between clear days, the various retailers did their parts to keep the visitors amused.

We got our first brief look at the airstrip when we dropped off our gear at the Hudson Air Service hangar. From there we walked into town to check into our rooms. At eleven o'clock, as the cool evening sun was finally touching the horizon, we enjoyed a second supper of grilled burgers and halibut sandwiches, deep-fried potatoes, and cold Alaskan Ambers.

Then, in the long twilight, we headed to the local tavern for a nightcap. Although the bar was in a nondescript clapboard building, the crowd inside was anything but dull—and did not fit the stereotype I had guessed would frequent a place like this. I saw no cohort of bearded, potbellied frontiersmen dressed in flannel shirts and suspenders, throwing beer glasses and punches at each other. The crowd was younger and more attractive than I'd imagined.

We had prearranged the next two nights' accommodations several months in advance, a necessity during the busy tourist season. The majority of us had chosen to sleep at the modest Talkeetna Motel, at the far end of town. It meant a longer walk to get back to the airport, but was farther away from town noise and, as a bonus, close to the river. A few members of our group stayed at the more visually appealing Roadhouse Inn—directly across the street from the noisy nocturnal revelers at the tavern.

Both locations were like the town itself, spartan but serviceable. At any rate, we weren't expecting this to be a pleasure vacation, and we wouldn't be staying in Talkeetna for long. Furthermore, since it had been twenty-two hours since my alarm clock awakened me in Chicago, I would have happily bedded down anywhere that offered me a pillow and a blanket.

I caught a glimpse of myself in the mirror as I got ready for bed. I had been scaling an ever-higher pyramid for the past six years. The decision to stop smoking had led to running; short races to two twenty-six milers. My love affair with mountains had led to Colorado, Nepal, Rainier, now here. Would my climbing résumé someday include even higher peaks? At this point I didn't even want to think about it. The current project was a huge undertaking in itself. It remained to be seen how I would do on a six-thousand-meter peak, much less an eight-thousand-meter one.

FINAL PREPARATIONS

—

SUNDAY, MAY 18

On our first day on Rainier, Angie and I had both been near tears because we had underestimated the size of our loads. With that memory fresh in my mind, I had vowed to be more prepared this time around. During my nine months preparing for Denali, rarely did two consecutive days go by where I didn't run or work out with a backpack. I ran the Chicago Marathon for the second time in October, and I continued running literally up until the day I left for Alaska. Even during the snows of February, I went out for long winter hikes in the park after work, repeatedly climbing any sort of incline I could find. When spring came around, I put even more weight in my pack and did it all again.

Now that I was finally here, idleness was the new norm. I was weary of sitting in airplanes and restaurants and hanging around airports and hotel rooms. I missed my little adrenaline fixes. In their absence I felt like a leopard methodically pacing back and forth in his zoo cage, nervously searching for a way to burn off steam. I was ready to meet the mountain. Tomorrow, I hoped, we would be on our way!

My internal clock was still set to central time, so I got up early and went down to the Susitna for a stroll. The sky to the northwest, where Denali should have been, was as opaque as the river itself. The mountain wasn't "out," as the locals say.

Later that morning, Jack hosted a team meeting at the Roadhouse Inn. The nine of us crammed into a large corner booth for a formal welcome to the Last Frontier by one of RMI's owners, Joe Horiskey, a seasoned Denali veteran. To me, he looked physically incapable of making it up Rainier, much less Denali—his rolling midsection detracted somewhat from his legendary status. And yet, I recalled that I had been barely capable of mowing my own lawn just a few years earlier.

Joe was a real peach of a guy. As he shared some of his own experiences with us, the waitress brought over several pots of steaming black coffee. When breakfast arrived, the portions seemed more appropriate for Alaskan lumberjacks than idle mountaineers. Rick ordered the full daily special: two Frisbee-sized cranberry-nut buckwheat pancakes saturated in butter and warm maple syrup. As he sopped up the last of the sticky syrup, the slight grin on his face twisted into a full smile. Even the half portion of the traditional breakfast was enough to fill my entire plate with scrambled eggs, country bacon, and fried potatoes. Slices of toast rested on top, just begging to be covered in spoonfuls of wild strawberry jam.

After Joe left, Jack went over the plans for the day. "First the bad news," he said. "If unsettled weather moves into the Talkeetna area, we could be stuck here for several more days. Entrance into the approach pass over the mouth of the Kahiltna Glacier and the landing on the glacier itself demand clear visual sightings, plus the pilots down at Hudson Air Service need a minimum of four round-trips to get us all there. In other words, we'll need six to eight hours of continuous cooperative weather to get it all done."

He was right. This was bad news. The last thing I wanted to hear right now was that we might have to sit around in Talkeetna for two or three more days.

"The good news," he said in a voice that was heavy with sarcasm, "is that there's still a ton of work to be done at the hangar, more than enough to keep idle hands occupied." The "ton" he referred to was only a slight exaggeration—in truth, our gear weighed 1,400 pounds (including the 500 pounds of food that had to be dealt with). "The bottom line is, good weather or not, I plan to have us mountain-ready in the next twenty-four hours."

Back at the hangar, each of us and our gear received twenty minutes of individualized attention from either Mike or Ryan. The equipment list that RMI mailed out months ago had told us what to bring, but we all needed some professional direction to fine-tune our stash. While the two guides invariably came to similar conclusions, their methods in getting there couldn't have differed more.

A typical comment from Mike was, "Well, you know, you probably won't need that. Maybe you should consider leaving it behind." Ryan would simply blurt, "Man, what the hell are you bringing *that* along for?" We invariably gravitated toward Mike, although a part of me got a kick out of Ryan's directness.

When Al hung his lunch sack on the scale, Ryan fumed, "Thirty pounds? Lose five!" The Alligator took Ryan's advice in stride. Although Al was accustomed to making these sorts of decisions and then living with the consequences, he readily accepted all of Ryan's suggestions—he had never been on an expedition this long and difficult before.

Bruce's pile was, by far, the neatest and best organized. He had almost everything right the first try. Keith and Armando had the most questions. Rick never seemed to be happy with his pile and constantly rearranged things.

When it was my turn, Ryan told me to forget the travel packs of Kleenex, the eyeglass cleaner, and every other grooming supply except for my toothbrush.

"One roll of toilet paper should do for a month," he insisted.

"But the RMI checklist recommended three," I said.

"On most days, a handful of snow will do me just fine. I save the paper for higher up, when it gets really cold." I compromised and took two.

Selecting the proper clothing used up most of my twenty minutes. Working methodically from underwear to parka, the two of us sorted through my pile one item at a time. Ryan hovered above me and either gave it a thumbs-up or a "Hell no!"

We began with the long underwear. These modern long johns had little in common with what I wore growing up in Indiana under my winter clothes. Made of synthetic polypropylene, they insulated surprisingly well, helped to protect me from sunburn, and wicked away perspiration. The only downside was that they held on to body odors.

On warm days low on the mountain, I planned to wear what had worked best for me on Rainier: long underwear bottoms covered with hiking pants. On subzero days up high, I would wear fleece pants under my trousers. For my top half, I would wear a long-sleeve underwear shirt as a base and add additional layers as needed.

I selected a variety of outerwear items, including a wind jacket and pants, to shelter my body from nastier weather. A fleece jacket was probably the single most versatile piece of clothing in my pack. I could quickly close its ventilating zippers when the sun went behind a cloud and then reopen them to release excess heat and moisture. My down parka, a heavier version of the one I had used on Rainier, was for periods of inactivity, either during rest breaks or in camp. Even in the foulest weather, I would still feel comfortably sheltered inside its protective cocoon.

I packed multiple weights of hand protection; an inexpensive combination of thin polypropylene liners plus fleece mittens ultimately worked best, although they made it harder to grasp ski poles and ice axes, and they were totally worthless during any activities that required fine dexterity. My more expensive ski gloves were a constant disappointment, as they never kept my fingers as warm as the mittens.

Headgear options included a baseball cap, stocking cap, bandana, and hoods. Climbing helmets were not mandated on McKinley, as the risk of rockfall was minimal and because we were in the land of the midnight sun, we didn't need headlamps. RMI did require all of their climbers to wear avalanche beacons when under way, even though avalanche risk was negligible. Jack told us that the RMI teams were the only ones on the mountain using them.

As for footwear, I had been instructed to bring plastic climbing boots, waterproof overboots for an additional layer of insulation, and down booties to wear in the tent. Finally, crampons and snowshoes would provide an extra degree of traction on ice and support in deep snow, respectively.

Lastly, we organized our personal food. Dried beef and fruit, as well as bagels, nuts, crackers, peanut butter, and cheese provided the bulk of my noncandy lunch calories. Bruce made a ham-and-cheese sandwich for each day. Al's monster lunch bag included a couple of pounds of tasty Alaskan salmon jerky. Armando brought his own ground coffee and a metal filter to brew it in.

For snacks, I had pocketfuls of Starburst, butterscotch candies, and Jolly Ranchers. Not only were they handy out on the trail, they helped us pass time while we lay around in the tents during storm days. I also carried lemonade powder to break up the monotony of plain water. I ditched the two-pound bag of spicy snack mix that wasn't traveling well.

In the end, most of the decisions Ryan and I made were the right ones, as there was nothing missing from my pack that I absolutely needed and only a handful of things that I didn't use.

Group gear added another forty pounds to each of our backpacks. First, there were nonconsumable items: three sleeping tents, a kitchen tent, two large aluminum cooking pots, three stoves, three ropes, a dozen snow pickets, three snow shovels, two snow saws, nine sleds, and a hundred bamboo wands (more on those later). Al and I worked out an arrangement to share a potty bag. It held some toilet paper, a package of baby wipes, and a bottle of hand disinfectant.

Then there were the heavier and bulkier consumable items—food and fuel. The total weight of all our food measured an impressive five hundred pounds. In the hangar, Ryan and Mike stuffed twenty kitchen-sized garbage bags full of dehydrated groceries. To conserve weight, they removed most of the individual wrapping and repackaged the items in bulk. Next, they bundled everything together into meals. This way, Jack could more easily track his remaining inventory.

Our breakfast menu was basic: cold cereal with reconstituted milk or hot cereal, and a large supply of granola bars. The evening meal was more complex. It invariably started with a mug of salty instant soup, either creamy chicken or split pea. RMI dogma stated that a daily salt ration was necessary to replenish what was lost out on the trail. The dry residue that built up on my skin every day and the heavy white stain on the bill of my ball cap by journey's end added credence to that hypothesis.

For the main dinner course, we packed ramen noodles, dehydrated potatoes, or instant rice. We also carried two meals' worth of Dinty Moore beef stew for special occasions. The few chunks of beef from the stew, as well as the contents of a half-dozen cans of minced chicken, represented the only meat (beyond the chicken soup) RMI provided us with for the month. To spice up the otherwise bland dishes, we carried a generous supply of soy sauce and Tabasco, but on the upper mountain they were mostly unusable, frozen solid inside their plastic dispensers.

Lastly, we carried supplies for one hot beverage—instant coffee, hot chocolate, raspberry herbal tea, or spiced cider—with each meal.

Of the five hundred pounds of food we packed up that day, none remained at the end.

After we repacked our backpacks for the fifth or sixth time, the guides led us through a refresher course on mountaineering equipment and the principles of crevasse rescue. I was reminded that the single most important piece of equipment I carried was my climbing harness, which fixed me to the climbing rope and, through that, to two or three other climbers. I was to carefully secure it and wear it at all times while we were under way.

Almost as vital was my ice ax. Its shaft measured almost thirty inches long with a point at the bottom that allowed it to be thrust easily into the snow. A head on the top had a serrated pick on one side for hammering into ice and an adz on the other for chopping through dense snow. If one of us fell, we were instructed to use our ax in a maneuver called the "self-arrest." We were to drive the pick end of the ice ax into the slope to brake. If we couldn't bring a fall under control, the accelerating force could pull everyone else on the rope off of the mountain, too.

To climb steep fixed rope, we each carried an ascender. The palm-sized ring of aluminum could be clipped onto the fixed rope and easily advanced in a forward direction, but its teeth would lock it in place whenever it was pulled downward. It assured us of at least one secure attachment to the rope all the way up a steep wall.

Along the same lines, but somewhat less technical in nature, are prusiks. Climbers tie these short sections of accessory cord into loops, which are then wrapped around the climbing rope. We each carried several. Like an ascender, they would slide easily up the rope but then hold fast when pulled downward. Using a prusik as a foothold and an ascender as a handhold, a climber could, in the event of a crevasse fall, theoretically shimmy up a rope under his own power. To do so while carrying a fully loaded pack would be extremely energy intensive, however—not impossible but very difficult.

Our trio of guides walked us through crevasse rescue techniques, which are designed to take the burden of extraction off of the fallen climber (who could be seriously injured or otherwise unable to rescue himself) and place it, instead, into the hands of the healthy members above. Depending on whether or not the fallen climber could assist, the team could drop down a second rope, which he would clip himself into. The other end would pass through a pulley system designed to increase the rescuers' mechanical advantage. Although I'd received an extensive tutorial on these rescue techniques while on Rainier, I'd need much more than this one additional afternoon's practice to become proficient in them.

Sometimes, for the sake of safety on hazardous sections, we would need to anchor the climbing rope directly to the mountain. For this purpose we carried several pickets—essentially aluminum fence stakes that we would pound deeply into the snow. We attached the rope to the tops of the pickets with carabiners. The last climber would remove the picket as he passed it. An important type of anchor that didn't need to be retrieved was the snow bollard. We carved it directly out of the glacier surface, and it resembled the ball end of a large trailer hitch. A climber could either loop the end of the rope around a bollard for protection while negotiating a hazard or use it as a fixed point to rappel down a steep slope.

At the end of our safety refresher course, we assembled all three tents and checked to see that they were mountain worthy. We fired up the stoves to assure that they, too, were in good working order, and attached red duct tape to the ends of several dozen bamboo wands. We would use them to mark buried caches or, should we be unfortunate enough to get caught out on the trail in a storm, our return route back to camp.

Long after we clients finished our chores, the guides went on preparing for a month of unsupported existence. As evening approached, their sense of urgency intensified. Our chief was taking his responsibilities seriously. He understood that as soon as we were on the mountain, it would be difficult or impossible to do anything about a broken stove, a damaged tent, or a missing kitchen item. Although each of us was ultimately responsible for himself and his gear, it would mean Jack's ass if something went wrong. We knew it and he knew it. So, while the afternoon dragged on, the guides agonized over the minutia. Everything had to be just right. Our success—and possibly even our lives—depended on it.

I couldn't help but notice one bit of friction, though. Something was bugging Mike Hamill. That first night in Talkeetna, when we had enjoyed our second dinner at the restaurant, he'd sat silently, slumped down in his chair, slowly nursing a beer. From what I could tell, the problem was related to hierarchies, specifically to his standing among the guides. Jack had made it clear to all of us that Ryan was to be his number one, even though Mike had more guiding experience on big glaciated mountains. Wasn't he, after all, the one who had recently returned from the summit of an eight-thousand-meter Himalayan giant?

It was impossible for me not to have a favorite. I knew Mike, and I liked and respected him a great deal. His calm presence came across as gentle confidence, the kind of confidence that comes from a host of experiences. Those experiences had already made him a capable leader. But it was not yet his time to lead. Jack was commander. And he wanted sergeants who would fall in line and follow his instructions unquestioningly. Between the two, Ryan was the one who would do just that. Mike, on the other hand, was a threat to Jack's authority.

While this bit of friction did nothing to hurt the team as a whole, we all felt a bit uncomfortable with Mike's situation. I was disappointed for him. Part of me also resented Jack. Did he not appreciate Mike's potential and recognize the need to nurture his abilities? Fortunately for us, Hamill quickly put the matter behind him, if for no other reason than that he knew he would be sharing a tent with the boss and his first officer.

When Jack noticed our idleness, he did what a leader does best. He gave us something to do—a decision to make. It turned out to be one of the biggest decisions we would have to make the entire trip. One of our tents was obviously for the guides. The six of us needed to break up into groups of three for the other two. The problem was that up until now, we had been pairing off into three groups of two: Rick and me, Al and Bruce, and Keith and Armando. The solution wasn't immediately obvious, so several awkward minutes of foot shuffling followed. In the end, Al and Bruce agreed to split up. Al would bunk with Rick and me, while Bruce went with Keith and Armando.

I resumed my watch of the afternoon sky, hoping it stayed clear, knowing that if it did, we would be saying our final goodbye to hot showers, flush toilets, and lumberjack breakfasts in the morning. What would take their place, however, would be an adventure beyond imagination.

▬

Before we could receive final clearance to fly, we had to take care of some important business at the ranger station. By far the nicest building in town, the park headquarters was attractively constructed of natural materials and designed to look sturdy and important. It was a mandatory stop for all climbers to pay a $150 climbing fee and listen to a presentation.

Ranger Joe led the discussion. "Much trouble," he began, "can be avoided if each of you work to minimize mistakes and take appropriate measures to stay healthy." He used a slideshow to illustrate our route, beginning with the standard ascent by way of the West Buttress. "On the way up you will make five camps, ranging in altitude from seven thousand to seventeen thousand feet. These camps are clearly marked and evenly spaced. All of this year's climbers on the Washburn route—and we expect that number to be around 1,200—will use these same camps."

His report on the mountain's north side was sketchier: "No defined camps exist over there because almost nobody climbs on that side."

Everyone on our expedition knew that that was precisely the purpose of the traverse—we wanted to do something different. But now it was clear that neither Jack nor the National Park Service knew exactly what the actual conditions were going to be like. Joe flashed a few of Bradford Washburn's wonderful aerial black-and-white photos on the screen to illustrate the path that would take us down. The mountain looked starkly isolated, ominously difficult, and above all, just freakishly *huge*. But these images didn't concern me too much; they merely further excited the sense of mystery and fascination I already felt about the quiet side of Denali.

"Your entire descent will follow a lonely, unbroken trail," Joe went on, "commencing at Denali Pass, at the top of the Harper Glacier at an elevation of over eighteen thousand feet. Then, since the Harper terminates in a precipitous icefall, you will mount the adjacent ridge to the east and descend it for approximately four thousand feet. Eventually this will land you on a second glacier, the Muldrow. The Muldrow has two nasty icefalls of its own as well as a multitude of treacherous hidden crevasses. You'll exit the Muldrow about two-thirds of the way down, at a natural weakness in the western wall called McGonagall Pass. That is where you'll start the eighteen-mile land crossing on terrain that is populated by nearly impenetrable thickets, a few dozen brown bears, and several million mosquitoes. Additionally, you will cross three unspanned rivers, climaxing with the mighty McKinley River itself."

"And remember, guys, you'll be doing all of this while carrying ninety pounds of gear on your backs," Jack added with a sarcastic smile.

My only negative thoughts as I listened to Joe's talk were that I was disappointed we wouldn't get to see the entire Muldrow and that the tundra crossing sounded like a bitch.

When Joe finished, Jack pulled a rabbit out of his hat. He leaned forward in his seat, tilted his chin down, and allowed a boyish grin to grow on his face. "No guided group, as far as I know, has ever climbed both of McKinley's summits on a single expedition." As if he didn't want the whole world to know his secret plan, he kept his voice barely above a whisper. "If we bag the taller south summit and I think you guys still have enough left in you, then we might just give the northern one a shot before heading down." His voice returned to normal as he added, "Of course, the main summit and the traverse will remain our main objectives."

To bag the north summit, I thought, would be an obvious feather in Jack's cap and icing on the cake for the rest of us. It was easy to support Jack's grandiose plans on that warm and pleasant afternoon inside the conference room. Why would we object? We didn't know enough to think differently. I hadn't even seen the mountain yet, and already I was imagining myself doing historic things on it.

Before we adjourned, Joe added, "You guys have a lot of hard work ahead of you, but not many people get a chance to do something like this. Don't ever forget that this mountain can be a dangerous beast. To make it through, you'll have to take care of yourselves and each other. This is a long expedition. It's likely that several storms will hit you. Your schedule will be disrupted. Things will threaten to knock down team morale and send some of you down in the dumps. But pay attention to Jack. He did this traverse two years ago. Listen to him. He'll get you through."

"Above all," he concluded, "you have to maintain a positive mental attitude. Don't let unexpected events threaten your own or the team's confidence. It will be your attention to details that determines whether or not you are successful up there."

Nothing I heard from either of them gave me reason to feel anything less than total confidence or to doubt our leaders' capability. And if Jack said that we looked strong enough to bag both of McKinley's summits, who was I to argue?

As we picked up some pizzas on the way back to the hangar, I continued to think of Denali simply as a bigger version of Rainier. Even better, since it meant a longer all-consuming adventure. I felt physically prepared. My gear was ready. And now, thanks to Joe and Jack, my mind was locked into the planned itinerary.

Whatever else I was thinking on May 18, I could not have begun to comprehend the reality of the next twenty-five days. The mountain would challenge all nine of us in many different ways. Our bodies and our wills—in fact, every bit of our essences— would be tested. Denali would nearly break us. Not one of us would escape from the upcoming ordeal unscathed.

But at that point I felt ready for anything. When I looked in the mirror that night before bed, I was almost certain I saw the face of a mountaineer staring back.

MEETING THE MOUNTAIN

—

We awoke on this second morning in Talkeetna to a bright and clear sky. There were no storms, either visible or forecasted. After a second gut-busting breakfast at the Roadhouse, we gathered up our belongings at the hotels and headed down to the hangar, where the planes and our destinies awaited us.

I felt great. The pulse oximeter reading I'd taken last night told me that here in Talkeetna, the oxygen saturation level of my blood was 98 percent and my heart was beating 54 times per minute. The nifty gadget clipped to my finger and sent a red beam of light through it, measuring the color change in the tissue. Down at sea level, the air was thick enough that almost all of my blood's hemoglobin molecules were bound by a molecule of oxygen, coloring my tissues pink. But we were headed up, and at altitude, where the air was thinner, less oxygen was available. Some of those hemoglobin molecules would remain unbound, giving my tissues a bluish tint and the sensor a lower reading.

To survive in this low-oxygen environment, our bodies would have to adapt. If a climber, even a very fit one, went quickly from sea level to twenty thousand feet, he would develop life-threatening altitude sickness. His brain would swell inside his skull, causing confusion and a severe headache. A frothy cough would signal pulmonary edema—water in the lungs. If he didn't immediately descend, he would eventually lose consciousness, his lungs would fill up with fluid, and he would die.

To prevent this kind of catastrophe, we would ascend the mountain slowly, giving our bodies the necessary time to make the essential physiologic adjustments, a process termed "acclimatization." Once my body sensed the need to adapt to thinner air, it would begin to sharply increase its capacity to carry oxygen through complex chemical changes and simpler mechanical ones like increased breathing and heart rate.

This extended acclimatization time is partly what makes mountaineering expeditions so lengthy. Consider that a well-trained athlete can run a marathon in under four hours or race up a hundred flights of stairs in only twelve minutes. It is not immediately obvious, therefore, why it should take a climber three weeks to get to the top of Denali when the distance from starting point to summit is several miles short of a marathon, and the elevation change is equal to the height of only thirteen New York–sized skyscrapers. The answer to the riddle lies with the need for acclimatization.

I planned to take additional pulse oximeter readings at each of our five camps as well as on the summit itself. Along the way I expected the saturation percentage to fall and my heart rate to rise. I might look a little bit blue on the summit and my heart and lungs might be struggling to keep up in the thin air, but if we did things right, I would be alive and functional.

On the tarmac sat a pair of bright-orange single-engine planes, each capable of carrying its pilot and three climbers (as well as their gear) from this concrete pad to a makeshift landing strip on the crevasse-ridden Kahiltna Glacier. Each round-trip would take the pilots a minimum of ninety minutes. Half the day would be gone before the nine of us were reassembled at base camp.

A casual bystander, if there had been any, might have thought the entire airport scene rather absurd, the nine of us strutting around all decked out in our climbing gear. As for myself, instead of yesterday's jeans, T-shirt, and tennis shoes (far more appropriate for Talkeetna), I was clad in cream-colored long underwear, khaki shorts, and clunky bright-yellow boots. Black gaiters, navy gloves, dark sunglasses, and a San Francisco Giants baseball cap completed the ensemble. But none of us cared the least bit about our unusual dress. Frankly, I didn't even consider us in Talkeetna at that moment. My mind was already inside the glaciated world of Denali.

Mike went alone on the first flight along with an extra allotment of gear. Ryan, Bruce, and Keith went on the second plane. Rick, Armando, and I would go out on the third run, after Mike's pilot finished refueling. Jack and Al would be on the final flight.

When our turn came, I buckled into my seat and, while we awaited takeoff, checked out the inside of our air taxi. There was just enough room to cram three backpacks, a couple of sleds, and a few incidentals into the rear of the fuselage. Randy, our pilot, was obviously accustomed to packing gear into places where it had no reasonable chance of fitting. We were wedged into similarly small spaces. The back of Armando's seat pressed uncomfortably against my knees and the space underneath was much too narrow to accommodate the toes of my boots.

My stomach fluttered as the plane sputtered down to the end of the runway. To help quell my uneasiness, I tried to imagine how great I would feel in an hour. The little puddle jumper quivered and rocked as we picked up speed.

For the next few seconds, I felt as unsettled as I had when our twin-engine Otter barreled down the runway of the tiny mountaintop airport in Lukla, Nepal. The short runway is inclined to slow arriving aircraft as they land uphill and help departing planes pick up the necessary speed as they approach the edge of the cliff and empty space. The lack of a cliff at the end of *this* runway—and Randy's calm profile—reassured me as the plane lifted off. He appeared to have everything under control. So I sat back and tried to relax.

No sooner had I become comfortable with the sight of Talkeetna receding into the distance several thousand feet below us than an urgent radio message came in from a passing flightseeing plane: a trail of vapor was emanating from the top of our right wing. Randy admitted that in his rush to get the aircraft turned around after his first run, he'd probably failed to secure the gas cap on the wing. At least he hoped that's all it was.

He quickly brought us around for an unscheduled landing. Randy did his best to maintain his composure, but it was obvious that his mind was racing a thousand miles an hour. Pilots, like surgeons, don't forget to perform crucial duties like closing the gas cap because they operate with a mental checklist. That was why Randy was so upset. His experience operating small aircraft in unforgiving places like Alaska had taught him that anything less than perfection was not tolerated.

A few minutes later, we parked outside the hangar and climbed out of the cockpit. Sure enough, the gas cap was dangling by its tether. Rick, who was himself a pilot, did his best to console Randy while the ground crew topped off the tanks and an FAA official filed a report. Then, at the end of a very uncomfortable twenty minutes, we taxied back out for a second attempt.

To add insult to injury, Randy failed to notice that the wind direction had changed. We were at the wrong end of the runway for takeoff! I thought that the best thing to do, while we sputtered down to the opposite end of the field, was to stare out the window and keep silent—and pray.

"No big deal, Randy," Rick said supportively. With that, the engine throttled up and we were off.

The plane steadily climbed to cruising altitude, and calmness returned to Randy's voice as he slipped back into his element. As the amazing panorama unfolded outside our windows, the four of us quickly forgot about gas caps and airport officials.

The aerial view of Alaska was vastly superior to the view from the highway. Wilderness dominated. I made out only two manmade structures in a hundred-mile radius—the sprawling compound of the Princess Lodges hotel and the meandering outline of the highway as it followed the serpentine form of the Susitna River. A pair of exaggerated sandbars flanked its central channels. Otherwise, there was nothing but an unbroken expanse of green all the way to the distant horizon where the snow-covered peaks of the Alaska Range stood watch. I recalled the map that I had been reviewing last night in the hotel room. The Alaska Range, which includes McKinley and the other peaks found within Denali National Park and Preserve, forms a horizontal arc across the southcentral portion of the state. The tallest of the peaks—the ones with monstrous glaciers and huge barren snowfields—run along the range's high central spine. Now I saw all of that laid out in front of my eyes.

After thirty minutes of gradually gaining altitude, Randy focused his attention on the new challenges just ahead, beginning at the narrow entrance to Kahiltna Pass.

"We're flying completely on my visual," Randy said through the onboard audio system. "Any sudden loss in visibility could send us crashing into the side of one of these mountains." And just as he finished saying "mountains," my heart jumped as he banked the plane sharply to the right and took us into the pass. It seemed that our wingtips really were only yards away from the sinister dark-granite faces of these sentinel peaks. My eyes told me we had just had the day's second near miss, but Randy's sly grin told me otherwise—we passengers were simply victims of a little practical joke.

We had already crossed the terminuses of two of Denali's southern glaciers: the Ruth and the Tokositna. We were now headed upstream in the turbulent air above a third: the Kahiltna. The soft cushion of spruce underneath our belly had disappeared. In its place was a dangerous landscape of hard ice and rock.

Unfortunately, I discovered too late that my camera batteries were frozen, leaving me unable to shoot even a single frame of our approach. It was obviously colder in the cabin than I'd realized. There was not enough time to rewarm them before landing. In fact, only a few minutes later—and all too soon for the happy flight-seer in me—Randy pointed the nose of our plane downward toward the rapidly approaching icescape. Our time as tourists was about to end.

As planes are not allowed to land within the boundaries of Denali Wilderness, the southeast fork of the Kahiltna Glacier was as close to the mountain's base as Randy could take us. And since this particular section of the glacier was historically stable and relatively crevasse-free, it was the ideal location for us to set down.

One problem remained for Randy to solve. Forty-five minutes earlier, he had taken off on rubber tires hardly suitable for landing on a glacier. So Randy performed a trick. Turning a pair of small cranks next to his knees, he lowered landing skis below the tires. On the return trip, he would reverse the process to expose the wheels again.

The terrain racing up toward us was featureless save for the collection of orange tents at base camp and some swirling ski tracks from other planes. The otherwise total absence of color and contrast prevented me from relying on my usual sense of depth perception. The disorientation became more pronounced the closer we got to the surface.

Besides my depth perception, my perspective was altered, too. Our significance relative to the scenery around us had shrunk from finite to miniscule, and it continued to diminish as the seconds ticked by. Only Randy's experience and keen instincts kept him undistracted by all this. He expertly planted the skis on the cloudlike surface while he simultaneously throttled back on the engine.

As in Lukla, the upward slope of the glacier assisted in our deceleration. Just short of a full stop, he spun the plane around and sped us part of the way back down the hill. A familiar figure stood there on the "runway."

"Welcome to Mount McKinley, gentlemen," Mike shouted over the buzzing of the propeller. "Hop out and grab your gear so Randy can be on his way."

We hurriedly dumped the packs and sleds on the snow. Then, without further delay, Randy set the throttle to full. Free of its burdensome cargo, the plane lifted quickly into the cold, crystalline air. Within the span of five minutes, Rick, Armando, and I had been transformed from comfortable flight-seers into figures marooned in a frozen wilderness.

We stood motionless as our sole link to civilization became a tiny speck against the enormous backdrop of Mount Foraker. The silence that remained was overwhelming. My ears were wide open but had no success gathering any sort of information regarding their new surroundings. My squinting eyes did no better; the glare from the glacier had turned my eyelids into slits and my pupils into pinpoints despite my dark sunglasses. Twenty minutes later, the fourth and final plane interrupted the silence for a little while.

We were now nine of perhaps three hundred individuals on the mountain. Roughly a third of them were milling around us here at base camp. Their presence comforted me to a degree—I did not feel totally alone at the start of this enormous undertaking—but at the same time this concentration of humanity displayed unpleasant side effects. Waste management was the first. The community's pee hole was a three-foot-wide ochre-stained depression that had been carved out by the spray of untold gallons of warm urine. It didn't take long for me to want to put this filthy frontier village behind us. Thankfully, our team was stopping for the night a few hours' walk away, down on the main body of the Kahiltna.

"Gather up, everybody," Jack ordered. "Ryan is going to give a brief lesson in sled management. After that, we'll be under way."

Ryan demonstrated the proper way to load the sleds and fasten them to the rope behind us, rather than to the bottoms of our packs, to avoid straining our backs. "Bulky, relatively lightweight items work best for the sleds: snowshoes, fuel cans, and tent sections," Ryan said. "Heavy items like food bags and clothing are best left in your packs, even though your first instinct will be to minimize the weight on your backs."

So we unloaded our packs once again and sorted their contents into two piles each. Ryan went on to explain that an overweight sled would tend to sink into the snow, whereas a lightweight one would glide along on the surface and offer minimal resistance. A top-heavy sled would more easily tip over when taken across a slope, whereas a lower-profile sled would stand a better chance of remaining upright.

Although we followed Ryan's advice to the letter, we all ended up hating the damned sleds before the day was done. Within a week I considered mine to be the bane of my existence. But sleds were as indispensable here on McKinley as yaks in the Khumbu. And since there were no hired porters or beasts of burden on Denali, we had to learn to live with them. The only other way we could have managed this much equipment (by Jack's reckoning, 133 pounds per man, including the clothing that we wore) would have been to increase the number of carries between camps. As it was, with double carries, we were already going to climb the mountain twice.

Today, when I look at the pictures of me and my teammates taken on that day, what impresses me most is the paleness of our skin and the naïveté behind our expressions. We look so eager and fresh. Our faces are not yet weathered and drawn. Supple lips, not yet scabbed and cracked, form our broad smiles. Our eyes have not yet seen the frightful things they would witness. Several extra pounds of fat fill out our features, pounds that are gone in the photos taken at the bottom of the Muldrow.

These early images accurately capture the sense of joy that was in my heart. I had worked incredibly hard to get to this place. It really was a dream come true that I was standing in that spot. I hadn't had time to start missing the things I usually took for granted. I hadn't yet stopped to consider how many days it would be before I could take my next shower or reach down and touch something that was alive and green. The smile in the photograph shows that I was simply thrilled to be there.

The sky overhead was sparkling clear and the air smelled fresh when I breathed it in. I admired the mind-emptying purity of the place. Out to my left the features of seventeen-thousand-foot Mount Foraker stood out crisply, and to my rear, fourteen-thousand-foot Mount Hunter radiated in the brilliant sunshine like one of those old backlit Kodak advertisement signs, the ones that displayed an immense enlargement of a high-definition Kodachrome image. Only now I was standing inside of the image looking out.

We headed out on the lone trail. It was even and compacted, created by all the climbers and sleds that had come before us that season. Just inches to either side of this narrow well was a much more irregular surface. If I walked off the trail, my feet plunged through the surface crust above my ankles. Early in the climbing season, there would have been no trail at all, and the entire route would have required snowshoes. Those pioneers would have had to probe every inch of the glacier looking for hidden crevasses. Now, well into this year's season, in the middle of May, an eighteen-inch-wide highway already stretched all the way from the landing strip to the top of Mount McKinley. The path was tried and true—or at least as safe as anything gets on a glacier. But Jack warned us that any deviation from it would head into the unknown, dramatically increasing the level of danger.

Crevasses (both visible and concealed) littered the glacier. For that reason we would stay roped together whenever in motion, each of us clipped into a knot (via our harnesses) evenly spaced along the climbing ropes, three people per rope, until we stepped onto the tundra—whenever that might be. Crevasse falls were a risk for everyone, not just pale-faced novices like us. Well-traveled mountaineers had died even this low on the mountain when they ignored the dangers and wandered about alone. Even in base camp, it was unlikely that anyone would survive a significant unroped fall. A serious head injury and multiple bone fractures would almost certainly result; rescue aircraft were less than an hour's flight away, but a minimum of several hours would elapse before the injured climber could be delivered to a qualified medical facility. Too much time to permit a happy outcome.

But, with a generous supply of cautious optimism, the nine of us tied into our ropes, each team led by a guide, and made our way down the hill toward Camp One. Yes, down. The climb to the top of McKinley actually begins with a descent of five hundred feet from the landing strip down onto the main Kahiltna itself. Those returning this way must climb *up* the final five hundred feet to get to the bottom of McKinley—hence this first little bump's nickname, Heartbreak Hill.

My pack was incredibly heavy but otherwise the early going was not particularly difficult. As silly as it sounds, this gave me the opportunity to learn the proper way to walk. The trick, I knew from Rainier, was to consistently match speeds with the man directly in front of me, in this case, Bruce. It was important to keep the rope between us slightly slack. If too loose, the rope would trip me; if too tight, it would tug on Bruce's sled, prompting him to look back to see what the problem was. The best solution, I found, was to maintain my focus not on Bruce, but on the sled itself. When it moved, I moved. The problem with that was the sled didn't always move in the same direction as Bruce. Gravity had a say in what line it followed. It also had an annoying tendency to tip onto its side whenever we cut across the slightest of slopes. Then everyone on our rope had to come to a standstill until I righted it.

If Bruce identified a potential trouble spot up ahead, he would try to communicate that back to me. However, the mass of his pack—the top of which rose twelve inches above his head— made his words frustratingly hard to understand.

After an hour of marching, we stopped for a rest. This routine rarely changed. Jack, who typically headed the forward team, would signal a break by pulling well off of the trail in a safe spot, yielding the right-of-way to any teams who wanted to pass. We were always tired (or "knackered," if you spoke Canadian like Al) at an hour's end. I looked forward to these opportunities to give my shoulders and hips a break. The rest periods also helped mentally by breaking down the day's work into manageable segments.

Starting with this first break and continuing over the next several days, Mike preached a packaged sermon to his client congregation of six. In it, Brother Hamill chastised us for not drinking enough, not eating enough, and not breathing deeply enough. Farther up the Kahiltna, he eventually grew tired of the mothering and—mercifully—decided to wash his hands of us. "You can all starve to death and die from dehydration as far as I'm concerned," he would say in his benediction. By then, we had all gotten the idea anyway.

The distance between the standard camps was always about two to three miles, with an altitude change of between two and three thousand feet. Any capable team would have no problem covering the distance in just a few hours. Our team generally broke the trip down into four one-hour segments, with three twenty-minute breaks in between. During these breaks we were to consume the majority of our two-liter water supply (Rick carried three) and consume our daily ration of lunch calories.

In between breaks I battled with the rope, learned to walk, righted my overturned sled, and fiddled with my pack. I adjusted the arm straps and played with the hip belt in an attempt to perfectly balance the pack's eighty pounds between my shoulders and hips. It took a constant and not insubstantial force to keep my sled moving. The work was hard, but I was relieved to find myself not immediately in over my head. My thoughts stayed focused on positive things. Instead of complaining about the backbreaking work, I rejoiced in the good fortune of finding myself in such a wondrous place.

I repeated simple phrases to sustain myself whenever I started feeling discouraged. "Smile every mile" was the first one I came up with. The smiling came easier when I daydreamed about pleasant past experiences. During that first day's climb, I thought about my first extreme altitude experience—Chukhung Ri in the Khumbu, 18,238 feet. The day my young Sherpa guide, Kancha, and I climbed to the top was relatively early in the trek, before I was well acclimated, and so I experienced the uncomfortable triad of high-altitude effects. First the excruciating headache, as if someone were tightening a vise inside the base of my skull. The pain was constant and penetrating. Second, an extreme sense of fatigue. Every step required monumental effort, and the next one more than its predecessor. Finally, the unbelievable shortness of breath that indicated oxygen starvation, like what an advanced emphysema patient must experience every day, I imagined.

Up switchbacks lined with dwarf rhododendrons, Kancha and I climbed on a trail of bare rock and brown dust. The two of us could barely communicate because of our labored breathing and the language barrier, but his congratulatory hug and smile at the top said it all. On a map Chukhung Ri doesn't seem to be anything special, only a minor ridge on the much larger Lhotse-Nuptse massif. But I was standing up close to that massive wall—and that was something special. From its base at fifteen thousand feet, the wall rises two miles to the summit of Lhotse, the world's fourth-highest mountain. Although I climbed only a fraction of the wall, I felt part of it, connected to greatness, somehow closer to knowing the extent of God's grace and majesty.

On a more terrestrial plane, I noted that the information my senses gathered was exaggerated and hyperfocused. The throbbing sensation in my cold hands was more intense, and I could almost palpate the texture of the rocks through the soles of my boots. The sounds of the wind and my breath were highly clarified. A feeling of calm, which came from accomplishing a difficult task and discovering something of the natural world that I hadn't known before, dominated it all. As when I ran, especially in marathons, I was stripped of all things superfluous. Only a life reduced to the basics remained.

But the transfiguring effects of Chukhung Ri were not sustainable. Eventually I noted that I was cold and the hour late. I began to worry. To avoid being stranded up there in the dark, we had to hurry back to camp. The desire for safety and comfort returned to dominate my thoughts.

Later, at camp, I asked our Nepali trip leader, Sunil, how the impoverished porters we saw on the trail every day were able to manage, wearing only thin shirts on their backs and flimsy sandals on their feet as they carried loads in excess of one hundred pounds. How was it possible for them to find happiness and satisfaction in their lives?

He responded in a Confucius-like fashion, saying that a man doesn't realize he is cold until he wears a warm jacket and then loses it. These porters had never worn an expensive down jacket like the one I owned, never lived the luxurious Western life that I had.

Now, as I made my way up the Kahiltna Glacier, I nodded in continued understanding of Sunil's statement. But my level of understanding about McKinley was still very naïve—I only felt secure out of ignorance. Later on, when I was missing the safety of my own metaphorical warm jacket, I would think back often to Sunil's wise saying.

I thought of the eighteen months between the end of the Nepal trek and today. At home I was surrounded by incredible riches by Nepali standards, and yet I understood less about myself there in Illinois than I had in the rarified air on top of Chukhung Ri. Now, with every breath, I was catching up with my lost self, reeling in the mountain air again.

Then, just as I was getting good at the glacier travel routine, Bruce rudely interrupted my thoughts by stopping completely.

"What's wrong, Bruce?" I said, knowing that it was too early for the next break.

Bruce responded with a point of his right-hand ski pole. Since my eyes had been down and my attention directed at his sled, I'd failed to notice a handful of abandoned tent sites with crumbling snow-block walls a hundred yards off the trail. Massive volumes of clean Arctic air continued to circulate in and out of my lungs as I followed Bruce and his sled off the main trail and into Camp One.

I had been uncomfortably warm ever since we left base camp. Once I removed my pack, though, I started feeling chilly. It was early evening, and a much more subdued light supplanted the intense brightness of the afternoon. Shadows stretched out across the mile-wide glacier, leaving only the tops of the eastern peaks illuminated by the evening's highly refracted light. It only further accentuated the finely sculpted details of their fluted ice walls.

I heard a sudden crackling, far to the western side of the glacier. It had taken several seconds for the event to register over here; a rising dust cloud and a pulverized heap of new debris at the base of the distant slope marked its location. The avalanche was a stark reminder to always keep a safe distance from the valley rim with its precarious overhangs.

As we were still low on the mountain and the weather was clear, we didn't need protective snow walls and bombproof snow caves. Still, there was much work to be done. Rick, Al, and I worked on setting up our tent. First, we leveled an area several yards square. Al and I shared the duty of breaking through the uneven surface crust and scooping away excess snow with an aluminum shovel. Then Rick trampled down the area with his snowshoes until it was smooth.

The snow was dry and surprisingly light. This would be true at the higher camps as well, except up there it was packed into dense stratified layers, requiring ice axes and snow saws to cut through. The only time we encountered heavy, wet Illinois-style snow was on the lower Muldrow, just before we hit the tundra.

While leveling a tent platform was not difficult, it was about as much fun as shoveling the driveway—not very satisfying business for an ambitious mountain man. After Rick was happy that the surface was smooth enough, we put up the tent and began stowing our gear. We laid out our sleeping pads and bags but kept the bulk of our gear outside on the ground in the packs. As it was, there was barely enough room in the tent for our three bodies.

The tent fly extended three feet beyond the structure itself, creating two semiprotected vestibules. In subsequent camps we would hollow out the floor of the front vestibule, which allowed us to comfortably sit on the edge of the door and remove our climbing boots. We used the rear vestibule very little at all.

To prevent a sudden gust of wind from blowing our light-weight home into a nearby crevasse, we lashed it securely to anything that could be used as an anchor: ski poles, ice axes, even a partially buried snowshoe. We had not seen more than a light breeze yet, but Jack warned us not to take any chances.

Next, we cleared a shallow semicircular area for the kitchen. Ryan set up his stoves along an embankment that protected his fires from turbulence. Only his head and shoulders were still visible on the other side as he went about the business of melting snow for drinking water.

Along that embankment we also carved out a row of snow benches. Although simple, the seats were ergonomically correct: their backs tilted gently away and the sitting surfaces were just the right height. The benches were not soft and cozy like the canvas-backed chairs the porters carried for us in the Khumbu, but under the circumstances, they were more than satisfactory.

Finally, no camp was complete without a latrine. This consisted of two areas. Several yards beyond the tents, Mike stuck a bamboo wand in the snow and declared it the pee hole. A little ways beyond that was the throne. Constructed so that it was partially submerged, shielding the user from the weather and curious eyes, it looked like a large armchair. Inside the hollowed-out middle we stuffed a heavy-gauge plastic garbage bag, its corners secured to the edge of the seat with bamboo-wand fragments.

No one ever dawdled on the throne. Speed and efficiency were of the utmost importance, especially at six o'clock in the morning, the time I typically visited it. The exposure of tender flesh for even a couple of minutes was undeniably unpleasant.

By the time the latrine was finished, Ryan signaled that dinner was ready. After eating our fill, we climbed into the tents and settled in for a well-deserved rest. I was content. As far as adventures went, I thought, this one had a pretty good beginning.

THE LOWER
KAHILTNA GLACIER

—

TUESDAY, MAY 20

My mind stayed busy through most of that first night. Between the lack of true darkness and my general excitement, I slept very little. Instead, I lay awake thinking about how far removed I was from my ordinary life.

When I had studied the globe in my office back at home, I found two things remarkable about this place: first, how far away Alaska is from everything else, and second, how close the state is to the top of the planet. Even by Alaskan standards, McKinley is remote, standing one hundred miles north of Anchorage, only three degrees south of the Arctic Circle. The tallest mountain in North America, it is also the largest mountain that is this close to one of the poles.

I thought about how different this Arctic landscape was from what I was accustomed to in the Midwest. Where I grew up in Indiana, green was the color of life. Cornfields, lawns, and shade trees displayed various shades of green each summer during the long, warm growing season. Even when the killing frosts of autumn arrived and everything turned brown, I knew that spring would bring green growing things back to dominate the landscape.

But the McKinley landscape is not the least bit green, and it remains almost entirely unchanged from season to season and year to year. I say *almost*. Each spring brings a new migration of a herd numbering well over a thousand, dragging their sleds and packing bowls of Dinty Moore stew. Only out on the periphery of the Alaska Range, many miles from where I now lay my head, will you find the color green. There on the tundra, between the end of the snowmelt in late May and the return of wintry storms in early September, the landscape briefly shows signs of life. Then hundreds of square miles of unspoiled and untamed territory thaw and become vibrant and wet. Prickly ground-covers artfully attire themselves with wildflowers. Impenetrable thickets of willows and alders sport new growth. A fresh carpet of green covers everything.

McKinley's tremendous altitude is not the only factor that interferes with flora and fauna. There is also the extreme latitude. Colorado's Rocky Mountain National Park sits at forty degrees north latitude, where tree line is at approximately eleven thousand feet. During the summer, you can find smaller plants near the tops of even fourteen-thousand-foot peaks. But Denali National Park is 1,500 miles farther north, at sixty-three degrees north latitude, where tree line is nearer to two thousand feet. Here, in the central spine of the Alaska Range, the entirety of fourteen-thousand-foot Mount Hunter is perpetually covered in ice. McKinley isn't merely sterile; it's dead. Nothing can possibly survive the extremes of this environment: subfreezing temperatures, lengthy periods of winter darkness, and incessant wind and storms. There is no fertile, black soil like what I am used to in the Midwest, and certainly nothing like what my farmer friends refer to as productive, timely rains.

Because of this absence, there are no large foragers and predators. There are no insects for birds to eat and no small mammals for larger carnivores to prey on. Only a few accidental life-forms wander onto McKinley: the occasional windblown insect, band of scavenging ravens, and troupe of odiferous mountaineers.

But while the mountain itself does not harbor life, it does play an important role in fostering life down below. Its immense bulk influences the local weather, encouraging formidable amounts of precipitation to fall nearby. On the mountain this precipitation is locked up for centuries within glaciers, ancient rivers of ice that scour the rocky slopes as they slowly slide downhill, grinding the underlying bed of granite and shale into a fine powder. These gritty inorganic components of new soil are eventually released from the glacier's terminus along with a regular volume of meltwater supplying the gray rivers that flow out into the valleys. Meanwhile, these rivers of ice, like the one where we were camping, provide several immediate benefits to mountaineering expeditions like ours. The Kahiltna is an easily climbable highway that gives access to the upper mountain. It also provides an inexhaustible source of drinking water.

I shifted in my sleeping bag. While our first day had been monumental, the first night seemed monumentally long. The air inside the tent was rank with the scent of wet socks, and my muscles were stiff from lying in an unnaturally straight position inside my sarcophaguslike sleeping bag. I was in the center of the tent with my head against the main door. Rick's feet were to my right and Al's to my left. There wasn't enough room for me to lie in a comfortable fetal position without getting in their spaces. And since we would be spending at least half the hours of each day confined to these limited quarters, it wasn't surprising that every bit of personal space had already been claimed and jealously guarded.

Throughout the long night of tossing and turning, I feared that I would accidentally migrate into their spaces. Periodically, I realigned myself along the ceiling's center seam. We had placed two rows of water bottles between us in order to prevent the water from freezing, and these helped me stay put, too. We could have kept the bottles inside our sleeping bags, but between a stiff pair of boot liners (the inner layer of my plastic climbing boots), my camera, and a bag of snack food, it was pretty crowded in mine already.

Another item I kept close at hand at night was my pee bottle, an empty saline bottle that I got from the operating room back in Springfield. Unfortunately, I found it to be inadequate—its narrow spout was scarcely large enough to urinate into without spilling and made it nearly impossible to empty out the frozen chunks of slush the next morning. I was not upset when it turned up missing after just a few days on the mountain, even though it took me nearly a week to find a substitute.

Although I had slept very little, I was anxious to get up and get moving. By six, I had had enough of the tent, so I sat up and started pulling on my gear.

Everyone else was still sleeping. The sky had already been bright for several hours, but because Jack didn't plan to have us out on the trail first thing, we weren't expected out of bed before seven. He wanted the other teams to go ahead of us, so that their feet, not ours, would pack down any newly fallen snow. Another reason for the late start was that he and his junior guides were night owls. That first night and each subsequent one, we heard them joking and telling stories in their tent until well past midnight.

The morning vista that greeted me outside was astonishing. I could see many miles down the glacier, past the turnoff at the southeast fork, and toward the Kahiltna's terminus. I admired the view—first from the pee hole and then from the throne. Antarctica must look much like this.

My brief period of solitude was too-soon interrupted by a buzz of activity from the other tents. It wasn't long before everyone was up and going about his business. Then, following a casual breakfast, we started loading up our packs in preparation for a carry to Camp Two. This second leg would take us three miles closer to the origin of the Kahiltna, to an elevation of nine thousand feet.

As we packed up, Jack dropped a bombshell. "Bruce and Ryan won't be going up with us. A problem has come up." He explained that as Ryan started preparing dinner last night, he'd found that the lids to our cooking pots were missing. Without them, melting snow or boiling water would consume an exorbitant amount of fuel—fuel that we didn't have. "Since we don't have anything else for a substitute, someone has to go back and get them."

Ryan and Bruce would return to base camp where RMI kept a cache of emergency supplies. If they couldn't find spare lids in the cache, then Ryan would radio Hudson Air Service and have them fly out the original lids as soon as possible. It sounded like a lot of trouble and expense for two lousy pot covers, but as Jack said, there were no other options. If he later discovered anything else missing, he never mentioned it.

Minus Ryan and Bruce, and with a few extra pounds of their gear thrown into our packs, the remaining seven of us headed up toward Camp Two for the first of two carries. Today's carry contained extra fuel cans, some of the food bags, and the portion of personal gear that we wouldn't need tonight. Tents, sleeping bags, kitchen supplies, and everything else would go up on the second carry tomorrow.

These double carries served two purposes. They assisted in the all-important process of acclimatization by allowing us to stick to the proven mountaineering adage: climb high and sleep low. And they kept us from having to transport the full weight of our equipment all at once (though the sum of the weights from the two was greater than what a single carry would have been, as some items like down parkas and storm clothing were in our packs on every trip). The second carry invariably proved to be the more difficult psychologically because we were not covering any new ground and had to overcome known hills or obstacles for a second time.

Camp Two was about three miles up the glacier. The gain in elevation was gradual at first, but the slope increased significantly as soon as we started up the prominence known as Ski Hill (so named because of the mode of descent preferred by many climbers). After three hour-long stretches of climbing and two rest breaks, we saw the telltale sign of a new grouping of tents. Once we arrived, we dug a pit large enough to hold the gear that we unloaded from our packs and sleds, tossed the gear in the hole, and then carefully covered it again with several feet of powder. Finally, we flagged the spot with wands.

This substantial amount of work—two hours to bury the load and two to dig it up again—was necessary to foil the intentions of McKinley's notorious scavengers, a pesky band of black ravens. Their only purpose in life, it seemed, was to search out and destroy poorly protected caches left behind by careless climbers. The ravens would rip open bags of food and clothing that were buried superficially in the snow, take what they wanted, and then leave the rest scattered indiscriminately over the glacier. None of us wanted to risk losing our gear or a chance at the summit to a bunch of damned birds, so we didn't complain about the work.

While it took us three hours to make the arduous ascent, the return trip took only an hour and fifteen minutes. On the way down, we pulled empty sleds and shouldered ridiculously light packs. Still, at the end of the day, when we pulled into our familiar home site, I was surprisingly spent. At these times I felt most thankful for our junior guides. While I headed to my tent to recover, Mike or Ryan went immediately to work melting snow and starting dinner. From the time they began to cook breakfast until the moment they scrubbed the last pot at night, these two stayed on the clock. The freedom that we clients enjoyed by not having to prepare our own meals was in itself worth every penny we paid.

On most days when we made a carry, the hours between four and six o'clock were special. The work of the day was done; I could enjoy being on holiday. My biggest challenge was resisting the temptation to spend that entire time recumbent inside the tent. Usually, I would sit outside on my overturned pack and read or chew the fat with my climbing mates while we admired the scenery. I'd write in my journal and, if the spirit moved me, draw a simple sketch. Since I hadn't seriously attempted to draw since high school art class, my expectations were modest. And while the results could hardly be construed as fine art, I found it to be worthwhile. Drawing forced me to spend several minutes studying the landscape, identifying its structure, and observing its various textures and contours. What I produced in the end was better than an exact copy—it was a personal interpretation of what I saw.

I find it interesting now to compare my sketches from the first half of the expedition with those I drew on the way down. The earlier ones reflect an inner optimism—I was aware of the vastness of the spaces and paid calm attention to detail. The later ones appear hastily made and narrower in focus. The subject is immediate—usually the most recent hazard we had overcome. Broken, angulated lines mirror the artist's fragile psyche—someone who was anxious to escape his surroundings.

But here in Camp One, after just two days on the Kahiltna, my comrades and I were just beginning to enjoy our new lives. We had already slipped into a mountain routine.

Ryan and Bruce returned to Camp One shortly before dinnertime with the missing pot covers in hand. Bruce came over to our tent after dropping off his pack and reported that they had found no spares in the buried RMI stash at base camp, so they had called Hudson Air Service and asked them to bring the originals out.

"Sure is nice not having to fight rush-hour traffic, answer emergency room calls, and struggle to keep the peace with four toddlers," I told Rick later as we lay in the tent.

"Can't say anything about the last two, but as for traffic, you should try Denver's sometime. The only thing worse than my weekday commute is the logjam on I-70 on Friday afternoons when everybody is heading out to their favorite mountain playground all at once."

As we chuckled about how foreign the ordinary sounded to us now, I felt an emotional release. Denali offered an entirely new reality: one of climbing and hauling, digging out and then filling back in again, eating and eliminating. It was a physically hard life but unmatched, even by Nepali standards, in its simplicity. I went to sleep that night wanting for nothing.

THE MIDDLE MOUNTAIN

—

WEDNESDAY, MAY 21

On Wednesday, we moved up to Camp Two. Following breakfast, we dismantled our camp completely. Each of us grabbed a portion of the tents and a share of the group gear—a bag of food and a snow shovel, a stove and a fuel can, or a cook pot and a handful of wands—to carry. We hustled to fit it into our packs so that we would be ready to get under way when Jack gave the signal.

The final duty before leaving a camp for good was to decommission the latrine by kicking down the throne and tossing the shit bag into a nearby crevasse. Because of our special route, we were exempt from carrying out our solid waste. All of the teams on the standard route were required to use the park service's new Clean Mountain Cans. To use a CMC, which looked like a plastic paint can, the owner would place the cylinder on end, unscrew the top, and squat over the Styrofoam-ringed opening. Teams were expected to return the same number of used CMCs at the end that they picked up at the beginning. I was relieved that we didn't have to transport those extra pounds of excrement all the way up this side of the mountain and down the other. Even so, after watching Mike handle that first garbage bag loaded with two days' worth of turds, it was clear to me that our method wasn't entirely pleasant either.

As expected, our second climb up to Camp Two was not as enjoyable as the first. My pack was noticeably heavier due to the larger amount of group gear. The weather was also partly to blame. In contrast to yesterday's crystal-clear sky, today's air was hazy. As a result, the architectural details of the mountainous cathedrals around us were not as crisp. It was as if I were viewing familiar scenery through a dirty windowpane.

But even on this second time up, each image on the trail was so unique and exciting that I wished I could have shared the experience with Angie. She had marveled at the beauty of Rainier; I felt certain that she would love it here, too. On the other hand, when I was dragging my sled up a steep incline or creeping along through a crevasse-laden snowfield while being crushed underneath a monster pack, I was sure she would have hated it.

Camp Two was nearly as simple in its construction as Camp One. We made a functional kitchen facility but did not dig out a shelter or build protective walls. The weather was a bit more unsettled here than at Camp One but hardly threatening. I tilted my head back. Higher up, it appeared completely clear.

"Good news," I said to myself. "It means we'll be able to keep moving."

Jack echoed that sentiment at dinner that night. "Guys, I've been staying up on current weather developments by listening to the evening report on my radio," he said as we slurped up our soup. "As long as conditions remain favorable, we'll stick to the original schedule of moving up every other day. And while I don't sense that we need one now, I'll insert a rest day whenever we need one."

We grumbled. His final statement was *not* good news. We were all fresh and eager, and the idea of wasting an entire day sitting idly around camp made us cringe.

But Jack was insistent. "Although the skies are still clear now, eventually we're going to have to deal with bad weather," he said. "Storm delays are a fact of life on McKinley. No team sticks to its prearranged schedule completely."

That evening I sat in the pleasant, shadowless haze and sketched Mount Hunter, now more than five miles away from us. The Kahiltna Glacier meandered down past Hunter and the southeast spur like a huge toboggan run, all the way out to the tundra on the horizon. I read a bit of the Hemingway short stories I'd brought, paged through my increasingly tattered copy of the *Economist*, and enjoyed some conversation with my two tent mates. My pulse oximeter readings that night showed an oxygen saturation of 89 percent and a heart rate of 71.

THURSDAY, MAY 22

On the fourth day, I added two more mantras to my repertoire: "Lord, give me strength and endurance to climb this mountain," and "Oh, give thanks unto the Lord for he is good and His mercy endureth forever." I repeated each phrase privately, three times in succession, while I was moving on the mountain. On the trail my breathing was heavy and rapid, so I could only whisper a few syllables at a time with each exhalation.

The first was a humble supplication asking the Almighty for the power to continue. It was just a phrase that I'd made up on the fly.

The second was an offering of praise to the One who provided me with all that I required. I had recited it countless times as a boy with my father, as an after-dinner prayer. On the flight up from Chicago, a version of the prayer printed on a photo of a spectacular Alaskan sunset had accompanied my meal service. I liked it so much I decided to carry the memento with me inside the pages of my journal, alongside four small drawings made by my kids.

As I said the mantras, I was able to refocus my attention on that specific moment in time. Usually, it was successful and boosted my positive energy. After only a brief time on McKinley, I was already feeling spiritually enriched. While I didn't literally hear the voice of God speaking to me or feel, directly, the touch of His hand, I did sense His presence in everything around me. When I reached out and touched the rocks, I felt their strength and I knew that He was there also.

Group morale was high. It was only day four and we were already about to make our first visit to Camp Three. At breakfast, even normally stoic Jack showed us signs of his contentment.

"These next few days on the schedule are some of my favorites," Jack said. "This middle section of McKinley is above the cloud layer that always hangs around nine thousand feet and yet well below the nasty weather that so often bombards the upper mountain. The work won't be too hard and the air will still be rich. You guys will have a chance to build up your mountaineering legs, to get stronger, so you can manage when we get up higher."

He went on to tell us how his team on a climb several years earlier had waited out a seven-day storm at seventeen thousand feet. Jeff, my lead guide on Rainier, was along as one of his junior guides. After the weather finally broke, they ran up and bagged the summit. As I imagined the unpleasantness of a weeklong storm, it became clearer why he relished the time down low. Later, we clients would also look back on those days with fondness. But at that particular moment, our ambitions would not allow us to be content with simply being on the lower mountain.

The first change of camps, from seven thousand to nine thousand feet, had taken us most of the way up Ski Hill. On a map, the "hill" appears as an insignificant undulation on the glacier, challenging enough that we had definitely noticed it, but an easy obstacle compared with what was to come.

The second change of camps would take us from nine thousand to eleven thousand feet—from the top of Ski Hill to the base of longer, steeper Motorcycle Hill.

After breakfast we set out. There was a fair amount of gentle grade on this part of the mountain. Had it not been for the damned sled, I would have even called the day's work pleasant. I had no complaints as long as we were on purely flat ground. There, the sled followed obediently behind me in the shallow trench of the trail. If the route went straight uphill, it required more effort to pull the weight up, but the situation remained tolerable. There were times, however, when we had to ascend or descend an incline that took us *across* the slope. At those times the sled would follow the laws of physics, instead of me, and hang down from the climbing rope like a pendulum. Having to drag it along sideways and then watch it tip over repeatedly every time it hit a little bump was maddening.

The skirting of Kahiltna Pass was the most memorable part of the day's journey. After leaving Camp Two we made a big right-hand turn at the top of Ski Hill and started up the long, straight incline that would take us into Camp Three. Part of the way up the incline, we stopped for a break. After pulling out a bagel half and my jar of peanut butter, I sat down on my pack to make my lunch. As I spread the peanut butter with my knife, I looked back down on Kahiltna Pass. Weather from the north channels through a narrow, U-shaped weakness in the Alaska Range on its way south. When we looked down on the pass from above, we could see a cloud bank literally pouring over its lip, as if someone were operating a gigantic dry-ice machine over on the Peters Glacier. It was one of the most striking visual features of the entire southern approach.

We buried the cache at eleven thousand feet in Camp Three and, on the descent, had a second long look at the spectacular

Kahiltna Pass cloud show. Back in Camp Two, the weather remained splendid. I relaxed near the tent while Mike and Ryan prepared our dinner. When they called us to come and eat, I went to my pack to retrieve my eating utensils. My heart sank. They were gone! The silverware set—a stainless-steel spoon, fork, and knife connected by a metal ring—was one of the least expensive pieces of equipment in my pack, but it was priceless to me because I carried no substitute. I mentally retraced my steps back to the morning break and realized that I must have set them down in the snow and then forgotten to pick them up again.

A highlighted statement from one of the pages of my RMI gear list flashed into my mind: "Bring two spoons; one will get lost in the first week." I could have kicked myself. Sure, I had a hundred things to keep track of and would inevitably lose something, but still, how could I have been so careless?

Fortunately for me, Bruce the Marine knew how to follow directions. He gave me his spare. If it hadn't been for this unselfish act, I would have been scooping oatmeal and ramen with my dirty fingers for the next three weeks. I was almost too embarrassed to say so, but the best I could offer him in return was the use of my toenail clippers that evening. I was indebted to Bruce for the first of many times.

As the daylight faded, so did what remained of our visibility. The clouds that had been pouring through the pass all day long were now running across the tops of our tents. Inside of ours, I closed my eyes and dozed off in comfort, enjoying the sensation of being wrapped in a cold, crystalline fog.

DIGGER MAN

—

If I were home that day, I would have been attending my daughter Emma's preschool graduation rather than slogging my way back up the Kahiltna Glacier toward Camp Three. The preschool's commencement program listed each child's intended profession beside his or her name. Four years earlier, our eldest daughter, Grace, had indicated she wanted to be an artist (which later became teacher, then veterinarian, and then pharmacist). Oldest son Will proclaimed that he wanted to be an "artiteck." Though he couldn't say the word properly, at least he had advanced beyond his aspirations to be a professional ant killer, the idea he had come up with the previous summer while beating insects to death with my hammer.

I already knew Emma's choice. She wanted to be a famous singer and dancer—or, as she said with a lisp, a "thooper-thtar." Naturally, this would require her to change her name, since "Emma Fenner" was not particularly flashy. Once I looked at Emma's program back home, I noticed an unusual choice among the typical policemen, firemen, teachers, and ballerinas: digger man. That little boy and I obviously shared a common interest. I had already spent many hours on Denali digging out tent platforms, kitchens, and latrines. Every day I was either digging a hole to bury a cache or digging a hole to retrieve one, and before this tour was over, I would dig snow caves and dig out tents during storms. I couldn't help wondering what the five-year-old boy had in mind for his digging career.

On our fifth day, we planned to do a second carry and move up to Camp Three. After breakfast we went about the business of filling in the holes we had dug out forty-eight hours earlier. A few swift kicks leveled the kitchen and latrine. This was likely the last of the "easy" camps. Soon we would have to build them sturdy enough to withstand the nastiest of Arctic storms. And before the day was done, Jack would demonstrate to us exactly how he defined a sturdy camp.

As was our custom, we did not hit the trail early. Just before leaving Camp Two, Jack paid us a rare compliment. "Guys, in comparison to the other teams I've seen up here, both guided and unguided ones, you look stronger and are moving up the mountain better." Whether he truly believed his statement was irrelevant. One of a leader's most important jobs, as I saw it, was to support his clients' fragile egos using whatever methods were necessary.

We completed the ascent in three hour-long stretches. The peak named Kahiltna Dome once again flanked us on the left as we approached the pass. Its nearly symmetrical, rounded top and heavily distressed icy surface make the mountain resemble a geodesic dome. That morning we spotted two climbing parties angling their way toward the 12,525-foot summit, apparently undergoing warm-up drills for the main climb of McKinley itself.

A bright sun sparkled overhead, giving a false impression of warmth. The air was actually quite cold. But even the cold was something of a contradiction. The sun's rays, as they reflected off of the snow, were penetrating and intense. I applied a liberal covering of sunscreen at each break, but by evening every inch of exposed flesh was swollen and tender.

As we made that giant right-hand turn at Kahiltna Pass for the second straight day and passed the rest area where I lost my silverware (it was nowhere to be found), we faced the bulky triangular terminus of the West Buttress. The massive geological structure that was our route's namesake is an unmistakable feature of McKinley's south side. Geologically speaking, a buttress is an incomplete rib, an appendage that helps support the mass of rock up above. But unlike a rib, a buttress doesn't extend all the way down to the mountain's base. We had already passed several examples of ribs: the West Rib of McKinley, just beyond Camp One, and the massively long ribs that hold up the bulk of Mount Foraker.

From a mountaineering standpoint, either a rib or a buttress can be used as a practical way to gain access to what it holds up. We, in fact, planned to scale the West Buttress in a few days' time but on its southern flank. Camp Four, positioned at the base of this flank, functions as the West Buttress route's advanced base camp, that is, the launching pad from which we'd attack the upper mountain. We would ascend the buttress's headwall—the mildest-sloped, easiest approach to the upper mountain. Easiest, yes, but hardly easy. It is a sharply inclined wall that rises unbroken for two thousand feet. But once we reached the top of the headwall, we would have a relatively easy walk along the ridgeline of the buttress to get to High Camp (Camp V). And from there, it would be only one more long day's push to the summit.

As I took one step after another up the glacier, each section of ground ahead looked identical to the ones we had just passed. I remembered Ranger Joe's discussion of the route: "The ascent of Denali really amounts to two separate climbs, the long twelve-mile glacier approach and the upper mountain." We were still in the middle of the laborious, unglamorous half—the necessary evil. I looked forward to reaching the Kahiltna Glacier's origin at the headwall of the West Buttress. That was when the "real" climbing would begin.

For the time being, though, the final push into Camp Three seemed plenty vertical. The stretch was physically draining and took longer to complete on both carries than I expected. We were at eleven thousand feet—altitude was starting to be a factor.

By the time we arrived at Camp Three, my water bottles were empty and my supply of positive attitude was nearly depleted. Getting the bottles refilled would take at least an hour. But to refresh my soul, all I had to do was look around. Camp Three sits in a level basin that is naturally sheltered on three sides, in an area that is easily large enough to accommodate the two dozen climbing teams that were there at the time. The smooth terrain conceals the fact that the entire basin is actually heavily crevassed. While I worked to catch my breath, I turned back to face the route we had just come up. A thousand feet below to my right was the perpetual cloud show at Kahiltna Pass. Straight ahead and roughly level with me was the summit of Kahiltna Dome. In the distance and to my left were the vertical faces and outstretched ribs of Mount Foraker, its eastern wall rising two miles above its base on the lower Kahiltna Glacier. Finally, in the foreground, I saw the top of the ridge that had been to our right during the ascent of Ski Hill. From down below it had appeared to be a solid wall, but I now saw it was anything but. Monstrous seracs leaned precariously on their sides, and huge clefts cut through the full thickness of covering ice. The whole wall looked highly unstable. I was glad that we were now above it, looking down.

Only far in the distance, out toward the western horizon, did I see something different, something other than ice, rock, and snow. Dozens of shimmering, silvery ponds punctuated the endless expanse of black tundra, which was nothing but pristine wilderness. In no direction did I see the slightest suggestion of human interference.

I was tired. I looked forward to getting the tent set up and then sitting back, relaxing, and studying the majestic scenery for several more hours. I wasn't the only one who felt deserving of some extended downtime after our strenuous climb. My fellow climbers were also sucking down oxygen. But Jack had other plans for us.

He selected the location of our camp so that we were well away from the main body of tents. Moving into one of the recently abandoned camps, with already completed snow-block walls and leveled tent sites, would have saved us many hours of labor. But that would have meant cutting corners from a safety stand-point. Those sites had been used by other teams and were con-taminated. Out here on the perimeter, we were assured of fresh snow and a clean house. As Mike put it, there was nothing more discouraging than digging up a previous camper's frozen turds while harvesting snow for drinking water. In spite of the park service's efforts to improve sanitation on the route by mandating the use of CMCs, they hadn't been in use for very long, so the top few feet of snow were still considered contaminated.

Most of us were already suffering from gastrointestinal symptoms ranging from mild nausea and stomach cramps to diarrhea. I was skeptical of Jack's rather hopeful explanation that our digestive systems had not yet fully adapted to a diet so high in carbohydrates. True, we were consuming next to no fruits, vegetables, and fiber, and only meager amounts of meat and other sources of protein. On the second day in Camp Two, I'd recorded in my journal that I'd eaten a western-style omelet (reconstituted from powdered mix), a granola bar, coffee, half of a bagel with peanut butter, Edam cheese (four slices), cheese-flavored crackers, a handful of mostly frozen carrots, two bowls of ramen noodles with peas, a split pea Cup-a-Soup, a Clif bar, and four quarts of water. None of us were accustomed to eating this kind of diet at home.

But I thought it was likely that our sour stomachs were the result of the inevitable exposure to bacterial contamination. We clearly lacked the facilities for proper hand washing and hygienic food preparation, and dirty snow could have easily tainted some of our drinking water. But as no one was seriously ill, there was no reason to belabor the point.

I saw Ryan harvesting a load of pure white snow for fresh drinking water and felt encouraged. The rest of us, in the meantime, began erecting the tents. We assembled ours in record time. Feeling rather smug, I thought that with a little more practice, Al, Rick, and I could make a pretty comfortable life for ourselves up here. I was especially pleased that today's efficiency would allow me additional time to relax and enjoy the scenery.

Jack made his way over to the two client tents. I imagined he was eager to congratulate us for today's fine efforts.

"Gather up, guys. Got a fun little project for ya," he said with a smirk. "Grab the shovels and the snow saw. You're going to dig us a kitchen." What he was asking for was anything but a "fun little project." He told us to dig a twelve-foot-square by ten-foot-deep hole in the ground, big enough to hold nine men at once. That was roughly the size of twenty cache pits! His little project would take the six of us clients the rest of the afternoon to complete.

The blast of reality hit me in the chest. Hot, tired, and more than a little grumpy, I was in absolutely no mood to hear that there was this much more work to be done. I tilted my head back again and looked up. The most unthreatening of blue skies stretched above us. Surely with no sign of a storm on the horizon, there was no need to go to the trouble of creating what in essence was a bomb shelter. The whole scheme smelled of busy work.

Jack saw my open-mouthed stare and smiled crookedly, "Fine job today, guys. I'm sure you'll do me proud with this, too."

"What-fucking-ever," I said under my breath. There was no point in protesting, so I grabbed one of the shovels and pressed it hard into the snow. Unlike me, Bruce didn't grumble. The Marine unhesitatingly dove into the work with his usual level of enthusiasm. The boss had asked for it and that was all he needed to hear. Rick, Al, and Keith shared my more muted response to Jack's challenge, but we all did our share. Armando, however, spent those hours fiddling with his pack.

The rest of us cleared a few inches of soft powder, exposing the denser layer underneath. This required a different excavating technique that Mike demonstrated. He first sliced through the four vertical sides of a block using an aluminum snow saw. The saw's large, sharp teeth made quick work of cutting through the Styrofoam-like stuff. Then he popped out the block from below using a flat-bladed shovel. For the dozens more we cut after that, we aimed for manageable-sized cubes of about eighteen inches square, each weighing roughly thirty pounds.

Two men shared the cutting and shoveling chores while the rest of us hauled the blocks out of the ever-deepening hole. The sweat really began to pour as the pit grew in diameter and depth. We saved the excavated material to construct protective walls around the kitchen and the clients' tents.

I say "clients" because curiously—despite Jack's repeated warnings about the potential damaging effects of storms—we never saw the guides put up any sort of protection around their own tent. Did this confirm my early suspicions that much of what we were doing was unnecessary, or were they simply being casual in regard to their own safety? Perhaps some of both. I concluded that if the weather turned really foul, Mike and Ryan would throw something together at the last minute.

Once we had dug down to a depth where even Rick could barely see out of the hole, we looked up at our leader for approval. He was clearly less impressed with the results than we were.

"You can go down another layer, can't you, boys?"

Out came another twenty blocks.

We kept three of the largest blocks stacked inside the hole to support the tent cap's center pole. We cut out steps for an entrance. Around the inside perimeter we carved benches to sit on and shelves for the guides to store their kitchen supplies on.

Finally, we set a ring of blocks around the outside perimeter to keep out the spindrift. In the end, we had something we were proud of.

In retrospect, I think Jack partly intended to demonstrate what we were capable of accomplishing. Once we reached the upper mountain, where things had the potential to get real nasty, we would know how to deal with weather contingencies. But at the time I was sorely pissed that we had wasted all of our remaining energy on one of his whims.

The evening was cold and fantastically clear. Through the tent door I watched the brightness of the day fade. Our encampment was undergoing a metamorphosis. A surreal dreamland of crystal and shadows replaced what had previously appeared concrete and substantial.

My camera batteries had frozen again, so I had to rewarm them inside my coat pockets before taking some shots. At times like this, when the sun was low and the light diffuse, my black-and-white film did a wonderful job of capturing the soul of Denali. When I look at those photos now, with some of the hard details of the landscape softened in the mist, I'm taken back to that airy and quiet magical world.

Alaska had wreaked havoc on our normal sleep patterns for two reasons. We had not seen a completely darkened sky for a week. Plus, frequent urinating (from drinking a gallon of water each day) meant our sleep was interrupted every hour or two. Furthermore, today's ascent had landed us at significant altitude and the workload required to make camp had been substantial. The bottom line: we were all feeling sapped. Jack seemed to recognize this and announced that tomorrow would be a rest day. The official reason he gave was that it would allow additional time for acclimatization. This time, the crowd didn't groan. On the two days after the rest day—May 25 and 26—we would do our two carries to Camp Four. Then we would be in position to begin the fun half of the climb.

Despite Jack's well-planned timetable, Denali had other plans for us.

The day started with one of my biggest gaffes of the climb so far. I wore my heavy fleece pants while sitting outside on a snow bench, not realizing until too late that they were never meant to be worn outside without a weatherproofing layer on top. When I stood up after a pleasant hour of writing in my journal, I discovered that a thick layer of ice crystals was stuck to my seat and the backs of my legs. The crystals would not brush off. They were inseparable from the material, like wool threads stuck to Velcro. When I tried to melt them off in the sun, the fabric just absorbed the free water. I left them on top of the tent to dry, but after staying out overnight, they were frozen stiff. It took two more days of laying the pants outside in the sun during the day and keeping them inside my sleeping bag at night to completely dry them out. I was so disgusted by the episode that I kept them out of sight in the bottom of my pack throughout the remainder of the expedition.

Jack did not schedule any formal group activities for our rest day. This not only gave our tired muscles a chance to recover, but provided our minds with an opportunity to reflect upon the first week's accomplishments. Soon enough we would have to reignite the fires as we began our assault on the upper mountain, but for the next twenty-four hours, we permitted ourselves to simply be content with where we were.

Throughout the day the weather remained clear and minimally windy. In contrast to the colors of snow, sky, granite, and slate, the camp itself was awash with crude brushstrokes of yellow, orange, and green—unnatural accents to an otherwise minimalist canvas. One neighboring campsite was especially colorful, with strands of Tibetan prayer flags hanging between two of their tents. Still, I saw a simply outlandish amount of white.

The guides discouraged us from wandering around due to the many crevasses, but fraternizing with other parties was uncommon on McKinley anyway. With such a large number of people concentrated in a handful of relatively small mountain camps, privacy was in short supply. To casually drop in on strangers would have been perceived as rude. For the most part, we also preferred being left alone.

The only outside interaction our group had at Camp Three was with a German couple that Rick had introduced himself to during a rest break yesterday. We would continue to bump into them as we ascended the mountain, as their schedule was nearly identical to ours. The couple wasn't hard to spot: they always wore matching yellow-and-black jackets. Rick's grasp of German exceeded the rest of ours combined, so he communicated with them the most. They replied in broken English, but clearly enough that we gained insight into their unique circumstances. The two had climbed extensively in Europe but were finding this current challenge surprisingly difficult. Because they were traveling alone, they had to do triple carries between camps to move up all of their gear; in their efforts to stay on schedule, they were denying themselves the luxury of even a single rest day.

Day after day we saw their distinctive jackets, him invariably in the lead, as they made their way along the trail. Up close, I saw that the young frau's forced smile only partially concealed an underlying look of exasperation. Her expression reminded me of a young, blonde Californian woman I met briefly on my Nepal trip. We were near Lobuche at sixteen thousand feet, only a day's walk from Everest base camp. She and her newlywed husband had been on the trail for three weeks. It had been his idea to spend their honeymoon trekking in Nepal, an idea she was now clearly regretting. I pitied both women.

Later in the day, while Rick and I were relaxing in the tent, we relived the events of what had been a perfect day and agreed the expedition had been going exceptionally smoothly. I went one step farther and righteously added that our group had been "blessed."

"Does that mean we've been singled out for more favorable treatment?" Rick asked me indignantly. "Doesn't that also imply that there are others up here who are receiving less-than-ideal treatment? Are some of them purposely being allowed to suffer?"

We moved on to other topics.

In the afternoon, I was outside picking ice crystals out of those damned fleece pants, one at a time. Suddenly, I heard a loud pop that sounded very close by and instinctively turned in that direction. A long series of crackling sounds followed, as if hundreds of cartons of firecrackers had been lit all at once. Finally, a long, low-pitched rumble vibrated through camp as several tons of shattered ice dropped from the eastern wall of the basin. It added to the growing cone of powder that rested against the wall's base, only a quarter mile away from the tents. High above the rubble hung many more tons of the tenuous stuff. I hadn't even bothered to notice the obvious clues to this nearby hazard when we first moved into camp.

That avalanche was history in a matter of seconds, but my thoughts continued to dwell on the subject. I couldn't help thinking of all of the four-wheel-drive GMC trucks named Avalanche or Denali that I saw in the Lower 48. I would think of the real thing every time I saw one in the future.

In contrast to the sunbaked, exquisitely sculpted eastern wall, the western wall was smothered in large shadowed mounds, the result of many years of accumulated snowfall. Absent the presence of direct sunlight, less of this snow had a chance to melt in between storms. The mogul mounds extended several hundred feet out from the wall, stopping just short of our campsite. The area also contained numerous broad crevasses.

Jack had heard that this entire western slope experienced a slab avalanche every few years, probably triggered by a sudden surge of the glacier. That would obviously be a very bad time to be standing where I was now.

In the center of the basin, we were bathed in pleasant sunshine. It was warm enough that Keith and Ryan had removed their shirts to sunbathe. I lazily spent the time reading, daydreaming, lounging in and around the tent, and chatting with Rick and Al.

Later in the afternoon, grand cloud formations passed us high in the stratosphere, blocking the sun intermittently. Finally, we lost its warming rays completely as it dropped behind the western ridge. The air took on a pronounced chill and a new, hushed version of the same landscape took over.

I lay in the tent after dinner, stuffed deep inside my sleeping bag, desperately trying to recapture something of the day's warmth. Before going to sleep, I wrote in my journal and admired the newest drawing of Foraker and Kahiltna Dome, from that afternoon. The past twelve hours of inactivity had left me feeling refreshed. It had been a delightfully boring day.

TUMULTS AND TWEAKS

—

SUNDAY, MAY 25

Shortly after two o'clock, morning began. There had been no true night. The morning only replaced a period of prolonged twilight. When I awoke for good at six o'clock, the new day's sky contained none of the clouds that the previous evening's had. Conditions were ideal for a carry.

I felt rested and anxious to be under way again. Jack told us at breakfast that this would be a challenging day, the most physically demanding of our young expedition. He planned for us to carry to Camp Four at fourteen thousand feet, a distance of approximately three miles, and then return to Camp Three for the night. He thought that four one-hour stretches broken up by three rest breaks should about do it.

Camp Three was at the base of Motorcycle Hill. From our position, the hill looked neither terribly high nor steep. Yet Jack knew its grade was actually quite severe and so had us strap on our crampons for the first time.

"Motorcycle Hill," Jack said, "is a shorter, steeper version of Ski Hill. Each year the specific path up the incline changes depending on snow and crevasse conditions. This year's route is as direct as it can be, straight up from the far edge of camp to the top of the hill."

An hour later we had topped Motorcycle Hill, and once on it immediately began to traverse a long slope. We stopped for a break partway across, near a feature known as Squirrel Point. As we sat down, Ryan warned, "Make sure to secure all loose items: packs, ski poles, water bottles, and anything else that can slide or roll. If you don't, they could end up on the Peters Glacier two thousand feet below."

His warning was prescient. Just minutes later, I set my peanut-butter jar down on an indentation I created for it in the snow, right between my legs. It was a careless move. The jar slipped easily out of its hold and careened down the steep hill, then disappeared beyond a grouping of rocks that appeared to be on the very edge of the precipice.

The smiles that the guides flashed at me were not difficult to interpret: *You idiot!* But this latest gaffe only gave Ryan an excuse to go exploring. Quickly but cautiously, he made his way down to the rocks and retrieved my precious jar as well as a pair of orphaned water bottles. I was happy to extend both hands as I took possession of not only the peanut butter but also a new pee bottle. Judging from the large number of items that Ryan reported seeing down there, I was not the first one to be careless at Squirrel Point.

The next hiking section provided us with some measure of relief as it followed a less extreme grade, coursing beneath the broad triangular base of the West Buttress. I would learn later that despite the area's benign appearance, it is a very dangerous spot. The south-facing wall is subjected to daily freeze/thaw cycles, and on a particularly warm day the following season, several murderous rocks were freed from previously stable positions and crashed down on unsuspecting climbers, killing and injuring several.

Ryan took a few minutes en route to examine the vertical face of the buttress and reported seeing several exciting climbing routes. The same physical feature seemed to impact each of us in totally different ways. When I looked up at the contorted face, I sensed no great danger in its rocks nor did I desire to climb on them. I simply saw our next obstacle.

Farther along this section were several slushy, shallow pools. The surface was slick and icy. The tips of my crampons failed to penetrate very far into the slippery ice, certainly not far enough to make my foot placement feel stable. It felt a little like walking on marbles. I had to be careful not to slip and fall down or twist an ankle. It also taught me a valuable lesson: even on sections that lacked obvious hazards, our path could be treacherous.

The third leg of the climb took us around the corner of the buttress, around the point referred to as Windy Corner. Exposure was the problem here. The path narrowed just at the point where the potential for powerful gusts of wind to strike was greatest. Several fatalities had been recorded here. Fortunately, on each of our three passes through the corner, the wind was absent.

The fourth leg of the day was the typical, longer-than-expected final push into camp. It wasn't steep; we had already gained the majority of the day's altitude. We needed to climb only eight hundred additional feet over the last mile. This otherwise pleasant and aesthetically pleasing section was disadvantaged simply by being at the end of a very taxing day.

We were above fourteen thousand feet, and physical activity was noticeably more difficult. Bruce, usually one of the strongest climbers, struggled the most on that final section heading into camp. When I sat with him during the final rest break, the wind seemed knocked out of his sails.

"You OK, Bruce?" I asked.

"Yeah, just a little winded. I'll be OK. Need to catch my breath, that's all," Bruce replied.

Mike Hamill also noticed Bruce wasn't his normal self. "The problem is your breathing, or rather your lack of it," Mike told him. Because Bruce had not climbed Rainier with RMI, he had not been introduced to the company's particular method of pressure breathing. I knew Mike's speech by heart already, having listened to it many times over the course of six days during our ascent of Rainier. Whenever he saw Angie struggling like Bruce was now, Mike would shout back at her, "Breathe, Angie, remember to breathe!" Brother Mike took advantage of this latest evangelical opportunity to make a convert out of the Marine.

"Bruce, when you exhale, blow the air out forcefully through tightly pursed lips, as if you are blowing out a candle you're holding at arm's length. This will empty out your lungs more completely. It will also allow the natural elastic recoil of your chest to pull in more oxygen during the subsequent breath in. The idea is to increase the absolute volume of air entering and exiting the lungs." Bruce's shallow huffing and puffing, much like a dog's panting, had not been getting the job done.

We never expected absolute solitude on this side of McKinley, but neither were we fully prepared for what awaited us at Camp Four. Because of the undulating terrain, Camp Four was hidden from our view until we were practically on top of it. In the broad basin now in front of us sprawled a tent city populated by at least two hundred climbers. Most of them, like us, were on their way up, positioning themselves for a move to High Camp. A few were stopping briefly here on their way back down.

Far over on the eastern edge of camp, a makeshift ranger station had been fashioned out of three large rectangular tents. Around a dozen semipermanent residents—a group of rangers and medical personnel who rotated onto the mountain every two weeks throughout the climbing season, each ready to provide assistance in the event of an emergency—were housed there.

One of the most practical day-to-day things the rangers did was maintaining a weather board. I remembered seeing something similar at the ranger's desk in Talkeetna. The weather board shared the most recent information available regarding the upper mountain: temperatures, wind speeds, and storm forecasts. We would have been very foolish to ignore the vital information there. Jack made the point early on that it would be equally foolish to rely too much on these rangers. Their presence here shouldn't allow us to become complacent.

The chief chose a campsite on the southern perimeter that had unobstructed views of Foraker and Hunter. Burying the cache was difficult because of a hard surface crust. The shovels wouldn't penetrate it. We had to hack through the stuff with our ice axes.

After covering up our supplies, we raced back down the hill to Camp Three in an hour and fifteen minutes. It had taken us a full five hours to cover the same distance on the ascent.

At dinner that night, Mike told me that in three months' time he was scheduled to be the lead guide on twenty-six-thousand-foot Cho Oyu—one of the world's fourteen eight-thousand-meter peaks, which I had seen from the Nepalese side standing proud next to its cousin, Mount Everest. I had been contemplating climbing Cho Oyu at some point in the future but hadn't mentioned this to Mike or even formally investigated the possibility.

I was flattered that Mike thought enough of my mountaineering skills to talk to me personally about climbing in the Himalayas. "How does that compare to what we're doing now?" I asked.

"Just like McKinley is a much bigger deal than Rainier, Cho Oyu is a bigger deal yet," said Mike. "Basically, more mountain to climb. But the biggest difference, and what I would say is the hardest part overall, is the much longer time commitment required. You have to be prepared to be gone for at least six weeks. Much of it is downtime, long stretches of days spent sitting around camp waiting for decent weather to arrive so we can move up. But from a technical standpoint, it's not much harder than what we're doing here." Then the salesman put the question to me straight: "Mike, are you considering doing Cho Oyu?"

The slight hesitancy I sensed in his question made me wonder if he was really so enamored with my mountaineering skills after all. "I honestly can't say," I replied. "I really don't want to look past McKinley. I want to see if I can handle this height before considering moving up. But I'm not ruling out the possibility."

"Well, here's something to consider while you're making up your mind. Several weeks into my expedition last year, the upper mountain was hit by a violent storm. Our tents up at High Camp were wrecked. Fortunately, the camp was uninhabited at the time. We were all down low, getting ready for our summit push. Everybody was OK. But if anyone *had* been up there during the storm, they probably would have been blown deep into Tibet."

"Sounds scary!" I replied. Part of me felt genuine concern for the danger those climbers had faced on Cho Oyu. Oddly, though, another part refused to feel sorry for them. *They knew what they were getting themselves into when they signed up, didn't they?*

Later, in the tent, I thought back to our discussion and found myself a bit ashamed by this last bit of callousness. I had reacted to their misfortune as if I were at home watching the synopsis of a tragic event on television—a naïve observer who was reacting hypercritically because he didn't understand the circumstances. I had reacted as an armchair mountaineer, as someone who wasn't there. But I *was* there—on an immense mountain at this very moment. Would people watching the news pity me if some disaster hit us while we were here? Or would they think, like I had just thought, "Hey, he knew what he was getting himself into"?

For the time being, listening to Mike tell stories about near misses in Tibet did nothing to dissuade me from thinking I would follow him there someday.

All of Mike's talk about storms was prophetic. Fierce winds began to blow at eleven that evening, signaling the beginning of a storm. We had no way to measure their strength, but I would guess they were somewhere in the range of forty to fifty miles per hour, strong enough to make the tent walls shake violently.

The air outside was in constant motion. A series of rocketing gusts periodically punctuated a monotone whistling, making it sound like artillery shells were exploding out in the moguls just beyond the western boundary of camp. Every ninety seconds a new volley struck our tents.

The tent's western sidewall bowed in noticeably from the wind, stealing precious volume from Al's already meager space. As the night went on, the wall sagged even farther as fresh snow accumulated and pressed in on it.

I didn't sleep at all until three o'clock, and even then for only a few minutes at a time. At eight o'clock, Jack unzipped the door and poked his head in. "I've got an update, guys. It's snowing!"

"No shit!" Rick, Al, and I chuckled in unison.

With continued emphasis on understatement, he added, "We aren't moving up to Camp Four today. Routefinding would be impossible in the whiteout, and we're likely to find the conditions worsening the higher we go. We're better off staying put." He reminded us that we had already cached a considerable portion of our extra food and fuel supplies up at fourteen thousand feet, so we would need to ration what remained with us down here. "I'm placing us all in survival mode. We have to maximally conserve our resources, as there's no way to know how long we'll be stuck here. Most storms last only for a day or two, but the rare one can drag on for a week."

Jack delivered his entire presentation with his customary patronizing smile. His voice held a large dose of mock enthusiasm for good measure. As always, his message was accurate but his delivery left me feeling cold.

"The idea of spending the next twenty-four hours confined in this tiny tent is discouraging, to say the least," I said, realizing even as I said it that there was absolutely nothing he or anyone else could do about it.

"Well, you're in luck then, Fenner," the chief said. "You and your pals can suit up, climb outside, and clear away these snowdrifts before they collapse your tent. And while you're at it, you should consider cutting some extra blocks to reinforce these walls."

So, on went the fleece jackets, Gore-Tex tops and bottoms, boots, gloves, and hats. The three of us climbed out of our warm tent and into the blizzard, joining Bruce, Keith, and Armando in a hopeless battle against the elements. As ordered, we cleared snow and patched holes in the barrier walls, but our rapidly diminishing store of enthusiasm kept us from even considering excavating additional blocks.

The outside temperature ranged from a high of twenty degrees Fahrenheit at midday to around zero at night. The wind made it feel much colder. By midafternoon there was a foot of fresh snow on the ground, and the wind had piled up even taller drifts against the two client tents. Fortunately, the snow was light and easy to move. But for every shovelful that I tossed to the side, the swirling wind blew half of it back in my face. The tiny icy crystals collected in every wrinkle of my clothing and stung like needle-sharp projectiles when they hit my tender, sunburned cheeks.

At breakfast that morning, I developed a new appreciation for our subterranean kitchen. Yes, it was the same kitchen whose construction I had so vehemently opposed only two days earlier. Sitting in it was not as warm and comfortable as lying inside of my sleeping bag back in the tent, but I could not imagine spending all day in the tent, and it sure beat the hell out of standing in the storm.

Inside the kitchen shelter, we felt safe and protected, but we were never completely isolated from the elements. Whirling clouds of spindrift continued to find their way inside the kitchen, either by way of the entrance steps or through minute gaps that had not been completely caulked around the tent cap's base.

I looked at the other members of the team. Everyone looked stressed. Faces that had been relaxed and carefree during our rest day now bore only empty looks. A crust of frost coated our jackets. Even the air in the center of the room looked thick and depressing. Wasn't I telling Rick how blessed I felt not two days earlier? That now sounded like a rude joke, one in which Rick had had the last laugh.

At the root of my disappointment was the fact that the storm was disrupting our schedule. It meant spending additional days waiting to move up, more precious days away from my family. Because of the empty hours, I had more time to think and worry. This storm day was proving to be tougher on me than any of the climbing days had been.

Between shoveling shifts, I passed the hours in the tent reading Hemingway's short stories and news articles from the *Economist*. I gave more attention to minor articles that had not seemed worthwhile on my first few reads; at least they represented fresh material. And although I found Hemingway to be sorely lacking in optimism, he did seem appropriate for the current conditions.

At least my book was readable. For some reason Rick had brought James Fenimore Cooper's *The Last of the Mohicans*. Nineteenth-century prose was painfully dry even at sea level and under the best of circumstances. Al was toting some esoteric treatise on Eastern spiritualism. I'm not sure if he actually planned to read the thing or not. Bruce had displayed remarkable insight by selecting Ben Bova's *Mars* as his literary companion. It proved to be the perfect therapy for our bored, oxygen-starved brains. By the end of the storm, his book had been disassembled into chapters and passed around. *The Last of the Mohicans* was saved from dismemberment, but I'm fairly certain that Rick ended up tossing it whole into a crevasse at some point along the way.

In the late afternoon, I fell asleep and let my dreams take me far away . . .

▄▄▄

Bang! A gun goes off.

I'm surrounded by a crowd of thirty thousand runners who slowly begin to inch forward. Sammy Hagar's voice blares from tall stacks of concert speakers on either side of me: "There's no tomorrow . . . Right now!"

It is a pure moment, a moment that has a singular purpose— running. I exist in a higher plane of spirituality, and yet I am grounded in a sense of intense physical self-awareness.

The logjam starts breaking up and I get some running room. My legs reach out in longer strides. My throat and lungs burn from gobbling up the crisp October air. I catch glimpses of other runners, their arms gliding neatly at their sides, their faces giving away little of the intensity of their inner thoughts. All of this adrenaline surging makes it impossible for me to resist the temptation to go out too fast. I feel the first nervous twitch in my chest. I cannot hope to maintain my pace.

A highly ordered flow of humanity fills Chicago's wide avenues, winding between skyscrapers. Warm-up T-shirts pile up in the gutters as the temperatures start climbing out of the forties. Overheated men and women are stripping down to only a few ounces of essential nylon and elastic.

Looping south, back toward downtown again. I follow my pace with my running watch. I feel good but there's that nervous twitch again. I'm still going too fast.

I did everything right to get ready: Pasta the night before—carb loading. Bagel and caffeine this morning—energy to keep me going. Now I'm drinking water and Gatorade from the refreshment tables at the end of each mile. Getting past the next station means that

I'm one more mile closer to finishing. So many miles! Wrigleyville, Lincoln Park, Greektown, Little Italy, Chinatown. Big loop out west and now back again, heading to the south side.

Wait. What's that? No, no, no! Something's wrong. I don't feel well. I've been running on pure instinct, but now my anxious mind is getting in the way. Only sixteen miles down, but my legs suddenly feel like lead. My hips feel the jar of every stride. That last mile was slower and this one feels slower yet.

I pass Comiskey Park, home of the White Sox, and am now on a bridge crossing the Dan Ryan Expressway. My hamstrings are cramping up. Need to stretch. I'll use that fence over there, the one on the other side of the bridge.

Down I go into a squat. My fingers grip the chain links while I stretch back and then forward. Boy, those muscles are tight! Glad I stopped next to this fence. I need it to claw myself back to an upright position. How can this be? There are so many miles yet to go, but I've hit the wall.

What have I done? What have I gotten myself into . . . ?

—

"Mike. You OK, Mike?" Rick shakes my shoulder. The sound of the wind blowing outside is as familiar as the face staring at me.

"Yeah, just dreaming. Wow! It seemed so real, too," I said. "I was dreaming about the marathon I ran two years ago. It was great fun but boy, did it kick my ass. When I finished that one, I promised myself never again. But do you know what? I went back and did it again the next year. Guess I'm crazy, eh?"

"Yeah, we're both crazy. Crazy enough to come up here!" Rick laughed.

During the storm we had only a handful of good reasons to leave the tent; breakfast and supper topped the list. The hot food and socializing were welcome changes from the stale air of the tent. As for shoveling, we took turns. In the beginning we went reluctantly into the storm every two hours to manage the drifts. Later, when I had run out of anything better to do but stare at the ceiling for hours at a time, I actually looked forward to taking my turn at the shovel.

For the first time on the expedition, I was glad to be the one in the middle of the tent, farthest away from the buffeting sidewalls. But it wasn't all gravy. Since my head was the one closest to the door, every time the zipper opened, a numbing blast of ice struck me in the face.

The snow didn't have to wait for the door to open to get inside, but snuck in through the two end doors and the single overhead window, which we were forced to leave slightly cracked. We didn't dare close them up all the way. The openings were as important for managing humidity as they were for providing fresh air. Water vapor produced from our breathing and sweating needed to be vented out. The majority of the moisture did rise up and escape from the cracks, but some ended up condensing on the ceiling. This delicate frost accumulated to a critical thickness and then fell back down all at once. The slightest provocation, either a timely gust of wind or an errant elbow, could trigger a mini snowstorm. The technique for collecting the frost was decidedly low-tech—a twenty-nine-cent Walmart sponge sopped the crystals off of the walls. It was just one more chore that helped alleviate the boredom.

In the end, we found the best way to deal with the situation was to sleep. Each of us ultimately succumbed to a desire to hibernate. I slept for hours at a time, not caring about the time of day and indifferent to the tumult that persisted outside.

During the storm, the twelve-hour stretches between meals were treated identically, whether they corresponded to nighttime or day. Clusters of naps were interrupted by short bursts of activity: shoveling, reading, and pissing into a bottle. The low level of activity suppressed my desire to eat, so I was not overly distressed by the fact that the majority of my snack food lay buried in a hole three thousand feet above me. When one of us did feel the need to snack, we shared what we had with each other. If nothing else, it gave us an excuse to mutter a few words.

I distinctly remember that I did not talk to Mike Hamill about climbing Cho Oyu at any time that day.

As evening became morning, the second day of the storm began. The continuing ferocity blowing outside prevented us from even considering a move up. Jack used the information at his disposal (a peek out of his door and a listen to the radio report) to come to the conclusion that we weren't going anywhere for at least another day. The snow was still coming down heavily and strong winds were continuing to pound camp.

When I went outside, I found that the storm had decommissioned the latrine. The throne was buried under two feet of fresh snow, and clearly there was no way to accomplish my business as usual. I thought back to yesterday morning, the last time I'd used it. Even then, only a few hours after the beginning of the storm, the latrine was barely usable. The bitter memory of stinging ice crystals and frostnipped fingers was still with me. I would hold off until I had a plan.

I came up with one while we were digging out the kitchen tent. It had collapsed during the night and required a couple of hours work to set it right. My plan had a logical basis. I explained it to Rick as we shoveled. "First, I'll zip myself inside the tent's rear vestibule. I'll drop my pants, squat down, do my thing, and get out. Three or four minutes tops."

He just smiled and shook his head. "Have you looked back there, Mike? Not a whole lot of room. Should be interesting."

When the time came, I unzipped the fly door and looked inside. Rick had a point. Since the floor had not been excavated, there was just barely enough room to squeeze myself into the cramped space. Between the tight quarters, the bulky boots, and the need to strip off multiple layers of clothing, it was a more cumbersome process than I'd imagined. My hands were clutching the handles of a plastic grocery bag to my bare bottom when it happened—the distinct pop sent waves of pain up and down my spine.

Still hunched over but now writhing in pain, I crawled out of the vestibule, pulled my clothes back on, and disposed of the bag at the throne. I then limped back to the tent and slid sideways into my sleeping bag. Rick was propped up on one elbow, still shaking his head.

Back strains were not new to me; I had experienced several similar episodes in the past. What concerned me was the time that it generally took me to recover from one: three or four days minimum. What if the group was ready to move out in the morning? I couldn't even stand erect, much less carry a pack! But there was very little I could do except be patient and hope for a better day tomorrow. I took a couple of ibuprofen, rested for a while, and then went back outside and tried to walk it off.

Ryan was down in the kitchen preparing breakfast. He looked up and saw me stooped over in pain. "You having issues?" he asked. I'd half expected him to say, *What the hell is your problem?*

"It's my back," I explained to him, and then to Jack when he wandered in a few minutes later.

The chief was calm and pragmatic. "We aren't going anywhere for the next twenty-four hours anyway," he said. "I would continue to take whatever pain meds you think are best, give it some rest, and we'll see how things look in the morning." His little pep talk over a bowl of hot oatmeal helped to boost my spirits. At least now I wouldn't mind so much being forced to spend another day lounging in the tent.

The rest of the guys wandered in. As we ate our breakfast, Jack reminded everyone to continue rationing his personal supplies, just in case we were forced to remain here for a third or fourth day. My lunch that afternoon consisted of half a bagel smeared with peanut butter (Bruce's loaner spoon was also my new knife) and a single coffee-flavored candy.

The storm drove our moods to new lows. None of us in the tent showed any interest in any activity, especially talking. As though keeping time with the winds outside, my back hurt continuously while volleys of excruciating spasms buffeted my spinal column every ninety seconds. Whatever direction tomorrow took us, whether shouldering the pack in a move up or spending a third consecutive day confined to the tent, I imagined only misery. We were only nine days into the expedition, only a few short miles from the landing strip—barely a third of the way *up* the mountain—and I had hit the wall. What had I gotten myself into now?

But damn it, I knew as I lay in my bag and silently stewed that quitting was not an option. The events of the morning only made me more resolute that nothing would keep me from finishing what I started. If I could just find a way to get through a few more hours of survival mode, then I would find a way to deal with tomorrow. I hoped for sunshine and a strong back in the morning.

GENET BASIN

—

The storm had ended, and with the dawn came calm, warmth, and sunshine—glorious sunshine! Wanting to check out the condition of my back, I got up early. While outside, I surveyed the situation. The tall, powdery incline of snow pressing high up against the western wall of the tent no longer looked like a crushing menace. Instead, I saw it as a delicate, intriguing sculpture. In spite of the many hours we had spent constructing those three-foot-high snow walls to act as barriers, piles of the white stuff—like bucketfuls of windblown desert sand—had found their way into every corner of the inner enclave. The other client tent was faring worse than ours, straining mightily under an even more massive drift.

A dozen feet beyond stood the guides' tent. The space around it was devoid of even the most rudimentary embankment. They had constructed no protection around it whatsoever. Not only was their tent undamaged, the entire area around it was pristine, scoured clean by the wind!

It would be another hour before Jack started his morning announcements, but I knew to expect a move up. And I was ready. While not completely pain-free, my back had improved to the point where I could stand up straight, and I was confident I could shoulder my pack.

Back in the tent I found Rick awake. He told me how he had strained his back, too, only a few weeks before the trip. He had been training on a thirteen-thousand footer, only a couple of hours' drive from Denver, when he injured it. As he limped back to his car, he worried that his upcoming climb might be in jeopardy. We agreed that our bodies could be remarkably fragile things and that what we were asking them to do here on McKinley was pushing the limits of human capacity. My near miss from twenty-four hours ago made me appreciate that much more my tenuous position up here and the need to do everything possible to remain healthy.

Al brought some levity to the situation when he awoke. He sat straight up, wearing a big smile. The first words out of his mouth were, "I dreamed that I was fingerin' the queen!"

"The queen of England?" Rick and I shouted back in unison.

"Yeah, she was a looker in her younger days," he insisted with a straight face. The three of us howled.

The scene was utterly preposterous: three grown men lying about in a putrid tent discussing each other's sexual exploits, both real and imagined. It was not unlike hanging around with my buddies when I was a pimple-faced adolescent. We whispered and giggled about all sorts of repulsive things, all the while behaving badly.

In fact, camp conversation was never highbrow. It varied from something approaching the broadest definition of intellectual all the way to downright crude. It all depended on the group's mood.

At breakfast Mike shared with us a humorous story from one of his previous expeditions. "So this guy, you see, he was traveling solo, and we asked him if he wouldn't mind sharing a tent with this very attractive young female climber because she was also traveling alone."

"Sweet!" we all responded, finding it hard to imagine this guy's amazing luck.

"Yeah, you would think so," Mike said, "but this poor guy suffered through three weeks of pure hell. She made him go outside in the cold at night so she wouldn't have to listen to him pee into a bottle. And he always had to be careful with his language. Hell, he wasn't even allowed to fart in the tent."

"Wow, the poor bastard! Not such a great deal after all."

While my dreams hadn't involved intimate relations with royalty, I noticed that my imagination was still running wild. The amazingly vivid marathon dream was just one example. I shared a pair of additional dreams with Rick and Al later that morning as we were packing up.

"The first one took place on an absolutely black night in Chicago. The whole family was riding in a cab to go out to pizza, traveling through downtown. Rain was pouring down. Once we were in the restaurant, I could smell the rich tomato sauce, garlic, and basil rising up off our freshly baked pie."

"Hey, you be sure to save me a piece of that the next time you're there, OK?" Al said.

"Sure, Al. Anyway, I was *so* looking forward to digging my teeth into it, but in the process of rolling over in my sleep, I woke up before I took the first bite. Have to say, I was pretty disappointed to find that I was still here in the tent with you two guys. I tried for the longest time to force myself back to sleep before the image disappeared, but no such luck."

Rick was still in the mood to give me some more crap about the rear vestibule incident. "So Al's doing it with the queen, and you're pooping in the tent and dreaming about going out for pizza with the family. What's that supposed to be telling me about my two roommates, huh?"

"Shut up, Rick!" The seventh grader in me suddenly surfaced again. "And who are you dreaming about, huh?" I continued my dream saga. "And then, on a different night, I was dreaming that I was standing at a distance from my wife, admiring her from across the room. Angie was looking great, dressed in a long, white satin gown. And no, the kids weren't in the room with us, in case you're wondering, Rick. But in the dream I'm up here in Alaska, and she's down there being pursued by my friend Greg, a very handsome surgical nurse at the hospital. He was being Bogart-smooth, all debonair. What's more, Angie seemed to be enjoying his advances tremendously!"

Rick kept going. "So you missed out on pizza and 'the other,' too, eh?"

It felt good to be laughing again.

These nocturnal titillations were the result of the liberating effects of altitude, Mike told us. I was just glad there weren't any psychiatrists among us. They would have had a grand time trying to attach some meaning to our dreams. It was enough to know that the sharing of the night's dreams was one more reason to look forward to getting out of bed in the morning.

Before we left, Jack made official what we already knew. We would indeed be moving up to Camp Four. After we cleaned out our bowls and mugs, we clients went about dismantling camp while the junior guides spent the next hour divvying up the remaining group gear. It was apparent from the large number of food bags they spread out that we had never been in danger of starving even if the storm had persisted for a full week. What we *were* running a bit low on was fuel. We had consumed more of it by this point than Jack had planned for. "No big deal," he said. "We'll get what we need once we're at advanced base camp."

He explained that when we got to the fourteen-thousand-foot camp, we would search out teams on the descent. They would be as delighted by the prospect of lightening their loads as we would be by acquiring the necessary fuel. The park service's rule stated only that teams were responsible for removing all of their fuel cans from the mountain; it didn't matter to them how much fuel was left in them. An empty can, depending on a team's circumstances, might actually be more valuable than a full one.

It made me wonder why the park service or one of the private concessionaires didn't maintain a sort of general store up at Camp Four to help teams manage things like extra fuel and food. Needy ascending teams could obtain additional supplies from the store while overburdened descending teams could unload their excess supplies. It would discourage them from dumping those unwanted items into a nearby crevasse. Wouldn't this be a more efficient way to manage limited resources? The advantage of the current system was, of course, that it kept the responsibility for a team's supplies solely in the hands of those individuals, but it seemed to encourage an unnecessary degree of redundancy.

If something as valuable as fuel was readily available for the asking, I wondered what else we might be able to pick up. Jack's morning talk had me looking forward to the opportunity to "work" our new neighborhood once we got settled at Camp Four. While it would feel awkward at first to ask a perfect stranger for food or fuel, I felt certain that I could adapt. I imagined a conversation going something like this: "Hi! How's it going? How's the climb? Excellent! By the way, you wouldn't happen to have an extra gallon of fuel, some coffee, and two rolls of toilet paper, would you?"

We moved up to Camp Four in five hours. We reascended Motorcycle Hill and then passed Squirrel Point and Windy Corner uneventfully. The day was a difficult one, but no one minded. The sun was shining, the wind was no longer howling, and the air contained some warmth again. Bruce sailed through the final section, the one that had exhausted him on our first carry, with the help of Mike's pressure-breathing technique and two additional days of acclimatization.

Once in camp, we began the processes of construction and assimilation. We located our cache and dug it out, leveled new tent platforms, erected the tents, and began to build fresh snow walls. My back was feeling better. And since my oxygen saturation remained a respectable 85 percent, I was enthusiastic about diving into the work. We were all thrilled by the opportunity to do something other than stare at the tent ceiling.

Camp Four was positioned on a broad glaciated plateau at the origin of the Kahiltna. The site is nicknamed Genet Basin in memory of Ray Genet, who pioneered the practice of guiding paying clients on McKinley. It was by far the largest of the formal camps and nicely protected on three sides by the West Buttress, the south face, and the West Rib. The open south end provided grand views out to Mount Foraker, Mount Hunter, and the lower Kahiltna Glacier.

At the basin's end is a sheer drop-off appropriately termed the Edge of the World. From the edge, we could gaze down on the origin of the West Rib, more than a mile below, to a position near the location of our first camp. It had taken us a week and a half to cover that short distance. I remembered back to what Mike Hamill had said about Denali on the way down from Rainier. Our present altitude was only two hundred feet lower than Washington State's highest summit, yet we still had more than a mile of mountain to climb to reach the top of Alaska.

As long as the bright sun shone overhead, we sweated in the afternoon's heat, even at rest. But as soon as the sun dropped behind the western wall of the buttress, the temperature in the basin plummeted, requiring us to pull out our down parkas. Even with the summer solstice approaching, solar movements still found a way to influence our lives in the land of the midnight sun. But rather than the onset of darkness, it was something subtle, like a sudden change in temperature or the rolling in of an evening fog, that told us the day was winding down.

Despite another intensely physical day, my appetite remained poor. I ate only one bowl of cereal for breakfast and a single bowl of noodles for dinner. Even my hand-selected personal snacks were disappearing at a slower rate than I had expected. Rarely did I experience the sensation of hunger. I ate because it was time to do so. The primary satisfaction I derived from mealtime was the socialization it provided. The rest of the clients were struggling to eat enough to keep their weight up as well, but Ryan said the loss of fullness in my face was more noticeable than it was in the others.

Paired with my general disinterest in food was a persistent feeling of nausea. It never progressed to the point where I vomited, nor did I skip entire meals because of the feeling, but it remained one of the more aggravating features of the climb. Since drinking more fluids seemed to be the remedy for most other ailments on the mountain, I accepted the guides' suggestion that it was the right thing to do for this one as well.

As I got into the tent that night, I hoped for continued clear weather so we could keep the expedition moving along and I could get back home. The downtime during the storm had left me with plenty of time to think about Angie and the kids. At the same time, I reminded myself of Ranger Joe's lecture, of the importance of remaining flexible. Unsettled weather was even more likely to interrupt our progress once we hit the upper mountain. Most of the two hundred climbers around us had, in fact, been sitting here for several days already, waiting for a long enough stretch of decent weather to move up. After all, it was still early in the season and only a handful of climbers had summited.

"Lord, give me strength and endurance to climb this mountain" was fast becoming my most often-recited prayer.

THURSDAY, MAY 29

Another scheduled rest day. It began as a sunny, shadowless morning. The brightness magnificently illuminated the details of our surroundings.

It was six o'clock, my usual rising time. Once I was outside, my eyes were attracted to a different part of this new encampment, beyond the ranger station, on the far eastern side of the basin—a large area of real estate that was noticeably devoid of tents. I wondered why. The explanation, as I soon realized, stood high above. A huge hanging glacier, made up of multiple pillars of fractured turquoise ice, clung tenuously to a vertical prominence of the West Rib. I turned my attention to Mount Foraker for a few minutes while I considered whether or not to make a trip over to the throne. The telltale crackling sound of shattering ice drew my gaze suddenly back to the hanging glacier. While I watched, several tons of the white stuff fell a thousand feet to the basin floor in a matter of only a few seconds. The resultant cloud blossomed upward and outward for a minute or longer, but its progress halted a safe distance away from the ranger station. When the dust cleared, a slightly taller debris pile stood at the base of the rib.

At breakfast, Jack announced to the group that we could spend anywhere from two days to a week here at Camp Four, depending on when the window of opportunity opened up. He reiterated that High Camp, on an exposed ridgeline at seventeen thousand feet, was not the place to be in a severe storm. And once we moved up to the upper mountain, we would be committed to proceed in one direction only: forward. Therefore, as long as the forecast stayed questionable, as it was now, we would stay put down here, where it was safer. Not surprisingly, he added that we needed to build a new kitchen facility.

Our efforts to accomplish the task were happier and more self-directed than they had been down at eleven thousand feet. Just in case we were going to be here for a week, we worked to make the shelter as comfortable as possible. We dug down as far as Jack would have asked us to go and then went one block deeper. We carved out enough bench space so that all nine of us could sit down at the same time. The cooking and storage areas were larger and more functional than they had been back at Camp Three. The steps leading down into the bunker were broader and less steep. We made the damn thing bombproof, capable of surviving even a full-fledged gale.

A cleanup area was designated outside, just beyond the steps, where the pots and bowls were scraped and cleaned. As it was impractical to wash dishes by the usual method, using soap and water, we did the only other thing possible: a thorough, mechanical cleansing using spoons and abrasive chunks of clean snow. Our plastic mugs were simply rinsed out with a couple of ounces of clean water to prepare them for their next use. Apart from sanitary issues, the main issue with a dirty cup was that it threatened to carry over the salty residue from last night's split pea soup into this morning's delicate chamomile tea. The rarity of wasted food made cleanup easier, too.

Early in the afternoon, after the deluxe alpine kitchen was complete, our leader surprised us with a special treat. He had been holding back a supply of peanut butter, strawberry jam, and pilot bread (large, indestructible soda crackers) for just the right occasion. To the celebration I added some thinly sliced salami and mixed nuts. Al provided a few strips of his tender salmon jerky.

We sat back on our packs and gorged ourselves on the lunch as we enjoyed the superb vista. Mount Foraker and Mount Hunter were still out there, but only their tops were poking through the carpeting cloud layer at twelve thousand feet.

Both my stomach and vision satiated, I didn't give a second thought to those poor saps who were down underneath those clouds, the climbers who were traveling a few days behind us on the lower Kahiltna. We had done our time down there, too. Being down there meant more than just being stuck in the cold and gray; it meant missing out on this magnificent high-altitude scenery. Today I was feeling selfish, content to enjoy this special moment that I had earned. Who could look at this scene, at what we had made for ourselves here in camp, and want for anything more?

I tried to put the afternoon's euphoria and the events of the recent two-day storm into context. Each day, in fact, we had been at risk from some outside danger: a brutal Arctic storm, a multitude of treacherous crevasses, and nearby avalanches. To dwell only on the dangers of McKinley would be paralyzing. Instead, on each of those days, I had worked to hold onto the sense of awe and innocence that I'd felt on the first day on the mountain. It had proved impossible during the storm days but now, on this most perfect of afternoons, I had my karma back on track again.

I can still look back on that afternoon's state of innocence thanks to a black-and-white photo I took of Mike Hamill's lone silhouette. His thin, shirtless frame rests atop an inverted aluminum stockpot. His climbing pants and boots provide his only protection from the elements. Snow in the basin merges seamlessly with a dense carpet of clouds extending from the edge of the basin far out to the horizon. Mike holds a snow shovel at a forty-five degree angle, making it look like an oar. It seems that he is paddling a tiny skiff on the frozen ocean. Despite his obviously vulnerable position, his calm posture and expression indicate control and serenity. He doesn't appear to have a care in the world. In the timeless moments of that afternoon, none of us did, either.

I wanted to call Angie. Since leaving Talkeetna, I had tried multiple times to reach her on my cell phone, but each time it failed to connect. In the first three camps, I'd hoped this was due to surrounding obstructions. But now we had a clear view out to the southeast, where the cell tower in Talkeetna should have been, and it still failed to work. Disappointed as much by the worthless extra ounces I had to carry on my back as by its inability to connect me to my wife's voice, I tossed it back into the pack in disgust.

Our resident telecommunications expert, Rick, thought the problem was in my phone's old analog design. It simply didn't have enough power to reach the distant tower. In support of this theory, Bruce's new digital phone had been working well all along. He used it frequently to check in on his sons back home in Connecticut. Even though Bruce knew that lending it to me now would consume valuable battery power, he unselfishly did just that.

It was so good to hear her voice but at the same time a shock to speak to someone in a different world altogether.

I couldn't think of a single interesting thing to say. "I'm fine," I told her.

"We're managing all right, too," she replied.

Hearing her voice made me start wanting for things I didn't have. "The climb is hard . . . very hard," I confessed. "It's fantastically beautiful up here, but I'm beginning to wonder whether all this is worthwhile." I was surprised to hear myself say that last bit, but those were the words that came out. Was I trying to say what I thought she wanted to hear, that I missed home that much? I tried to be upbeat, as did she, but by the end we both were crying. "I miss you, you and all the kids."

I was teary-eyed for fifteen minutes after our conversation. My mind was going crazy. Things had seemed fine until the phone call. Now, just like that, I was down in the dumps again. A wave of intense loneliness passed though me.

I needed a diversion, and Al's suggestion of a walk through "town" sounded like just the ticket. We were, after all, vacationers with an excess of time on our hands. Shouldn't we do what tourists do—go sightseeing?

Jack told us that Camp Four was a partial exception to the rule of no socializing between teams on the mountain. Since it functioned as a staging platform, some climbers tended to be more social, faced with plenty of time on their hands.

The layout of advanced base camp included dozens of individual compounds separated by an integrated network of trampled "streets." Some were broad avenues, such as the path that led to the rangers' tents and the two that led in and out of town.

Others were no more than back alleyways, where the sparseness of boot prints indicated only a few had passed that way.

We started the tour by traveling over to the ranger station, a quarter mile away, out in the "suburb" opposite ours. There we found three large tents, which served as living quarters, administrative offices, and medical clinic. I was curious to see how they lived, but we weren't invited in for a look. We checked out the weather board. The short-term forecast for seventeen thousand feet called for high temperatures in the negative teens and continued high winds. It seemed we would be lucky to squeeze in even a first carry to Camp Five over the next several days.

The remainder of the town was a hodgepodge of tent compounds, each encircled by protective storm walls. None of the sites looked as fresh and tidy as ours did. In fact, from the dilapidated appearance of many of the walls, it looked like some of these camps had housed multiple tenants during this season already.

Al recognized a compatriot from the group just across the "street" from our tents, Barry Blanchard, a renowned Canadian ice climber. Every other person we encountered was a stranger, although we had common destinies. Over half were North Americans, but some contingents also represented France, Great Britain, and Germany, as well as various countries in Asia.

Each camp had its own idiosyncrasies, in large part based on the country of origin of its occupants, but on this day all of the occupants were behaving similarly. As we passed, they gazed back at us watchfully, I'd say even suspiciously. Stocking caps and pairs of dark sunglasses masked their faces. Their unevenly sunburned faces, greasy hair, and quirky, hermitlike mannerisms indicated they were suffering from a prolonged separation from social norms. Where were the social ones Jack had spoken of? Maybe they were all just tired. Only a minority still looked fresh (as fresh as I imagined myself looking), still capable of feeling awe regarding their surroundings. Most looked haggard.

Who were these people and why had they come? Did any of them have histories similar to my own? I would never know. Instead of reciprocal inquisitiveness, I sensed only defensiveness in their return stares—understandable, really. We were here to do our thing; and they, theirs. They didn't know if I could be trusted in a pinch. And honestly, I wasn't sure who of them could negatively impact my chances up here. As for those who could actually improve my chances of success—like Al's friend Barry—the risk to me was different. If I wasn't careful, they might see through my flimsy veneer and recognize my inadequacies.

As there was only so much entertainment value in a self-guided tour of Genet Basin, we soon returned to our private space. What I found back at our compound provided the solution to my recent foul mood. The tent was home and my teammates were my family, the only things that would be truly secure during my time on the mountain. The events of the day, the feeling of emptiness after talking to my wife, and the plethora of glaring stares from our neighbors had left me with a new appreciation for familiarity, something that could now be provided only by my teammates.

To hell with all those other climbers out there. Whatever my fate was to be, I would face it with my teammates and only them. Those climbing ropes that tethered us together during the day had also bound us together in less tangible ways. We were a microcosm, a tiny world within a world—nine men among hundreds, on one mountain in one terribly vast wilderness. The massive block of granite and ice we were engaging could sometimes be generous and at other times violent. The fact that I was doing so with eight people I now considered my friends gave the expedition a nobler purpose. I felt pleasure in knowing that we had become a cohesive group. We had come to trust each other. We *had* to trust each other. Together, I knew that we would succeed in conquering this magnificent mountain.

Strangely enough, I had even begun to like the way Rick's socks smelled.

The evening meal provided another much-needed lift to my mood. Earlier in the afternoon, when I was down in the dumps, I was willing to bet money that dinner would consist of everyone's least favorite entrée: ramen. By this time in the expedition, I considered us to be a band of Israelites from a lost tribe. We were wandering endlessly in a frozen wilderness, and ramen was our equivalent of manna. Like in the original story, we bitched about it constantly. The difference was that our frustration was directed at Joe Horiskey, not Moses.

But Jack surprised me: dinner was Dinty Moore stew. At home one of the little bowls would barely raise an eyebrow, an after-school snack that could be quickly heated up in the microwave. In the Arctic backcountry, the stew was a culinary masterpiece, but preparing it represented a significant challenge.

To cook them, Mike piled the sealed plastic bowls into his biggest pot filled with boiling water. It took him thirty minutes to boil the water and another thirty minutes to thaw out the bowls, but it took the nine of us only seconds to devour their piping-hot contents—savory bites of tender meat and chunks of potatoes and carrots. Like a starving pack of wild dogs, we licked every drop of gravy from the sides and bottoms of the bowls.

I went to sleep contented.

LOSING IT

—

Before the twelfth day even began, I knew that it was going to be difficult. Each of the previous eleven had been challenging in its own way, but this one would take us into the thin air of seventeen thousand feet for the first time.

The air at fourteen thousand feet was quite cold, but it was clear enough for Jack to recommend a carry to Camp Five. His plan had us returning to Genet Basin to wait for a long stretch of good weather. When that time came, we would move up for good. So it was with heavy packs and high spirits that we roped up and headed out for the north side of "town."

The West Buttress headwall that we were about to engage was the most practical way to gain access to the upper mountain from the basin, but as I've said, nothing about it was easy. In fact, what we were about to do represented the crux of the entire Washburn route. On its upper portion, where the pitch was as great as fifty-five degrees, several hundred feet of fixed rope were anchored. It marked the biggest technical challenge we would face on the entire south side.

At the back of the basin, the incline began. Its lowest portion was straightforward. The base of the headwall rose easily enough for the first couple of hundred feet. The next thousand were no worse than Motorcycle Hill, only longer.

Although still straightforward, the steepening incline of this middle section required that I significantly alter my walking pattern to advance up. Instead of pointing my toes straight ahead, I tilted them out at forty-five-degree angles. This simple adjustment took much of the pressure off of my heel cords and calf muscles. Pointing both toes in the same direction for a while and then switching to the opposite direction also helped. These two techniques were termed the "duck step" and "French pointing," respectively. Their downside was that they were less efficient in terms of distance traveled for each given stride. Even so, it was hard work. After an hour of waddling and zigzagging, my calves were protesting loudly—and this was still the *easy* part, a gentle thirty-degree slope. At least the snowfield we were moving on was safe and relatively crevasse-free.

When we took a break at the end of the first hour, Jack pulled us together in tight formation to assess the group's condition. Most of us were doing well. Armando was noticeably less jubilant than normal, although he too reported feeling fine.

"I'm just a little tired," he said.

Looking back to where we had started, I saw several trails, each originating from various compounds in Camp Four, all converging to form a solitary path. All the climbers on the headwall now followed that single line up toward the bottom of the fixed ropes.

As we continued our move up, the tent city grew ever smaller. Now *we* were some of those tiny black specks creeping up the headwall. When I had watched climbers from down at Camp

Four, it reminded me of the minute hand on a very large tower clock. You could tell that there was movement but only barely so.

After another two full hours of climbing, we reached the bergschrund at the bottom of the fixed ropes. A bergschrund is the place where a glacier begins, where its end abuts the rock of the mountainside. The persistent downward force from the glacier's mass causes the ice to pull away from the rock wall, creating a horizontal crevasse.

Mike and his rope team were the first to arrive at the 'schrund. When Keith and I got there on Jack's rope, the six of us gathered on a narrow icy ledge to await Ryan and his crew. We stood against a sheer wall of ice. When other climbers wanted to pass, we pressed our backs firmly into it, giving them just enough room to squeeze by. I looked to my right where several pairs of skis were planted in the snow. Their owners were obviously planning a quick descent to the basin after they returned from High Camp later in the day. Seeing those skis made me briefly think that we were merely standing in line at a ski resort.

My legs had not yet fully recovered from the strain of today's first stages, so they wobbled beneath me as I gingerly peeled off my seventy-five-pound pack. I was desperate to give my spine and hips a breather, if only for a few minutes, but this was hardly the place to lose my balance. A fall would send me tumbling several hundred feet back down the hill.

When Ryan's team arrived ten minutes later, I reversed the process with my pack and moved over toward the fixed rope. The lowest portion was attached to the wall that we had been standing against, on a dozen feet of vertical ice beginning just a step across the broad crack of the bergschrund. It continued up beyond that for several hundred feet, but I couldn't see the rest of it just yet.

"On fine, clear days like this one," Jack had said before we left camp that morning, "bottlenecks tend to form at the entrance points to the ropes. Everyone wants to move out at once. Climbers can wait a long time just to get on the rope. Then, once clipped into it, they're stuck behind the same people for its entire length, and their pace is subject to the speed of the slowest climber. That better not happen to me today. Heaven help the inconsiderate bastard who waits until today to figure out how his ascender works. I tell you right now that I'll have zero tolerance for that kind of bullshit."

Now that I was staring at these two ropes up close (the right one for climbers going up and the left for those who were coming back down), I understood Jack's meaning a little better. They represented a limited resource, one that all of us were forced to share. Everyone's cooperation was necessary to keep things running smoothly.

As it was, today we were fortunate. The mountain was very active, just as Jack had predicted, but he had gotten us to the bergschrund at just the right moment. We were spared the inconvenience and inherent dangers of battling a large crowd on the rope.

Jack led my rope and Keith followed him. When it was my turn to climb, I reached across the crack and clipped my ascender onto the rope. With one hand grasping the ascender and the other holding the shaft of my ice ax, I kicked the front points of my crampon into the ice and stepped onto the headwall. My crampons supported all of my weight when I advanced my hand positions. Then, while my hands steadied me, I moved my feet up one at a time. After the short vertical section, I could better appreciate what lay in store for us up ahead. We had a long way to go.

The climbing ritual itself was a simple, repetitive loop. First, I advanced my ascender to arm's length. Then, with a sharp swing of the ax, I thrust its pick side into the wall, just opposite the fixed rope from the ascender. My feet then followed, one after the other, until I was back in a slightly crouched, neutral position.

I climbed slowly and rhythmically, breaking the long wall down into short, manageable sections, partly for psychological reasons and partly to ration the immense energy required. The air was thin and the work hard. I averaged one upward movement for every three breaths. Excepting the guides, Al was the only one of us who had previous experience on fixed lines. Jack, knowing this, had held two practice sessions, first in the hangar back in Talkeetna and then again during yesterday's rest day. Although I was still hitting the rope as a greenhorn, the sessions allowed me to establish the necessary skills. Now that I was working on the real thing, my confidence was building quickly. This was part of the adventure I came here for. My heart and lungs were racing to keep pace with the level of excitement.

After fifty feet we arrived at the first of many spots where the rope was tied into an anchor (there were a little more than a dozen other fixed points at similar intervals for the next eight hundred feet). Even though the line functioned as a single long rope, it was actually a series of short ropes all tied together. From a safety standpoint, as long as my harness carabiner remained attached to the fixed rope, the next anchor below would stop a fall, meaning I would drop no farther than fifty feet.

When I came to the first anchor, I briefly detached my ascender from the rope and then reattached it above the knot. After two more steps up, I did the same with the carabiner that fixed my harness to the rope. During these transitions, my exposure to a fall was greatest. However, as an extra safety measure, Jack, Keith, and I stayed connected to each other by way of our climbing rope. If one of us fell while detached from the fixed rope, the other two would still, theoretically, be in a position to arrest his fall. This also meant that the three of us always had to move at the exact same pace. At the end of the rope, I was subject to frequent delays while the pair above me clipped themselves in and out of the rope. I took advantage of these minibreaks to rest my calves, switching my weight back and forth between my feet.

But being on the end, particularly when I passed the anchors, had its disadvantages. At the second anchor, I hadn't yet clipped my harness back into the fixed rope when the climbing rope suddenly went taut as Jack and Keith advanced. The sharp tug momentarily knocked me off balance. I recovered my poise in time, moving three quick steps up the ice until a little slack developed between Keith and me. Only then could I finish reattaching the carabiner. The trick, I deduced by the time I reached the third anchor, was to speed up my pace as I approached the next tie-in. Then I would have all the time I needed.

Down on the ledge, we had gone over a system of calls. "Anchor" meant that all of us on that particular rope should halt. "Climbing" meant that we could proceed again. But in practice it was impossible to hear any of my partners' commands. They were both facing away from me, and Keith was forty-five feet up the rope and Jack was twice that far. I don't think Jack even bothered to use the calls after the first anchor.

Had we been here in the early spring, we would have found a much different headwall, an icy surface that was smooth and unbroken. Now, at least, we could climb in fairly well-formed steps that had been kicked in by this year's teams. When available, the steps allowed for more stable footing and provided a small platform for me to stand on. More of my crampon points were in contact with the wall, and my weight was distributed across a larger surface area. Even so, a smattering of smooth patches—sections of blue ice so dense they resisted all attempts at significant penetration—remained. Those areas were greatly respected, and when on them we were especially glad that we had the fixed rope. When only my toe points were in contact, climbing was far more dangerous and considerably less comfortable. I could only imagine how much more time and energy we would have needed if we'd had to climb the entire way without any steps.

I tried, as much as possible, to avoid relying too heavily on my ascender and using it to pull myself up the rope. Rather, for several reasons I wanted it to be a guide, something that kept my movements aligned. It was much better to use my larger leg muscles to push me up the wall than my weaker arm muscles to pull me up. Also, I wanted to get a feel for what it would have been like to climb this section without aid. Finally, the fixed rope was someone else's. Throughout its life it had most likely been kicked by crampons and swiped at by ice axes. Had the trauma of age and abuse critically weakened it? I wasn't willing to bet my life on it.

An hour and a half after we stepped across the bergschrund, the angle of our ascent began to flatten out. The end was in sight. Only one final anchor remained, with no more fixed rope above it.

Another fifty feet after unclipping from the rope, we reached a small level spot on an otherwise narrow ridge. Looking around, I saw nothing but openness. Everything about this part of the mountain looked significantly more dangerous. It was breathtaking just to be standing there, both because of the sheer beauty and because of the sudden rattling of my nerves from the severe exposure.

We were at sixteen thousand feet. The ridge ran the full length of the buttress, ahead of us angling up toward High Camp 1,200 feet above us, and behind us terminating at the face Ryan had found so fascinating on our first trip around Windy Corner five days ago. Down to the right, advanced base camp looked quite tiny. The Edge of the World and the debris from yesterday's avalanche were clearly identifiable landmarks around the basin's perimeter. To our left, 1,500 feet straight down the other side of the ridge, we got our first good look at the pristine surface of the Peters Glacier. The glacier's origin pressed up against the black rocks of the north summit. The Peters exemplified Arctic purity even more than the Kahiltna. It was an untouched river of ice, one that I had nearly defiled with my runaway peanut-butter jar back at Squirrel Point. Farther down, on the side of Kahiltna Pass where the cloud show was being produced, the Peters made a sharp right-angle turn and then ran out the rest of its course beneath the gigantic form of the Wickersham Wall—that severe, eminently recognizable feature of McKinley's north side. The Wickersham Wall was McKinley's equivalent of the Everest area's Lhotse-Nuptse massif. They were similar in that they both rose unbroken for two miles above their respective valley floors.

I studied the scene intently, trying to absorb what I saw. No photograph could come close to capturing the scene. The entire Denali ecosystem was visible from up here, from the sterile charcoal-gray shale and white ice of the north summit to the flat green-black expanse of the tundra wilderness far out on the horizon. From the highest glacial basins to the lowest meltwater pools shimmering out on the plain, everything came together in a single geological equation.

Still standing on the small platform, we had nearly finished catching our breath when we met up again with Rick's friends, the German couple. Jack stood nearby talking with an oddly dressed gentleman. He looked better suited for a stroll in the Bavarian Alps than a climb on Denali.

"You know what?" Jack said to our group after the man had moved on. "That guy claimed to be the mayor of Prague. What a bunch of bullshit. Can you believe the nerve of these fucking foreigners? They're such a huge waste of my time."

We all looked at each other, not sure what to say.

Jack also informed us that the area we had been standing on was occasionally used as an intermediate camp, but it seemed to me that there was barely enough room for a pair of tents. If climbers chose to camp here, they had better hope that no storms were due to strike, and if one did, digging a snow cave would be their only hope of survival.

Our destination for the day was still another mile away. The route promised to be spectacularly beautiful (as I imagined High Camp would be, too). The air was noticeably thinner up here, so even the gentle climb—most welcome after the unbroken steepness of the headwall—made for a breathless experience.

Jack led us along this easy section until we reached a rock outcropping dominated by a huge square block of granite. This feature was large enough to be visible from Camp Four and carried the name Washburns Thumb. A short section of fixed rope led up the moderate rise on the approach to the thumb. The section was not terribly steep or significantly exposed, so I guessed that the rope's main purpose was to provide a convenience for tired climbers.

We made our way to a narrow ledge that circumvented the left side of the thumb. This spot *did* feel exposed. I looked at the rock face on my right. It was smooth and vertical. No handholds. To my immediate left was a precipitous drop down to the Peters Glacier. I moved my right foot onto the ledge. As I brought my left foot forward, the back side of my pack (where I had attached an empty sled—one of the three that we were going to use on the traverse) snagged on the edge of the rock, threatening to knock me off balance. I spun my torso around the corner and pressed my chest against the rock. At the same time, I moved both feet into secure positions on the ledge. My pulse raced even higher in a brief moment of panic.

"Fucking pack!" I whispered, hoping no one had seen my clumsiness.

After the ledge, the ridge broadened. More snow, less rock. The path undulated slightly but was easy, allowing me to climb unhampered by concern until we reached a second obstacle. Large, jagged boulders broke up the smooth snow of the ridgecap. To get through, we had to drop down onto a shadowy, icy trail on the Peters Glacier side. The path was so narrow that we were forced to travel in single file. As we made our way on the trail, a group of French climbers with funny wool caps and industrial-style dark goggles came marching down from High Camp at a blistering pace. Protocol, as well as common sense, dictated that they (the descending group) should wait at the top of the narrows for us (the ascending group) to safely pass. But they had other plans. They barreled straight through our line, not even bothering to pause their conversation.

Jack was furious. "Jesus, did you see those guys?" But his anger had little to do with their odd looks or concern for his own team's safety. "Those fucking *Frenchies* are fucking with *me* on *my* fucking *mountain!*" We all stood there wide-eyed, more so due to Jack's latest tirade than from the other team's inappropriate actions.

As the trail rose out of the shadows, I noted that the knifelike ridge was broadening into a plain. Whereas I had been overjoyed at the first sight of tents on our approach to the first four camps, what I saw here repulsed and disappointed me. The plain was nearly featureless, a barren Arctic wasteland. In its center stood some dilapidated snow walls and piles of exposed frozen excrement. A constant wind blew away any fresh snow that might have tried to hide the filth.

But by this point, we were so exhausted that we would have been happy to drop our packs, grab our shovels, and bury our cache right here in the middle of this shit hole. Fortunately, Jack did not stop. For twenty more minutes we marched up to a much more aesthetically pleasing location. The larger number of tents suggested this was the principal camp. It was far superior to the first spot, but still much less inviting than Camp Four.

To think Jack and his band had the misfortune of spending a week up here during a raging tempest—that experience would have been enough to test anyone's nerve. I wondered which direction the storm hit them from. It was hard to imagine how a storm from the south wouldn't have devastated their camp. Worse still, winds from a storm from the north would have intensified as they traveled through the narrows of Denali Pass a thousand feet above and hammered their tents mercilessly. Either way, they'd have had nothing but a few anchoring threads of nylon to keep them and their tents from being blown clear off of the ridge, all the way down to Genet Basin.

Even if the weather conditions were favorable during our time up here, and clearly that wasn't very often, the place was wholly uninviting. Unlike at the lower camps, no soft, fluffy snow cushioned the ground. Every surface that our crampons touched was scoured and hard. I imagined the difficulties we would have in setting up Camp Five once we returned. The thin air made any work harder. Hell, even standing still was difficult.

Only its position at 17,200 feet made this a desirable place to be. It was the only logical place on the south side to launch a summit attempt from. Only from here could teams reach the top and then return to their tents all in a single day. I understood the mountaineering logic, but that didn't make me look forward any more to our next visit.

Our prudent leader selected a site well away from the center of camp for us to bury the cache. We peeled off our packs and then had to stand still a few minutes to catch our breaths again. My God, the air was thin! Before we had a chance to fully recover, Jack barked out that there was work left to be done. We had to find a way to penetrate the top layer of snow prior to burying the cache. As I stomped on it with my crampon, I noted it had the consistency of concrete. My thoughts migrated to wishing for comfortable things, like my sleeping bag in a warm tent. But comfort was a long time off. We still had two hours' work here and then the not-inconsequential trip back down to fourteen thousand feet.

As I stood there with shovel in hand, pulling in lungfuls of rarified air and trying to extract what oxygen I could from it, I was interested in one thing only: all of us working together to finish our business here so we could start down as quickly as possible. But, as when we had dug out that first submerged kitchen back at Camp Three, Armando found some urgent issue on his pack to deal with. Under less stressful conditions, I would have had the sense to mind my own business.

In a tone heavily laced with sarcasm, I said, "Hey, Armando, instead of standing there pretending to look busy, why don't you come help us bury this load so we can get the hell out of here?"

He just looked at me. And I should have stopped there.

"You know what," I continued, "I think you've been slacking all along. You never pitch in and do your share of the work. We're stuck having to do your work as well as our own."

"Fuck you!" he shouted.

"Wait a minute," I said curtly. "I'm not the one slacking, but yet you're getting pissed at me? What the . . ." I looked around at my teammates, expecting at least one of the seven to add something to support my case. I got only silent stares from them.

Mike Hamill interrupted the painful seconds of silence that followed. "Hey, come on, guys . . ."

Realizing where this was going, I slammed on the brakes and reversed course. "Sorry, guys. I'm not sure what got into me. I'm sorry, Armando."

I'm pretty sure no one believed any of it.

The disruption was over in less than a minute. Privately, though, I went on steaming long after we were back on the trail. I was justified in what I had said, wasn't I? He *hadn't* been doing his share. And yet, no one else seemed to understand. Was it me who was failing to understand something here?

In the meantime, Armando was having his own difficulties with the descent. He had admitted to feeling fatigued early in the day, but his real troubles started shortly after we left High Camp. Only then did his waning confidence and glaring liabilities become obvious. Even on very modest grades on easy parts of the ridge, he was overly cautious. He literally tiptoed down the slopes. When faced with more severe inclines, especially in areas that had dangerous drop-offs, he was struck by paralyzing indecisiveness that repeatedly brought his entire rope team to a standstill. His uncertain steps and perpetual fear of falling led him to develop a dangerously timid posture. His feet went too far ahead of his body. His stride was unsure and unsteady. At times he even resorted to going downhill on all fours, belly up—crabwalk style. Time after time he allowed the rope in front of him to go slack. Time and again Ryan, at the lead, cursed him for stepping on it with his crampons.

Jack initially stopped every few minutes to allow them to catch up, but when what was left of the chief's small store of patience disappeared, he pressed us on ahead. Ryan was left to manage the best he could.

Before we moved out of range, we could hear Ryan's shouts behind us: "Armando! Careful with that rope. You're stepping on it, damn it. You've got to watch where you're going!" The longer it went on, the more frustrated Ryan became. His screams made all of us cringe, but no one was critical. In Ryan's defense, we knew what Armando was doing to that climbing rope. If his crampons broke through the rope's stiff outer casing, they could harm the delicate central fibers within. If damaged enough, that lifeline could fail under stress, perhaps a week from now, just when it was needed most—when one of us tumbled off of a ridgeline or dropped into a hidden crevasse.

The descent on the ropes gave me additional time to dwell on my own imperfect actions and by the time we got down to the bergschrund—into noticeably thicker air—I was kicking myself, wishing that I had never opened my big fat mouth in the first place. Everyone would have enjoyed the day a little bit more, and I wouldn't have come across looking like such a jerk. What had happened to that peaceful, mountain-Zen attitude I had been working on? Why had I let outside pettiness drift in?

Once we were past the bergschrund, my rope team practically flew. Jack pulled Keith; Keith pulled me. Taking full advantage of gravity's positive effects, our empty packs, and the ever-richening air, Jack drove us down the next eight hundred feet.

He then tore through the final section at an even more furious pace. We practically had to jog to keep up. The afternoon sun had softened the top few inches of snow, making for poor footing at any pace. To further complicate matters, the heels of my high-stepping crampons kept snagging on a loose sling of rope dangling from the bottom of my pack. I started feeling additional compassion for Armando as he wasn't the only one struggling on parts of the descent. I lunged forward and fell on my face a first time, and then a second, and then a third. In each instance a firm tug from my mates in front snapped me back to my feet. By the fourth fall, I was beyond humiliated—I was pissed. Quietly, I slung the most unimaginably foul curses back at the sling and forward at our speedy leader.

And then came the coup de grâce. At the bottom of the hill, just a few minutes away from the comforts of camp, I looked down and discovered that one of my crampons was missing. My heart sank. As we carried no spares, my options were limited; I either had to retrieve the lost crampon or my climb was over. So I did the only thing I could do. I unceremoniously unclipped from the rope and shouted ahead to Jack that I was going back up to find it.

I had no idea how far I would need to go, but I was prepared to retrace my steps all the way to the bergschrund if necessary. Before Jack could shake the dumbfounded look off his face and come up with some sort of scathing remark, Mike pulled alongside with his second rope team. He had a huge grin on his face and something dangling from the index finger of his right hand.

"Lose something?" he said, chuckling as he held out my crampon.

A few minutes later, I collapsed on top of my bag inside the warm, oxygen-rich atmosphere of the tent. As I lay there, I was forced to admit once again how fortunate I had been and how great my debt was to my teammates. I knew I had little chance of repaying it.

MINUS ONE

—

Day thirteen. Even though there was no sign of a storm within the protective confines of Genet Basin, word had it that high winds had returned to the upper mountain. Although other teams were up on the headwall this morning, we were staying put. After the physically and—surprisingly—emotionally difficult experience up high yesterday, no one expected or wanted to move up so soon. We weren't disappointed when Jack gave the official word.

"You guys are getting a breather today. That's the good news," Jack said at breakfast. "The bad news is that based on the forecast, there's a strong possibility we could spend two to four more days here."

I did the math. Taking into account that we would almost certainly face additional weather delays up high, I calculated that we would be on McKinley for at least seven to ten more days. I let out a deep sigh.

All of us groaned when we heard his report, but in the bigger scheme of things, this pause represented merely another short-term delay. Jack knew this and so did we. Everyone was still optimistic regarding our chances for the summit and traverse. Everyone, that is, except Armando. He was being unusually quiet, and no one had to guess why. I had realized much too late yesterday that he failed to help dig in the cache at seventeen thousand feet because he simply lacked the energy to partici-pate. He was twelve years older than I was and a full twenty-three years older than Keith. My excuse for my short temper was the thin air, but I had no excuse for my cheap name-calling. I hadn't even thought to reason through an explanation for his behavior. It had hardly been my finest hour.

But what kind of liability would Armando represent when we hit the north side? Jack could tolerate a certain degree of hesitancy from Armando here on the populated West Buttress route, but what about the lonely descent of Karstens Ridge? No one broached the subject with Jack. We didn't want to go on record as being further critical of Armando. And certainly no one felt it was his place to tell Jack what to do.

At the same time, I think each of us quietly considered the implications of Armando's remaining with the team. No one would be surprised if Jack sent him home. But we didn't know what it would take for Jack to dismiss him (or any of us, for that matter). There were multiple levels of responsibility to think of: the responsibilities of RMI, the guides, and Armando himself.

RMI had accepted Armando's money. Neither he nor any of us had been required to do more than pay the $4,500 fee, complete the equivalent of a five-day Rainier expedition course, and submit an application. Didn't the fact that RMI had accepted his application mean that they were responsible for providing him with every reasonable opportunity to complete his climb? The company knew it wasn't getting clients who were professional mountaineers. At best we were intermediate-grade novices with differing skill levels. While the Rainier course had been eye-opening and challenging for me, I didn't consider it to be anything more than an introduction to serious mountaineering. My three RMI guides could not have exposed me to every possible contingency that I might face on an expedition of this magnitude. Nor could they thoroughly evaluate me, to really know if I was capable of tackling something as big as a McKinley traverse. But Ryan had been there on Rainier with Armando. Wouldn't he have noticed Armando's shortcomings or come away from the experience with at least some concerns?

As RMI's representative here on McKinley, Jack had the ultimate responsibility of determining Armando's immediate future. I couldn't remember the exact wording of the waiver we had signed, but the gist was that anyone *could* be removed from the expedition at any time, at the discretion of the leader. Still, how was that to be decided exactly? Also, I wondered what would happen if Armando fought a dismissal.

Breakfast was over and Jack hadn't yet made an announcement, nor had he asked the junior guides or any of the rest of us clients for input. Back in the tent, Al, Rick, and I could only guess how things would turn out. The one thing we did know was that continued speculation and rumor were not healthy for the team, so we were relieved when Jack summoned us back to the kitchen tent for a group meeting less than an hour later.

It was Armando, rather than Jack, who stepped forward and requested our attention. "Guys, what I have to say is difficult for me. I have thought long and hard, staying up through much of the night." He paused briefly. "I'm sorry. I really wanted to see this thing through to the end, but I think it's best for everyone if I leave the team."

He was an absolute gentleman. He never said or implied that Jack had asked him to quit. I don't recall that he even mentioned Jack's name during his remarks. The chief just sat there quietly and watched as Armando spoke.

"What I tried to do, what we have all been trying to do . . . it's an incredibly hard thing," said Armando. "In the end, I'm forced to admit that it's not in my power to complete it. You guys will have to finish this mountain for me."

He then turned to his favorite guide. "Ryan, you know how I feel about you. I wouldn't be here now if it weren't for you. You have been my guardian angel."

But as it turned out, even this young giant of a guide wasn't capable of carrying one of us up and down McKinley on his back.

By impeccably handling a difficult situation, Armando gained a huge measure of my respect that day. He admirably maintained his composure throughout his presentation. His voice never once quavered, and he always held his head high as he addressed us.

After Armando was finished, Bruce asked, "What are your plans?"

"I'm thinking about heading south, down to the Kenai Peninsula, to do some fishing before returning home. Might as well, since I'm up here."

"I'll take care of your equipment that you cached yesterday up at seventeen thousand feet," Bruce promised. "I'll ship the items to you once we get out."

"Thanks, Bruce," he said. And with that, he wished all of us luck and then headed up the steps to pack up his belongings.

On his way out, I asked for a word. "Armando, I'm sorry for what I said up there. I wish I had those words back."

"Don't worry about it," he answered. "Good luck to you. Good luck to all of you." We shook hands and wished each other well. I was relieved that we had taken a minute to bury the hatchet and say goodbye as friends.

▬

Although blowing clouds indicated that the weather up high was less than ideal, the calm conditions here at fourteen thousand feet and below permitted Armando a safe retreat. Once his pack was loaded, he tied himself into the rope between the towering bookends of Ryan Sorsdahl and Mike Hamill. The remaining six of us watched silently as they headed out in the direction of Windy Corner. Ten minutes later, their three figures vanished behind the mounds on the western edge of the basin, and we saw Armando no more.

Mike and Ryan would take Armando all the way down to base camp. It wouldn't have been safe for just one of them to travel back up alone because of the crevasse risk. The only other option would have been to make Ryan's or Mike's trip one-way—precisely how Ryan had lost the summit the year before.

Once there, they would radio for a plane to pick him up (at Armando's extra expense). Then the two guides would hustle back up to fourteen thousand feet in hopes that the eight of us could move to High Camp the following day. For the junior guides, this represented a round-trip of twenty-four miles and fourteen thousand total vertical feet, all in a span of twenty-four hours. Whatever RMI was paying them, it clearly wasn't enough.

As for Jack and the rest of us, we would stay put at advanced base camp until the others returned. The chief, of course, would be a bit out of his element without Ryan and Mike to jaw around with. We five remaining clients would fill in as his audience, expected to endure his nonstop mountain litany. Jack would assume the duties of camp cook, with us as assistants, of course.

When the high clouds cleared away that afternoon, I took full advantage of the opportunity to savor some more spectacular views. From this lower perspective, I reviewed the features we passed on the trail yesterday. Two thousand feet above, I spotted a tiny chip of granite that I could now identify by name as Washburns Thumb. Camp Five itself remained hidden behind the edge of the ridge, where it joined with the south face. I could far better appreciate the details of that face from down here than from up high. But by combining the two perspectives, I was better able to piece together this portion of the mountain's anatomy.

Yesterday's exciting vertical mountaineering experience made me anxious to exchange the monotony of the two-week-long glacier approach for the "real climb" with its more variable features: an exciting world of steeply pitched ice, wind-scoured snow, and crampon-grating rock.

We had glimpsed something else at High Camp, the next formidable obstacle: the thousand-foot path along a long icy slope that led up to Denali Pass. I had read that more falls were recorded on that section of the mountain than anywhere else, and that was only the *beginning* of summit day! But the traverse portion of the expedition continued to intrigue me more than even summit day itself. Yesterday while on the ridge, I had my first taste of that highly anticipated sense of isolation, and it whet my appetite for the north side.

My thoughts turned back to the present. Activity was clearly increasing in our part of camp. The conditions had improved up high and several teams had completed their descents from High Camp. They were now milling around Genet Basin. Some climbers weren't just finishing a carry; they were finished, period. They were heading down either because they had successfully summited or because they were simply ready to go home. But before they descended farther, they wanted to unload as much dead weight from their packs as possible. Throughout the afternoon we watched this pack of domestic climbers and their more intriguing European counterparts go door-to-door with their food bags open. When they hit our doorstep, it felt like Christmastime, or at least a reversed version of Halloween.

From the English we took custody of two enormous blocks of cheese, each easily weighing four pounds. The Scots gave us hard candies and shortbread biscuits. Even Jack's nemesis, team France, paid us a visit (I wish I had thought to ask them whether they'd summited).

"If this is their discards," I said to Rick as I rummaged through their goodie bags, "then I would have liked to see the good stuff!

Just look at this: sardines in mustard sauce and fruity granola bars, chamomile tea, and little tubes of Nescafé!" The last two items excited me most. We had long since run out of coffee and hot chocolate, and I was sick to death of our seemingly inexhaustible supply of cider and raspberry tea.

The cold smorgasbord we set up for lunch was a welcome change from the usual fare. But dinner that night took us straight back to reality: the entrée du jour was ramen à la Jack. In two decades of climbing mountains, Jack undoubtedly had produced hundreds of similar camp meals, and at this stage in his career, he was clearly not interested in preparing anything more than the basics. His ultrabland cooking style gave me one more reason to anticipate our junior guides' return from their unexpected detour.

Before it turned cold for the night, I sketched what I had studied earlier in the day. I began with the far left-hand side of the headwall, drawing the inverse view of what I had seen from that first break yesterday, noting again the crow's foot of multiple footpaths coalescing into a single path that eventually led to a pair of barely discernible parallel threads. The ropes began just above a horizontal shadow, the detail that I now knew was the bergschrund. Again I recognized that we had taken the easiest path to the top. To the right and extending over to the prominence of the West Rib, the buttress's slope was noticeably more severe. Scattered rock outcroppings interrupted what was an otherwise-seamless wall of white. Here and there were linear tracks formed by tumbling boulders that had broken free of their icy moorings. No doubt they had careened violently down the slope before eventually coming to rest in the soft powder at the back of the basin.

I identified several of the other named routes on the buttress, none of which showed any evidence of recent use. The reason was clear even to my novice eyes. They all appeared damned difficult. The next potential route to the right is Rescue Gully, a steep, icy slide used in emergencies to expedite the lowering of incapacitated climbers from High Camp. Farther over to the east is Messner Couloir, a mile-long, forty- to fifty-degree slope that bypasses High Camp altogether, rising directly to the top of the south face to a point very near the summit. Finally, there is the long, technically demanding route of the West Rib itself. It begins on the lower Kahiltna Glacier and continues uninterrupted for two vertical miles.

Just short of the rib, one final route descends through a dangerously icy couloir. It has been given the crass nickname of Orient Express. A number of climbers, including a disproportionate number of Asian climbers, have fallen all the way down the south face to their deaths while trying to use this shortcut.

When I finished the sketch, I packed my pencils away deep inside the pack. The upper mountain was hardly the place to be doing plein air drawings, I thought.

I spent the last warm minutes of the afternoon reflecting. Like on that transcending sunny afternoon when I looked out from Cathedral Rocks high up on Rainier, my high current level of contentment was, in great part, related to the severity of the effort it had taken to get here. Except for the highly emotional times during the long storm and the brief phone call with my wife, I considered that effort to be worthwhile. We had successfully established all but one of the camps on the south side and made a first carry to the fifth. I had experienced remarkable things: the fog show at Kahiltna Pass, those exhilarating hours on the headwall ropes, and the majestic beauty of the upper mountain. I saw no reason to be pessimistic about the rest of the climb.

I had successfully done everything required of me except the actual climb to the summit. All that would remain after that was the simple matter of the walk out.

I thought about Armando. Remembering my behavior from yesterday made my chest tighten again. I had revealed a dark side of myself to the group. But it had taught me two valuable lessons. First, obviously, was to keep my big mouth shut. Equally important was the need to always appear strong, to never show any signs of weakness. Armando had, and now he was gone.

I took a satisfying deep breath. What I had seen and experienced already on this adventure was enough to provide me with memories to last a lifetime.

But the truth was, I hadn't really seen anything yet. In four days' time, I would start discovering just how terrifying a place this mountain could be. And the weaknesses I would eventually expose about myself would be ten times greater than anything I'd let slip out so far, beyond anything I'd dreamed to be possible—truths about myself that only the dark side of Denali could bring out.

GETTING INTO POSITION

—

SUNDAY, JUNE 1

Perhaps it was the altitude, but I responded apathetically when Jack summoned us out of our cozy tents to do some rope training on what was otherwise a perfectly lazy Sunday afternoon. I had been thinking of my youngest son, Calvin, who was two-and-a-half years old. During my trip in Nepal, he had taken his first steps. I wondered what he was learning to do this time around. When I got home, Angie and I were going to buy a set of bunk beds for him and his brother Will. The two boys were already close. When I left, Will had been teaching Calvin his favorite war game and how to use his particular brand of bow—a clothes hanger. My daydream had them rampaging around the house shooting pretend arrows at goblins and each other.

But Jack was interfering. I wished he would go away, but he refused to leave. He reminded me of myself when I woke the kids up for school. He had no intention of leaving that spot until he saw that we were actually out of bed. He told us to dress and get outside. So much for my pleasant fantasy.

"Mike and Ryan should be back by now, but they still haven't returned," said the crouching figure outside the tent. "We need something to do while we wait for them," he added.

"OK, OK, Jack. We'll be right out," the three of us mumbled.

I thought it was unreasonable for Jack to expect them to be back this soon. They had left less than twenty-four hours ago and had twenty-four miles to cover on their journey. They also had to arrange that rendezvous with Hudson Air Service once they got down to base camp.

Jack understood that his two junior guides were capable of taking care of themselves. Safety wasn't his concern. His tone implied that he thought they were loafing. He was worried that this current window of opportunity for getting up to High Camp was going to close while we sat here waiting for them. His agitation had everything to do with having to entrust them with our fate.

As I prepared to crawl out of the warm tent, I went through some calculations. I assumed that it would take the three of them (assuming good weather) two hours to descend to Camp Three at eleven thousand feet and another four to six to complete the descent to Kahiltna base camp. Once there, they would have to arrange for a plane to fly in from Talkeetna. Even if conditions were clear and a pilot and plane were readily available, it still would take several hours to make it all happen. Mike and Ryan would then want to rest for a few hours before embarking on the return journey, so would likely not set out again until early this morning. The uphill return would be a slower ordeal taking a minimum of eight to twelve hours to complete. If they pushed themselves too hard, they would hardly be in shape to move up to High Camp tomorrow, as Jack had planned. I didn't think it was reasonable to expect them back before later tonight.

Jack must have reached the same conclusion, because he soon stopped fretting about them and shifted his full attention to the things he could control—namely, us. At least he could make sure *we* stayed sharp while we waited. So back on went the boots, crampons, and Gore-Tex as we prepared for a trek out to the Edge of the World.

On an exceptional day, one without the cloud layer that perpetually hangs around at twelve thousand feet, standing on the edge would be a dizzying ordeal. This day, unfortunately, was more typical. The only sight we saw, once we arrived an hour later, was what we had already seen from camp: the tops of the clouds.

Jack wanted to head straight back, but Al added a line to the agenda. Spotting a four-foot-tall boulder on the absolute edge of the precipice, he said, "Wouldn't it be great to get a picture of each of us standing on top of that rock? Put *that* on your Christmas card next year."

Not wanting to disappoint Al, each of us agreed to take turns posing for the camera. First Al, then Keith and then Bruce each calmly hopped up on the perch while Jack snapped their photos. My clumsy ascent of the rock—crampons grappling for traction on the uneven granite surface with nothing but a mile of air below them—and my quivering posture suggested I was a terrified elderly man grasping for a handrail that wasn't there.

After surviving the scary photo shoot, I stared out toward the serene forms of Foraker and Hunter, near the area where we had landed on the southeast fork of the Kahiltna two weeks ago.

Jack gave us a news update. "I heard on the radio that a small plane crashed into Mount Hunter last week, just a few days after our arrival. The pilot and all three passengers were killed."

The news made me recall how harrowing our flight through the approach pass had been. From the moment Randy turned us into the pass until we landed on the Kahiltna a quarter of an hour later, I had thought mostly about how small the margin for error was. But while this news was tragic, it had taken place outside the realm of our little universe and had no direct bearing on our expedition. No one seemed upset by the news or dwelled on it for long.

Later, when I had more time, I thought about how dismissive I had been about those deaths. It was more of the same sort of crassness that I had displayed when Mike and I discussed the violent storm on Cho Oyu. Was this becoming a pattern?

In this case, I had flown past the very spot where those four people died. We had admired the same scenery that they had, flying in low over the Kahiltna Glacier. We lived to tell the story, and they hadn't.

If I had been in a normal state of mind, I might have continued to dwell not only on those four but also on my own mortality—thinking that it could have been me. I would have stewed about all of the other things that could go wrong up here. After all, we had experienced a number of glitches ourselves, beginning with the gas cap incident. To begin asking "what if" would open up all sorts of unhappy possibilities—being thrown off balance by a freakish blast of wind while passing Windy Corner or being knocked off the ledge while navigating Washburns Thumb. A single false step on an exposed ridge could end any of our lives.

But I was not in my normal state of mind. I was in the middle of an extraordinary fantasy. We were traveling through dangerous country. For me to survive, I had to act selfishly and restrict the use of my energy to manage my own affairs. So, as loathsome as it sounds, we had enough problems of our own to consider without dwelling for long on the problems of others.

On the way back to camp, Jack spotted a small team of climbers struggling on a high, difficult section of the West Rib. It was getting late in the day and they appeared to be in a tenuous position, seemingly unable to advance and having nowhere to safely retreat.

"I think those guys are in trouble," Jack said. "I wouldn't be surprised if they call in for a rescue. Didn't they even stop to think about who else they'd be putting at risk if they screwed up? Now what? The rangers are supposed to jump right in and save their asses and maybe get themselves killed?"

The rest of us nodded in agreement. Plain and simple, they had overreached. From our position of relative safety, it was easy to be critical. They had allowed themselves to get in trouble, where an outside force had to intervene—indeed, the climbers did call in for a helicopter rescue the next morning. We weren't perfect, but at least we had been self-reliant. I remember thinking, *The nerve of those guys*. More on that later.

Once back in the tent, having seen all there was to see on the lower mountain and frankly a bit tired of all the time I had for contemplation, I was anxious for the next carry—to return to the world of simple laboring. The fixed ropes and everything else beyond awaited us.

As we turned in for the night, there was still no sign of Mike and Ryan. Patience was indeed a hard lesson on McKinley. What plans would unfold in the morning and what direction they would take us depended entirely on them—and, of course, the weather.

MONDAY, JUNE 2

"Monday morning, you sure look fine." I couldn't get the words of the Fleetwood Mac song out of my head. Monday was glorious indeed! I peered outside the tent and heard the call of another clear bluebird day.

At some point during the long twilight, Mike and Ryan had returned home. We had awakened to overhear the sounds of them talking in their tent, describing the details of their foray to Jack, but we couldn't hear well enough to know what had actually transpired.

An hour before breakfast, Mike resumed his duties in the kitchen. The hissing of the stoves and the clanking of pots woke me up, so I got dressed and went out to see him. One look at his face told me the past thirty-six hours had been physically wearing. Mike's expression was similar to the one he had had the first night, back in Talkeetna. What had Jack done now, I wondered? I liked Mike a great deal, but I often struggled to find the right things to say to him. Our conversations usually ended with me wishing I had said more. This morning was no different. I came close to asking Mike what he thought Jack's problem was and why he didn't say something to him, but I didn't.

My relationships with the guides and my fellow climbers reminded me of relationships during my residency years with the senior surgeons and other residents. Protocol demanded that interactions with the senior surgeons remain brief and formal. I was careful to keep my thoughts to myself, especially early in my training. I understood that saying too much risked them discovering just how little I really knew. At the same time, I felt completely comfortable saying absolutely anything to my fellow residents in training. Such was the case when I talked to Rick in our tent. We were just a couple of normal guys, freely willing to admit to each other that we were just barely able to do this sort of thing without getting ourselves killed. With the guides, it wasn't that easy.

At breakfast we learned the details of Mike and Ryan's trip. They had gotten Armando back down to base camp in good time, but then yesterday a storm dumped a foot of fresh powder on the trail (our tents received only a heavy dusting), making for slower-than-expected progress on the return trip.

After breakfast, Jack announced his plans for the day. Our two seemingly invincible mountain warriors were no doubt hoping for a rest day to get caught up. Unfortunately for them, that wasn't to be. However, in a conciliatory move, Jack set the morning pace even more leisurely than usual. Methodically, we made preparations to get under way. To dismantle the kitchen, we first removed the tepeelike tent covering and then, to prevent future climbers from accidentally stumbling into the hole that we had worked so hard to excavate, we filled it back in again. The individual snow blocks had, over the past five days, fused into a single unit. Still, it took only a few hard kicks to bring the whole thing tumbling down. We took the tents down and divided the group gear, but this time into only eight piles, not nine. Our packs were heavier than ever.

The morning's slower pace continued once we were out on the trail. Jack's mood was both exuberant and apprehensive—he was happy to be back on the road again, but he was also the only one of us who had any personal experience on the mountain beyond High Camp. Did he know something we didn't?

The work was at least as hard as I remembered from the first carry. After we had climbed for an hour, the tent city began to fade into insignificance. For my part, I looked anxiously ahead, wanting to hit the ropes one final time. My back felt fine. And my legs, thanks to the extra day of rest, had rediscovered their strength.

But only halfway up to the bergschrund, I saw—out of the corner of my eye—something terrible happening. One of the strongest men I had ever met was on his knees, grimacing in pain.

Ryan was screaming. "Damned leg! Son of a bitch!"

Our stupefied leader crept over for a closer look.

"I was going along just fine when I felt a sudden pain in my right hip, like something popped," Ryan explained to Jack. Ryan tossed off his pack and lay down on his back, writhing in pain. He drew his right knee up to his chest. His face was contorted.

The rest of us gathered in. "What do you think, Doc?" Jack asked, turning his attention to me.

I put my pack down in the snow and bent down to ask Ryan some questions and poke around on his hip.

I turned back to Jack. "I'm not an orthopedic surgeon, but here's what I can tell you. It's pretty obvious that the problem isn't a fracture or a dislocation. That leaves a muscle strain or some sort of acute tendonitis as the most likely diagnosis."

I didn't add my opinion on what could have caused the injury, but I was certain that the junior guides' two-day marathon journey had played a role. As was the case with my back strain, Ryan's injury itself didn't appear to be very serious, but there was no way of telling how long it would take him to fully recover.

"It's your call, Doc," Jack said.

"It's a no-brainer. Ryan isn't going anywhere but down."

What that meant for the rest of us, I was less sure. Our leader spent another thirty minutes ruminating. We knew his options were limited. In the meantime, I periodically reevaluated Ryan's condition. His pain had diminished enough that he could stand and put partial weight on the leg, but when he took a few trial steps, it was clear that he couldn't walk without a significant limp and couldn't walk *uphill* at all.

Jack was apparently considering whether we should all return to Camp Four with Ryan and stay there for another day or two until he had recovered. But that was not an attractive option for several reasons. First, we were on the move again. Backtracking would be demoralizing at the very least, and if a long-enough stretch of bad weather moved in, it might even jeopardize the remainder of our climb. Also, Ryan might take several days to fully recover. What if he still couldn't go up after that? But wasn't the only other option—the rest of us going on without him—even more daunting? Not once had I imagined that we might lose one of the guides.

It was only after Ryan assured him that he could get himself down to the medical tent without assistance that Jack realized that his mind was made up, or more accurately, that it was made up for him.

"Ryan is going down to Camp Four alone," he announced without fanfare. "He's finished. We're moving on."

The seven of us got right down to business without further delay. Moving carefully on the thirty-degree slope, we gathered to raid Ryan's pack, scavenging everything of value: food, fuel, stove parts, tent parts, snow pickets, and a shovel. After each of us found room in our already very full packs to stow our portion of his things, we stared at the big man, hardly able to believe it. We were saying goodbye to the guy who was supposed to carry *us* off of the mountain if we got banged up.

Ryan's expression showed little of what was going through his mind. I would think that he was devastated that for the second year in a row he was turning back well short of the summit, but the only thing we saw was more of his no-nonsense stoicism.

A few minutes later, with his crampons strapped to the top of his pack and his weight leaning back on his remaining good leg, he began glissading down the slope. Minutes later he, like Armando only two days earlier, passed beyond a mogul and out of our sight for good.

▄

Now we were suddenly down to a party of seven. As such, we ceased being a three-rope expedition. Jack fashioned a fourth tie-in on his rope so he could lead three climbers while Mike claimed the other two. By default, Mike was now Jack's number one. Bruce's stature was also elevated to guide number two and a half. Rick took up permanent residence behind Jack, riding shotgun. Al's, Bruce's, Keith's, and my positions on the ropes would vary from time to time. Today, Keith and I followed Mike in that order. Al slipped in between Rick and Bruce.

We didn't need to be told that losing a single guide was far more significant than losing any number of clients, but the bottom line was that none of us wanted to quit now. Jack's confidence in us obviously hadn't wavered. As far as I could tell, he and Hamill had only briefly discussed whether we should go forward. I didn't feel uneasy about continuing—if anything, I was relieved that Ryan's loss wasn't the end for us, too.

It remained unsaid that going forward, everything about our routine was to become more structured, with far less variation. We would be forced to sharpen our focus. As for me, I cinched my hip belt a little tighter and made a mental note to be even more careful. I took my next step with the understanding that my responsibility to the group had just grown a bit larger, and that the tolerance for screw ups had gone from very small to infinitesimal.

We didn't make High Camp until eight o'clock. Once there, we dug out the cache and set up our tents beside a short embankment. I had learned to keep my mouth shut and my mind on my work, but Jack had not stopped being Jack. He was not satisfied with the way I was leveling my platform, so he ripped the shovel out of my hands and started whacking furiously at the snow. I bit my lip and just stood there until he finished venting. We were back at 17,200 feet, where each breath contained only 50 percent of the oxygen of one at sea level. If tempers flared again, I wasn't going to be the one wasting my breath arguing.

We excavated only one block down for the kitchen tent. The ground was too hard to easily dig farther, and we weren't planning to be here very long anyway. The latrine was of the most basic design for the same reasons.

No one talked of the summit or the traverse that night. Our concerns were more immediate, centering on staying warm and getting enough oxygen. The temperature had dropped to minus twenty degrees Fahrenheit, and my pulse-oximeter reading was down to 76 percent. I buried myself deep down into my sleeping bag.

The forecast called for at least two more days of clear weather. We assumed that Jack planned for us to make a summit bid during that time, but at the moment I was too tired to care. If we went to the top of McKinley tomorrow, fine. If we didn't, that was fine, too.

SURREALISM AT 20,310 FEET

—

TUESDAY, JUNE 3

When I awoke at eight in the morning, the air entering the tent from the cracks in the doors was cold and crisp, but the tent walls themselves were perfectly still. As I dressed, I peeked outside and looked up. Although it is impossible to actually see the summit from High Camp, the beginning of the route up the icy traverse appeared reassuringly calm. Just then Jack walked up to the tent.

"Summit day, guys! Do you feel up to it?"

Rather than invite a giddy wave of enthusiasm and celebratory rounds of high fives, Jack's announcement effectively switched everyone's mood to sober and businesslike. On McKinley, climbers have the luxury of time on summit day. There is no need for the kind of midnight awakening and predawn start required in the Himalayas. On long Arctic summer days, there is plenty of light for the descent, even if it doesn't begin until late evening.

Everything we did now took on special significance. We took extra care to be well hydrated; then, when we were done drinking, we carefully topped off our water bottles, zipped them into their insulating jackets, and tucked them deep inside of our packs. We pulled out the clean, dry pair of "summit socks" that we had saved for this occasion. Overboots went on over the plastic boots. By the time I'd strapped crampons on, I had spent the better part of an hour just getting my feet ready to go.

When I had finished dressing, I checked everything once more: long underwear bottoms, climbing pants, and Gore-Tex bibs; long underwear shirt, zippered T-shirt, fleece jacket, and Gore-Tex coat; liner gloves and fleece mitts; glacier glasses and stocking cap . . . my oxygen-starved mind went through each body section systematically to be sure it was covered.

For the first time in sixteen days, our packs were light for the move uphill. All we carried in them were ski poles, ice ax, down parka, ski goggles, heavy mitts, camera, food, and water. Rick, Keith, and I each tied a sled to the outsides of our packs to cache at Denali Pass. We would retrieve them before we began the traverse.

If any of us didn't already sense the importance of the moment, Jack's breakfast speech reinforced it. "We're in full battle mode, guys. We are about to go to a dangerous place, not the kind of place where any of us can afford to be either hesitant *or* overconfident. This is what we came here for—the summit of Denali! Have fun today but don't fuck up. It might just get you killed."

Mike added his two cents: "It's going to be a seriously long day, eight to ten hours going up and four more getting back down. Because of that and the thinness of the air, we'll proceed extra slowly in order to conserve our energy."

A glaring sun beat down on the hard, compacted whiteness of the snowfield. Although the day was bright and calm, the air possessed little warmth. At eleven thirty, when we moved out, Bruce's pack thermometer registered ten degrees above zero.

After leaving High Camp, we began climbing a long ramp, traveling across the notorious slope that leads up to Denali Pass. For two hours we followed a narrow indentation in the massive hill. The trail was icy and treacherous looking, and I saw a few exposed areas where I thought one of us could easily fall. But my pack was light and my legs fresh, so I felt no uneasiness when we passed by them.

We didn't stop for our first real break until we reached the top of the traverse. As we were gathering together, Rick suddenly lost control of a package of food that he had been fiddling with. He and Jack exchanged glances, and then the two stood silently as the package tumbled a hundred feet down the slope. I was reminded of my errant peanut-butter jar back at Squirrel Point. But this time Jack did not smile and playfully shake his head.

"What the hell was that, Rick?" he fumed. "If you can't be more careful than that, we're all fucked. Jesus Christ! Go down and get it. As far as I'm concerned, it's not my problem."

Rick took the sudden outburst in stride. The reprimand was certainly more severe than circumstances called for, but he knew enough not to provoke Jack further. "Sorry, Jack," was all he said. It was all Jack expected him to say.

"Hey, let's both go down and get it. No big deal," I said as I came alongside him at the end of Mike's rope. The two of us unclipped, dropped down, and retrieved the bag. With the item safely in hand, we took a moment to survey the landscape, something we had been unjustly ignoring.

"Whoa!" Rick crowed. "Just look at this place."

I had seen pictures of Denali Pass, the saddle between the north and south summits, and instantly recognized the scene. "That north summit looks close enough to reach out and touch," I said.

"Guess Jack has probably changed his mind about us climbing that one, huh? Yeah, oh well." Rick didn't look the least bit disappointed as he answered his own question.

On each of our three passes through this spot (up and down today, and then when we crossed over to the north side), I somehow knew that this was as close as we would get to the north summit. We would never set foot on it. Jack never said another word about his grand idea. We assumed that with the loss of Armando and Ryan, the rest of us needed to stick to the basics. What a shame. It was right there.

"Come on. Let's get back up to the others," I said to Rick when we'd had our fill of the view.

Above Denali Pass, the standard path continued up to the right, putting the north summit at our backs, and followed beside a lip of rock that ran across the top of the south face. I knew what was on the other side of that lip—a sheer fall of two miles back to Camp One. But because the barrier prevented me from seeing that drop, I felt neither exposed nor in danger as we advanced along the trail. In fact, the next two-hour section was remarkably pleasant.

"Welcome to the Football Field," Mike announced at the end of the two hours. The nickname was fitting. We stood on a surprisingly spacious horizontal expanse in the middle of otherwise purely vertical terrain. The broad patch of snow reminded me of the inside of the crater on Mount Rainier. And like that crater, it was the perfect staging area for the assault on the summit itself.

This was our first look at the summit pyramid. The trail to the top had been hidden from our view until now. There was no escaping the fact that going beyond this point *was* going to leave us feeling exposed. At least the air was calm. This would be a terrible place to be in a storm.

Jack said, "Have a seat on your packs and dig out your parkas. Grab some food and start hydrating." We relaxed for a few minutes and caught our breath while Jack went over our final instructions.

"First," he said, "we will ascend the short headwall just in front of us. That will put us onto the summit ridge. Then all we'll need to do is follow that ridge right on up to the summit. We're leaving the packs here. Take your ice axes and your cameras."

At the end of his pep talk, we joined the two dozen colorful spots that were already on the headwall. It took the seven of us one full hour just to climb its five hundred feet due to the painfully slow pace. Even at this crawl, my lungs burned as they struggled to extract enough oxygen out of the lean air. It was barely enough to keep my muscles working. At some unmarked point along that wall, we passed the twenty-thousand-foot barrier.

Once on the ridge proper, I felt even more breathless due to the incredible panoramic views that the perch afforded. We were still roped together and I had to keep moving along, but during one particularly long rest step, I took the time to appreciate this newest perspective of McKinley itself. There was no mistaking its overwhelming preeminence among the peaks of the Alaska Range.

Many of the sensations I had felt over the past sixteen days had reminded me of past experiences: the sharply focused thoughts that sifted through my mind while I ran in marathons, the intense spirituality I felt from the Everest-viewing peaks in Nepal, and the fresh excitement of high-altitude mountaineering adventure as I worked my way up Mount Rainier. But what I felt now was unlike anything I had experienced before. I was in a dream world, feeling as if we had just stepped from the Impressionist gallery in the Art Institute of Chicago—where the idyllic landscapes had pacified my mood—into a chamber showcasing bizarre surrealist paintings. Like a Salvador Dalí canvas, everything around me felt detached from reality. Even my own body seemed an abstraction. When I looked at my fellow climbers, it was as though they were fictional characters in this dream as well.

The evidence all around me suggested that I was in an incredibly dangerous place, but knowing that did nothing to raise my level of concern. My hypoxic daydream kept me spiraling up toward the objective ahead. The rope connecting Jack, Rick, Keith, and me together forced us along a singular path. I felt like a Jimmy Stewart character in a Hitchcock film, a bewildered man working tirelessly to make sense of the clues around him. *Why was I climbing up the side of an iceberg in Alaska?*

But I never lost sight of the feeling of breathlessness. I had to take four or five breaths before taking a step and earn every meter slowly and painfully.

Halfway up the ridge, I saw something familiar. Among the collection of faces and colorful parkas were the telltale yellow-and-black jackets of the German couple. They were ecstatic, having just come down from the summit. Rick shared one final congratulatory moment with them, and then he, along with the rest of us, moved on to capture his own piece of glory.

None of the other peaks of the Alaska Range even came close to approaching the height we were at now. Foraker still appeared large, even from a distance of twelve miles, but its majestic top halted a half mile below us. Even the area around McKinley's north summit seemed small and inconsequential, nothing like how it appeared when Rick and I had looked up at it from Denali Pass. As for the other peaks in the range, they were so much lower that they represented only nameless ripples in the vast, windblown snowfield that ran out at our feet in all directions.

Jack and Mike maneuvered our rope teams so that we stayed well to the left of the heavily corniced summit ridge. The incline was otherwise nondescript, an unbroken slab that went on for what seemed to be a very long time. It was difficult to say how much time had elapsed since we left camp, or even the Football Field. I had stopped checking my watch. Time no longer had any meaning. The sky looked the same as it did when we began. There were no shadows to follow, hardly any landscape features at all—nothing that might have helped break the day down into manageable time segments.

Then, without warning, the incline ended. I was standing on a flat perch with nowhere higher to climb. The sight was incomprehensible to me at first. What did this mean? Was this just the end of another section? I looked over at Jack as if to say, *Where do we go from here?*

After studying the scene for another minute, I came to understand that there could be only one plausible explanation. We were at the top!

We stood at 20,310 feet above sea level—the summit of Mount McKinley. It was 6:15 p.m. on Tuesday, the third of June, the sixteenth day of the expedition. *One final mile, one final smile.*

I needed to continue to breathe deeply even at rest. We wrapped our arms as far as they would go around each other's thick parkas. In my heart I felt something that wasn't exactly joy but was much more than relief. I didn't look at Bruce's thermometer, but it was obviously very cold. I did take a moment to remove my gloves and retrieve the pulse oximeter from around my neck. It showed an oxygen saturation level of 69 percent.

I felt fine.

I shot individual, group, and panoramic photos with my second camera, an inexpensive disposable one, until all the film was used up. One photo of Jack and Mike shows Mike's triumphant smile framed by an icy beard. He is bundled up inside his down parka. A wool stocking cap covers his ears. He holds his ice ax above his head in celebration. Jack stands beside him. Only a ball cap covers the top of his head, and his parka is fully unzipped in front. He appears weirdly unfazed. He's smiling and actually looks pleased.

For all the time we invested in getting to the summit, we spent surprisingly little time on it. After an hour, we were ready to descend. Any profound statements and attachments of deeper meaning to our accomplishment would have to wait. At the end of the hour, I was no longer hungering for breath, and I had full control of my faculties again, but the intense cold penetrating my hands and my chest core told me that I was on the verge of hypothermia.

The descent of the summit ridge and headwall went smoothly. Gravity did most of the work. My odd dreamlike sensations vanished. I no longer saw the summit ridge as anything but the latest obstacle we had overcome. Less than an hour later, we were back at our packs eating a snack and drinking icy water from our bottles. I took only small sips. Camp was still potentially several hours away, and I was anxious that the water last until we were the rest of the way down. It didn't. Even with severe rationing, it ran out long before we reached the tents.

The downward going continued to be easy until we reached the icy traverse. By now we had been on the trail for more than nine hours, and if ever the time was ripe for an accident, it was now. The guides continued to move us along at an ambitious pace. I didn't complain. My tired legs were anxious for the final mile of the descent to be over. Still, all of us took extra care on this section to lessen the risk of a fall.

We finished retracing our route at nine thirty. We five clients went immediately to our tents and collapsed. Mike went on working. Exactly sixty minutes later, he came to the door asking for our empty bottles and returned a few minutes later with full ones. His room service continued with hot water for soup followed by the last of the containers of Dinty Moore beef stew. God, it tasted good!

The skin of my face was tight from the sun. My feet, still covered in sweat-soaked summit socks, were struggling to keep warm at the bottom of my sleeping bag. The tired muscles of my back and legs spasmed intermittently. I tossed and turned, hoping desperately to land in a comfortable position. I tried to sleep, but the air in camp was bitterly cold and filled with the sound of barking coughs. Sleep did come, but slowly.

I had thought that summit night would be an evening worthy of celebration, but I could barely imagine moving from this bag. We had been to the top. Mission one accomplished. Now it was time to get the hell out of here.

THE HARPER GLACIER

—

WEDNESDAY, JUNE 4

Although Jack had told us to sleep in as long as we wanted, by ten o'clock everyone was ready to get up and moving. Our tired legs and backs were only getting stiffer by lying around. The clear weather was holding, presenting an ideal opportunity for us to move out. Had we been going back down the West Buttress route, I could have been looking forward to sitting in a cushioned booth at the Roadhouse, eating a well-deserved lumberjack breakfast, in three days tops.

We took almost as much time and care getting ready this morning as we did on summit day. Almost everything in camp had to find a way into our packs. There would be no more double carries, and we would make very limited use of the sleds from this point forward.

Each of us carefully sorted our gear and pulled out nonessential items. This process did very little to lighten my load, however. I was carrying next to the bare minimum as it was. The small cache that we ended up burying at High Camp, the one that another RMI team would pick up, included four of the seven sleds, several of the duffels, and a small collection of personal gear. As for my contribution, only a couple of minor clothing articles, my sled, and my own duffel went in the hole. Everything else went back in my pack.

Without a sled to handle some of the load my pack weighed an impressive ninety pounds. It was hard enough to lift it onto my shoulders, to say nothing of walking underneath it. Still, I felt content as I gazed up the thousand feet to the crest of Denali Pass. At the top was the beginning of the way out. I don't believe I went so far as to tell Rick how blessed I was feeling, but the sun was shining and the memory of the summit was still fresh in my mind. I certainly felt that life could treat me worse. And I was confident that we would be standing on the tundra in seventy-two hours. The tremendous effort we had invested in getting ourselves and this ton of gear to altitude was now spent; the double carries that took us to progressively higher camps, the lengthy adjustments to progressively thinner air—all that was behind us. The hardest work was history. Gravity would be on our side. Each step down would mean more oxygen and with it a chance to get stronger again.

Both my misjudgment of the timeline and the fact that I was less concerned about the glacier portion of the descent than the long tundra walk clearly demonstrated my lack of understanding of what we were about to do.

What I would also come to understand very quickly was that beginning today, except for the repeat climb up to Denali Pass, our itinerary would be largely unknown. We would move until Jack told us to make camp. Then we would sleep until it was time to get up and do it all again. Then we'd do it again . . . each day until we hit the road. The fact that I had stood on McKinley's summit yesterday meant nothing at this point. Only when I got down off of the mountain would any of this mean anything at all.

Because our packs were sixty pounds heavier today than on summit day, this second climb up to Denali Pass took a full hour longer. To lose my balance on this glassy-smooth path would spell disaster, so I carefully contemplated and executed each of the thousands of steps I took with summit-weary legs, my eyes focused on every detail as I balanced the crushing burden on my back. I spent even less time looking at the scenery than I had on summit day. We completed the entire stretch with only the briefest of stops, just as we had yesterday.

Three hours after leaving camp, we arrived at the crest of the pass. While my lungs worked to catch my muscles up on deferred oxygen demands, my eyes finally caught up with the landscape. But what captured most of my attention today was not the high things up close, but the low things so far out in the distance, beyond the massive glaciers and the foothills beyond, out to the tundra on the horizon. It looked like much more than a two-day journey. The dark, flat land was very, very far away. I recalled some of Ranger Joe's talk. "Immediately after Denali Pass," he had said, "you will start cutting a fresh trail. Yours will be the only human marks in the snow, probably the only ones you will see all the way down to McGonagall Pass." I found myself longing to be out there on the tundra, that much closer to the warm, safe confines of home. For the first time that day, I felt uneasy. It wouldn't be the last.

The path ahead showed no signs of trails or markings whatsoever. We had taken our well-traveled route mostly for granted so far, but now I realized that the tried-and-true path had always given me a sense of structure and confidence. As I looked down on the unbroken expanse of the Harper Glacier, I sensed something entirely foreign—disorder bordering on recklessness. And that disorder was precisely where we were headed.

We dug out the three sleds and piled a few light articles into them. Then Keith, Al, and Bruce lashed the sleds behind them on the ropes.

"Everybody ready? Let's do this!" the chief exclaimed. Jack took the first step onto the virgin powder, and with that, the real adventure began. We had begun the crossing of Denali.

■

Walking on the edge of a knife, balancing a fine line between success and failure, was not unfamiliar territory for me. During the course of any difficult surgical procedure, especially one in which the organs are deranged with cancer or inflammation, normally familiar anatomy can be distorted, even hostile. Tissues will fall to pieces in my hands. I know the general direction I intend the operation to go, but I must work out the exact route to get there. A stable situation can deteriorate very quickly if a large blood vessel encased in disease is unintentionally cut. Blood will well up in the wound. Only seconds remain before massive hemorrhage fills the entire cavity. At that instant, hesitation and panic are my enemies. I buy time by moving my finger quickly to cover the opening in the vessel while suction removes the pool of blood. I slowly pull back my finger until I identify the spout of high pressure and then apply a hemostat and a suture. And then I must press ahead. Once I've begun the operation and started to remove the affected organ, there can be no going back. I must find a way to finish.

So when Jack's boot plunged into soft snow halfway up his calf, I understood something of the nature of the beast we were engaging. We would walk a fine line all the way down, all the way out to the McKinley River, seventeen thousand feet below.

Jack took a second step and then a third. Rick followed Jack, and the rest of us followed Rick. We did not tear down the slope like we had when descending the West Buttress headwall, because there was no speedy way to determine the safest path. Each step our leader took required an evaluation of the local environment followed by a leap of faith as he went forward. As I stepped onto the Harper on Mike's rope, I sensed that whatever remained of my safety net had just been yanked away.

Zigzagging down through the fine powder, we had only the pair of summits as company. I looked up and tried to see the twin tops. The black rock of the north summit to our left peeked in patches through its icy covering. The south summit was, strictly speaking, out of view, but the steep slope that went up to it was covered in a continuous layer of white.

The Harper was home to enormous crevasses, far larger than any we had seen on the south side. To get past the first one, we traveled sideways for a mile, all the way over to the north side of the glacier, before Jack found solid ground to pass on. A narrower crevasse might have had snow bridges to walk across, but I didn't expect one as large as this one to have any.

I thought back to the brief crevasse rescue training we had received on Rainier. Just above Cathedral Rocks at Ingraham Flats, the site of our highest camp, were many broad, deep crevasses, and we spent the better part of a day climbing in and out of one of them. "Ours" measured a good twenty feet across and one hundred feet long. Its sheer crystalline walls plunged another one hundred feet toward an irregular bottom with a random collection of blue ice blocks, arches, and pillars. Beyond that were patches of black emptiness where even sunlight couldn't reach.

Throughout that afternoon, each of us took turns learning what it was like to dangle at the end of a rope. Those left on top learned how to set up a rescue system and then use it to haul up a fallen climber.

When it was my turn to go down in the hole, I double-checked the security of my harness straps and clipped my carabiner into the rope. I then watched anxiously as my teammates disappeared from view above the lip of the crevasse. My first look down nearly caused me to panic. If the rope broke, I would free-fall to an almost certain death.

The rescue process seemed to take forever. My groin ached from the pressure of the harness, first merely uncomfortably, then painfully. After thirty more minutes, both of my legs were numb.

It was perfectly quiet inside the hole. I could hear my own nervous panting and the glass-chandelier sound of ice crystals falling whenever I inadvertently brushed up against the wall. But I could hear nothing of the goings-on up above unless our lead guide, Jeff, leaned over the lip and shouted directly down at me. Not quite a tomb, not quite a prison. It was confining, but I found the sense of freedom and isolation from the world above thrilling. Of course, if I hadn't been completely confident that my teammates would eventually pull me out, I would have felt much differently.

When I did eventually emerge from the hole, my throat was dry from hyperventilating and my voice cracked from the hour-long adrenaline rush. My legs began burning as soon as the pressure of the harness was released. I was smiling, happy that my one-time experience of a "crevasse fall" was over.

—

This side of Denali appeared to receive heavier amounts of snowfall. Some of that freshly fallen snow tended to accumulate along the edges of crevasses, and if the snow was thick enough, the growing edges would eventually meet, creating a bridge.

A snow bridge might be sturdy enough to support a climber's weight, but then again, it might collapse the moment he steps on it. The trick is knowing which of them can be trusted. Choose poorly, and you could suddenly find yourself falling into empty space—not a very desirable thing, since the crevasses on the Harper can be well over one hundred feet deep.

Still, in order to proceed, we had to find a way past the crevasses, and crossing snow bridges was one of only a handful of ways to do that—more new territory for us.

This wild side of Denali was also bitterly cold. On the mountain's south side, we'd enjoyed afternoons baking in the sunlight. On the north side, the mountain was covered in shadows—and in the shadows at eighteen thousand feet, Alaska is a very cold place. Our new, slower pace made the cold seem even more penetrating. Our travel times were significantly longer than what we were accustomed to on the ascent because of routefinding.

After going around the first, thirty-foot-wide crevasse, Jack brought us to a full stop while he surveyed the terrain ahead. Many minutes later he decided to bring us back toward the center of the glacier again, basing his decision on visual readings and a reference to his GPS device, which contained the stored details from his traverse route two years earlier. He referred to it often. An hour later, we still had not found a suitable snow bridge on which to cross over a second, slightly narrower crevasse. We continued across the glacier, all the way back to the south edge. In the end, it took two full hours to circumvent this single crevasse, and during that time we gained less than a quarter mile of ground.

Especially when we were traveling downhill, every movement was slow and methodical, because we were much more likely to find new dangers going downward than sideways. Mike and Keith created footprints in front of me, but I didn't always use their indentations to plant my own feet. Sometimes the spacing was not right or cutting across a corner in the trail seemed easier. But wrong choices had me postholing, that is, plunging a snowshoe-clad leg deeply into uncompacted snow. Although there was nothing alarming or dangerous about postholing, it was an exhausting nuisance.

Mike and Keith passed a harmless-appearing section of snow and stopped to wait for Jack to direct them which way to go next. As I worked to catch up to them, I stepped my right foot into the center one of Keith's footprints. I suddenly felt the ground underneath my snowshoe give way. This was no posthole. I felt nothing at all under my foot when it came to a stop, mid-thigh deep! My heart leaped up into my throat as my leg hung suspended in midair. I held my breath and held very still as I waited to see if the rest of me was going to fall through. But because this was a narrow crevasse, only a little wider than the length of the snowshoe, my left leg remained on solid ground and held the rest of me up. I saw now that I had never been in any danger. Nevertheless, my hands shook as I pulled my wedged-in foot out of the hole.

Only moments later, just as I'd stopped shaking, I looked up to see Al plant his left leg on a patch of absolutely level snow and then plunge as quickly as a hiccup into a slightly larger crevasse than mine, up to his hip. A second rush of adrenaline raced through my chest as I anticipated the worst—seeing Al disappear before my eyes. He pushed down hard with both of his ski poles and pried his leg out of the hole.

Twenty minutes later, it happened again. Keith's leg popped through the surface crust right in front of me. I stopped with a jerk and carefully surveyed the ground before taking my next step. Each of these plunges sent my heart racing and eroded my confidence a little bit more. I was clearly not in control of this operation—and no one else was, either. In every case the ground had appeared solid, and the area around the crevasse had already carried the weight of at least one other climber. In every case the sense of safety was an illusion.

By the end of the next hour, Rick and Jack had also plunged into small crevasses up to their hips. As the plunges became commonplace, we all quickly learned not to trust the ground in front of us—no matter how safe it appeared. The next step could result in a free fall into a much larger crevasse. And since we had tens of thousands of steps yet to go, it began to seem like a crevasse fall was inevitable. The calmness of the morning had evaporated. I stopped being a sightseer and ignored, except at break times, the alpine beauty that surrounded us. Instead, I obsessed about the few feet of snow in front of me, poking at it incessantly with my walking poles, always wondering what lay beneath the surface.

Although menacing to look at, the huge open crevasses, like the two we had spent half the afternoon circumventing, weren't the problem. They were easy enough to avoid. The dangers were in the ones concealed by a continuous snow bridge. The surface covering is strong enough to support its own weight but not the additional weight of a climber and his pack. Not even the faintest hint of a depression had alerted us to the existence of these first five crevasses. When my leg had plunged into one, there had been no time to react by pulling back or jumping forward. I knew that even the fastest reaction time would be too slow to overcome the speed of gravity. Even so, with each step I took, I tried to hold back some of my weight until I was sure there was no hidden defect. Of course, there was no possible way to make myself lighter by stepping lightly, but this was one of the ways I was expressing my growing sense of paranoia.

On any other day, the distance we'd traveled since leaving High Camp would have taken only four or five hours. Today it took twelve. My body was tired. The constant downward pounding caused a substantial impact that reverberated up through my aching legs and into my spine. When I plunged into soft snow or a minor crevasse, it required even more effort to keep going. And I was relying on thigh and calf muscles that still hadn't recovered fully from the previous two days, each of them *big* days.

I breathed a sigh of relief when Jack announced that we were stopping to make camp for the night. The spot was as level and safe looking as we had seen all day, and its location appeared to be within a couple of hours' walk of Browne Tower, the prominent landmark that marked the beginning of Karstens Ridge. After Jack's announcement, Mike extensively probed the area of Camp Six with a long pole to search for hidden crevasses. Only when Mike was satisfied did he allow the tents to go up.

We ate a late dinner and went to sleep at two o'clock in the morning, exhausted.

I had plenty of time to think, catch up on sleep, and relax on the second day after summiting. In the night a new storm struck the upper mountain. With the bad weather came a bit of much-needed recovery time. Thirty-eight hours had passed between our departure from High Camp for the summit and our arrival at Camp Six. We had spent twenty-four of them on the trail, and we had been above seventeen thousand feet for almost that entire time. The few hours that we *had* spent in the tents, on post-summit night, were restless ones. So, oddly, the fresh blizzard with its fifty-mile-per-hour winds was not entirely unwelcome.

Lying in my tent that morning, I started thinking about our guides and my appreciation for them. Even having guides put our group in the minority. In any given year, only a quarter of the climbers on McKinley are led by guides. The other 75 percent go it alone. However, with the possible exception of Al, none of us would have felt comfortable taking on the West Buttress ascent without guides. And even Al admitted he would never have considered doing the traverse without guides. Jack, Mike, and Ryan provided us with essential necessities: experience with routefinding, superior safety in glacier travel, and (in case of a full-fledged crevasse fall) the know-how to accomplish a rescue operation. We had already taken advantage of much of their expertise on a regular basis.

But there were some significant drawbacks to being on a guided expedition. From the minute we got up in the morning until we went to bed at night, we were told when to move and when to stop, where to camp, and what to eat. Often it seemed that these three young men, two of whom were nearly half our age, were trying to be our parents. The more I thought about it, the more the analogy rang true; while we clients each possessed a healthy independent streak, that didn't mean we weren't in need of constant supervision. I'd go so far as to say that we even needed a bit of discipline and nurturing from time to time. But we weren't adolescent boys; we were already middle-aged men, men with other careers who were climbing glaciated mountains only on an infrequent basis. We accepted that we would never possess enough mountaineering experience to function independently on big peaks like Denali.

The RMI trio had nicely met our needs except, perhaps, for the nurturing part. Jack had not turned out to be the type of kindly fellow I had hoped we would have along, the type of fatherly figure I imagined Joe Horiskey would have been. Jack was good at shepherding but didn't give a hoot whether his sheep loved him, or even liked him.

As the commanding officer, Jack was dogmatic and self-assured. He didn't see the need to ask his clients for an opinion. Hell, he rarely even solicited a view from his own staff, at least not publicly. When he did occasionally ask for a junior guide's opinion, he would usually follow up his answer with a pained grimace on his face, looking down at his feet while shaking his head slowly from side to side. Then he would go to great lengths to explain to everyone listening why that would be the absolute *worst* thing to do. After spending almost three weeks with Jack, we'd all come to accept that this is what we could expect from him. We'd learned to live with it.

But for all of the fantastic things that these guides *were*, there were many things that they were *not*. They were certainly not hired porters. And they weren't guarantors of anything, not success and not absolute safety. Yes, they did allow us to do more than we were capable of doing alone, but as was the case with the rangers in Genet Basin, it was crucial that we didn't become overconfident just because they were there.

Guide service websites are loaded with testimonials like "I trustingly put myself in the guide's hands" or "I feel like I could have climbed anything with him." More than just expressing goodwill and confidence, these accolades almost suggest that these climbers' guides possessed superhuman powers, that they were somehow able to ensure that client's success and wellbeing. On Denali, I'd seen no evidence for this sort of omnipotent guide force. In fact, my experience—for example, with Ryan and Armando—led me to accept the opposite: no individual had the capacity to provide a continuous safe haven for another. And when anyone placed inappropriate reliance on another, it encouraged the overreaching of abilities. I thought of the climbing team on the West Rib calling for a rescue. Poorly prepared climbers and teams consumed a disproportionate amount of valuable limited resources while putting others at risk. I very much appreciated everything our guides were doing for us, and I understood the gist of what the testimonials were saying; I just felt that anyone who went to a mountain like Denali had to accept ultimate responsibility for himself.

Taking this self-reliance argument one step further, many serious mountaineers feel it is inappropriate to carry a cell phone or satellite phone on a major expedition. The thinking goes that having the option to use one in case of trouble could, again, encourage irresponsible behavior. This not only increases their risk of harm but the risk of harm to their rescuers as well. Our group carried several cell phones (which mostly didn't work) but not a satellite phone. Jack's official explanation was that it was too expensive. So whether by intention or coincidence, our band complied with this mountaineering code. But there would be times ahead when I would wish we could have called for help.

Jack's shout to Al, Rick, and me from outside the tent interrupted my daydream. "We aren't going anywhere for at least another day," he said.

I waited for him to continue, to follow up with his typical stern set of instructions, or to even ask if everyone inside was all right, but instead I heard only the squeak of his boots as he walked over to deliver an identical message to Keith and Bruce.

Maybe his rapid retreat was meant as a compliment indicating that he knew we had reached a certain level of self-reliance. We didn't need to be told what to do—or be coddled. He made no mention of shoveling snow or building elaborate snow walls. His silence could have been saying that the time had come for us to function more independently. Or possibly he was just being a jerk. At any rate, one of the first independent decisions we made was that the two clients' tents would go as bare as the guides' tent always had.

Shortly after Jack left, tired of doing nothing but listening to the wind batter the tents, the three of us suited up and went outside to shovel. Anytime we stepped outside that day, we dressed in our warmest clothes, including down parkas. With the addition of wind and snow, the Harper was absolutely frigid. Even inside the tent, tucked deeply into my thick down bag, keeping warm was next to impossible.

Later in the afternoon, Al and I discussed the events of the previous twenty-four hours and the unknowns of our going forward.

"Based on what we ran into yesterday, I can't help thinking we're facing a pretty serious situation over here," I said. "And it's only going to get worse the farther down we go. We'll be even more removed from the crowds and the known elements of the south side. If we run into trouble right here, we can get back up to Denali Pass pretty easily, but what about two days from now? Then backtracking might be just as dangerous as going forward. Don't get me wrong, I'm still excited about the trailblazing stuff; hell, it's why I signed up for the traverse in the first place. It's just that I'm afraid we might get backed against a wall, in a situation where we've run out of options."

"Sure, things are tough over here," Al said. "I don't doubt for a minute that they'll get even tougher, but don't worry so much about it, Mike. I've been in stickier situations and made it out all right. I've never been on a mountain as big as this or on an expedition as long as this, but I've always found a way to manage. We'll do the same here."

Al's reassurances made me feel a little better, but it was clear we saw the situation differently. His experience and personality made him better able to take these sorts of unknowns in stride. In fact, all along he had found it easier to accept the less pleasant features of this climb. He knew they were a part of any serious expedition. He chalked up the crevasse risks we'd seen yesterday as just another day on the mountain. Whereas I was seeing these types of hazards for the first time, they had been a regular part of Al's climbing life for as long as he could remember.

"Yeah, I get you," I continued, "but I'm starting to recognize that there are limits to how far I'm willing to go to satisfy my hunger for adventure. I'm not willing to risk getting injured in a bad crevasse fall, for example. And what about the fall risk on Karstens Ridge? There are going to be much more dangerous things down there than what we're seeing now." I didn't say it aloud, but I couldn't help thinking it was easy for him to say that he wasn't overly concerned: he was single and living a carefree life. I had my wife and kids to think of.

I saw that I hadn't convinced him of anything, so I continued. "Look, Al, it's clear we both have this insatiable desire for adventure, but just because I want to do something extraordinary once in a while doesn't change the fact that I have responsibilities waiting for me at home. It's because of my family that I have a very low tolerance for something going terribly wrong. And now I see myself getting in over my head."

Al was becoming equally frustrated. "Look, just relax. Jack has been on this route before. He said it took them only two days to get down to the tundra and then one long push to get out to the road. He's got that very route locked into his GPS, and we're following it. Trust me, we'll be down and looking at wild-flowers before you know it."

While Rick fidgeted and Al and I philosophized, I pulled out some lunch from my food bag: frozen cheese, frozen beef jerky, some stale sesame crackers, and mixed nuts. The menu hadn't improved but at least my appetite seemed to be improving.

That evening I dreamed again about eating pizza, that is, until the blowing racket outside woke me up. I was disappointed when I found myself still on Denali, still in our stinking tent. It was peaceful inside, though. Al and Rick were asleep. I looked down at myself inside my sleeping bag. My body looked so thin. I shook my head as I stared up at those all-to-familiar seam lines on the tent ceiling. I was tired and cold. On the south side, I'd looked forward to the end of the storm days so we could get moving again. Now staying here another day or fighting our way through crevasse fields both sounded like lousy options.

I thought about a morose, tongue-in-cheek comment that we residents liked to say back in training: "All bleeding stops eventually."

Yep, I thought with a bitter smile, *one way or another, this expedition will be finished, too.*

As I drifted back to sleep, I chose to concentrate on what Ranger Joe had said about staying focused and remaining positive. He was right.

Once the storm cleared, we were only about two or three days from the road—or so I thought.

KARSTENS RIDGE

—

FRIDAY, JUNE 6

When I awoke that morning, I felt like the night had been restful. It really wasn't. I had been awakened two or three times an hour. Maybe I was finally accepting that this was the type of night I should expect on Denali: short periods of rest interrupted by wicked winds, wild dreams, hacking coughs, a full bladder, the need to change sleeping positions, and the need to remove snowdrifts from around the base of the tent.

I peeked out the door. The morning was clear and the wind quiet.

Mike had done limited excavation to set up the kitchen tent, as he had at High Camp. He was inside getting the stoves fired up when I finished at the latrine.

"Hey, Mike," I said. "What's for breakfast—French toast or waffles?"

"Yeah, right, you *know* what's for breakfast!"

Our cold cereal, milk, and granola supplies had long since run out but I knew what hadn't—the oatmeal. From what I could tell, it *never would*! And it turns out that instant-oatmeal burnout is a permanent condition. To this day, I can't stand to even smell the stuff.

After a few more of the guys wandered over, he said, "Hey, look at this." His spoon pointed to a blue-lined crack in the snow, in the back of the tent. "I didn't even know this was here. I probed every inch of this snow last night, but when I get up this morning, I find that there's a crevasse *inside* of my kitchen tent!"

When Jack appeared a minute later, he just smiled and shook his head. He was speechless, just like the rest of us—no scathing remarks, no public criticisms of his junior guide. It wasn't the only surprise we got from him this morning. The rest of the guys gathered to see what was going on, toting their cups and bowls.

"Since we've got everybody together, I want to put a question to the group," Jack said as Mike started pouring hot water into the cups.

What? The chief was about to ask us for our opinion? This was a first.

"We need to decide whether to move out this morning or stay put. I'm not sure I like what's going on with the weather. I don't have a lot of data to go on. I haven't been able to get a report on my radio since we left High Camp, and we obviously don't have access to the weather board at the ranger station. On one hand, the wind has died down and it has stopped snowing. But I feel like the air is still pretty unsettled. What do you guys think?"

What we thought was that it was shocking to hear him ask our thoughts after eighteen days of living under a dictatorship. Perhaps, though, we should not have been so surprised. Jack had always been extremely conservative, especially when he was making up his mind to move, even more so if there were questions about the weather. His hesitation now made perfect sense. It was just odd to hear him say it out loud and in the form of a question.

My knee-jerk response was to move, if for no other reason than I wanted to get the hell out of here as soon as possible. I didn't say that exactly, but I nodded my head when others suggested that moving out would be OK with them. Apparently, no one else was interested in prolonging this thing, either.

The morning stayed clear until just before we were ready to rope up. Then, sure enough, we saw that Jack had reason to be concerned after all. A dense fog was creeping up toward us from the lower Harper, exactly in the direction we were headed. It made no difference. Camp was packed up; there was no changing our minds now. At noon we moved out toward Browne Tower and the fog.

Because the Harper Glacier ends at an impassable icefall just a few hundred yards below Camp Six, we had to bypass it by going down the adjacent ridgeline, Karstens Ridge, which starts at Browne Tower. More than four thousand feet below where we now stood at the tower lay our next objective, the Muldrow Glacier.

The descent of Karstens Ridge represented a significant technical challenge. It was totally unlike the high ridgeline we had climbed above the fixed ropes on the south side. Over there, there had been a few tricky spots to pass, like the ledge I struggled on at Washburns Thumb and the icy path where we first met the French team. But for the most part, the path had been broad and moved along mild slopes. Not so over here. Karstens was a sharp-edged monster with harrowingly steep portions inclined up to forty-five degrees.

To understand what the descent of the ridge was like, imagine a staircase that is two-and-a-half times the height of the Sears Tower (now officially the Willis Tower). Incline it so that its minimal angle of descent is about thirty degrees, the typical angle of a flight of stairs, but rather than giving it individual steps, make it a continuous ramp from six inches to ten feet wide. Put the top of that ramp three miles above sea level. Now, fold the ramp down its long axis so that the entire thing is pitched like a roof. Instead of giving these rooflines the gentle pitch of a typical house, have them drop away more steeply, at angles of fifty degrees. And beyond the edges of those roofs, place sheer drop-offs—to the left, two thousand feet to the jumbled blocks of the Harper Icefall; to the right, a falloff of even more staggering proportions, a full mile to the bottom of the desolate east face. Now spray the ramp with water and chill it until it is frozen. On top of that thick layer of ice, pile a variable amount of snow, between three inches and three feet. Remove the handrails. Finally, surround the whole thing with persistently thick fog, throw in a bit of Arctic turbulence, and set it out in the middle of nowhere.

To add to the feeling of unsettledness, the minute we stepped onto the ridge, it began to snow. Fortunately, the air remained calm and there was no evidence that the fierceness of yesterday's storm was returning. Still, the snow further compromised visibility, especially in terms of our line of sight straight ahead.

We moved at a comfortably slow pace, averaging about ten to fifteen strides per minute. You may think that I worried with every movement about tumbling down this steep, slippery incline, but I did not. With each downward step, I plunged calf-deep into the snow, so that both the bite from my crampon's teeth and the heavy mass of powder that accumulated around the front and sides of my boot arrested my forward progress. What's more, my foot stopped in a nearly horizontal position (although the powdery, dry stuff never did form into solid, well-compacted steps). The end result was that I was feeling surprisingly confident in my stride.

Jack signaled a rest break. "There is a section of fixed rope along here somewhere, about five hundred feet's worth," he said as we all happily peeled off our packs. "At least I remember there being one when I came down here two years ago." He had said this at least a dozen times already in our first two hours on Karstens.

As we continued down the ridge, he dug around and eventually found the rope, buried under two feet of snow, but by then we had already descended the greater portion of its length. Had we been going up the ridge, we would have spent more time looking for it because it would have provided an extra measure of security as a handhold. As it was, none of us regretted not finding it sooner, and no one used it for the remaining hundred feet of its length.

Past the end of the fixed rope, the slope didn't show any signs of leveling off. And it was still tough to figure out much about our path beyond our current position. With the heavy fog and thick curtain of falling snow, we couldn't see more than twenty yards ahead of us. We saw nothing down the treacherous east face and very little down the Harper side. Not being able to see the drop-offs wasn't necessarily a bad thing—out of sight, out of mind. But not being able to see far ahead *was* distressing. How far did we have left to go? Would it get more difficult down there or less so? Where exactly was this route taking us? These questions and more circulated through my mind as we descended on little more than a hope and a prayer.

I thought about Al's reassuring words to me during the storm day back at Camp Six. Once again, among all the clients, he was the one who appeared most confident now. The rest of us were moving more tentatively.

Although none of us was doing highly technical chores like placing pitons or ice screws, we were still involved in some pretty serious mountaineering. I wondered why Jack hadn't given us some basic training before bringing us down, just a few tips. How about an encouraging word, even? If one guy took a fall here, an entire rope team might never be heard from again. Sure, the chief's routefinding skills were beyond reproach. I never once worried that he would get us lost or knowingly put us in harm's way. But I continued to need something more from him.

Step after step, we continued down. As I walked, I found it helpful to mentally break the day down into shorter time periods—focusing on only the next quarter of an hour, the next foggy horizon, and then the next, and so on. Completing each time block meant we had covered another one hundred feet . . . or was it two hundred? It was impossible to be sure. Then I started counting steps. First ten, then ten more. That makes ten tens . . . one hundred. After a while it was no longer necessary to check my watch or count steps. I knew instinctively that another section was done. What I understood even better was that we still had a vast distance to cover and that I needed to continue to distract myself from that truth. It was too overwhelming and too distressing to try to guess where the ridge might end or when the next rest break might happen. And as the afternoon crept on, it became clear that neither would arrive anytime soon.

During these fifteen-minute sections, my mind worked— and not totally successfully—to purge all negative ideas and emotions. On the south side, my mantras had nicely supported me. Over here, I kept it even simpler. I told myself that I had chosen to do something this tough because I was a tough person.

Right foot down . . . my crampon glided forward until it met firm resistance. I waited briefly for a feeling of stability, ensuring that the rest of me would remain stable and vertical when I picked the other foot up. Left foot down . . . wait, that foot rotated out a bit more than I wanted; I need to shift the weight of the pack slightly to my right shoulder to compensate . . . There, stabilized again. Now, inwardly rotate that left one. Ready for my right foot again . . .

We had been on the ridge for a very long time, but had it been two hours or four? As the case had been on the summit ridge, in that Salvador Dalí world, time had no real meaning, except that at *some* time this ridge would have to come to an end. I snickered. Yeah, and all bleeding eventually stops, too.

The crest of the ridge grew so narrow and the slope so severe that we could barely stand on it, so Jack dropped us down a few yards to the left. It was a good move. With the improved safety and confidence in my stride came an increased level of appreciation of our surroundings; in between steps I looked up and found that the fog had lifted somewhat and the snowfall had lessened. It was a relief to be able to see the direction our route was taking us.

Four hours after mounting the ridge, I finally began to enjoy the day. Looking around, I could see we were in a magical place, more intoxicatingly beautiful than anything we had experienced on Denali's south side. The minimalist canvas laid out in front of me was striking: the black of the shale, the white of the glacier, and the gray of the mist. The fractures in the icefall created massive hunks of ice, some the size of city blocks. The mist touched my face, the only part of my skin that was exposed. In that moment, there was no place I would have rather been, and *nothing* I would have rather been doing.

The eerily wonderful sensation continued to build until it became so strong that I felt I needed to tell someone about it, someone important. I wanted them to know how vital this place was, how its national status should be elevated further. I started composing a mental letter to the president about this wonderful spot on Karstens Ridge, a place where time stood still, where its unimaginable beauty transcended self. Places like this, I would tell him, represented America's true wealth!

Just then I saw that the easy path we were on had ended. Jack stood facing an impasse—a deep V-shaped notch in the ice that was too wide to jump across. He looked farther down to the left. There was no snow bridge to cross over the crevasse, and the slope down there was too steep anyway. There was no other choice. Like it or not, we had to go back up. We first backtracked a few yards in order to have a better angle to reascend the slope. Then we moved up, following a diagonal path to the narrow crest. We were relieved to find that the V-shaped crevasse stopped just short of the crest itself.

Now back on top, I appreciated all the more why we hadn't been traveling up here. Like on Al's perch at the Edge of the

World, I strongly desired some sort of handhold. The knifelike crest was so narrow that my feet wouldn't fit side by side on it. It was obviously not a place we should be for any longer than absolutely necessary. Too much could happen—a fall, a twisted ankle. But it was the only way. The right side was out of the question: it was a terribly steep slope covered by wind-scoured ice and bare rock for the first twenty feet, and in the mist beyond that there was nothing except, presumably, a sheer drop-off.

We tiptoed along the crest, aiming for a slightly broader section just ahead, only two rope lengths in front of where Jack now stood. Yet at this pace, covering that short distance might take us half an hour.

When I looked down at my feet, I noted that the wind had blown much of the fresh snow away. And the thin layer of powder that remained compacted very poorly around my crampons. But because the incline remained a modest thirty degrees, I didn't feel overly concerned. I thought I'd be fine as long as I paid careful enough attention to my footing.

As I had for the thousand steps that preceded this one, I stepped down with my right foot and shifted my weight to bring my left foot forward. As I lifted the toes of my left foot, I saw that my right crampon had come to rest on a patch of smooth blue ice. The teeth didn't even scratch the diamond-hard surface.

In the next heartbeat my ankle was rotating outward and my foot was rolling to the side.

I was falling.

Landing hard on my stomach, I began sliding sideways down the wind-scoured east face. Two rapid heartbeats later my body rotated ninety degrees so that my feet were now going first. I was picking up speed, sliding down the unknown part of the slope toward the edge of the "roof"—and oblivion.

Instinctively, I drove my ice ax into the snow in an attempt to arrest the slide. No good; I was still accelerating. I rolled on top of the ax, trying to use the weight of the pack to drive the pick in deeper. It bounced off of the hard surface. The slope continued to rush past my face.

I know I have to stop! I have to stop now!

Finally, the ax bit deeper into the ice and the ground moving past my face began moving slower.

I stopped.

But now what? Where am I?

Panting like a frightened dog, I stayed completely still for several seconds. The pick side of my ice ax was dug deeply into the ice, nearly up to the handle. I wiggled my feet. Thankfully, my toes were resting on solid ground, not hanging over the edge of a cliff. I began to shift into a more stable position, but the slope felt very steep. I was afraid that if I moved too much, I might start sliding again. I couldn't see anything. My face was still buried in the snow, shoved into it by the weight of the pack.

I tried to remember what had happened. *Crampon slipped on the ice . . . the overwhelming inertia of the pack as I started falling sideways . . . feeling nothing but air all around me.*

And then hitting the ground with my body.

"Mike!" Jack yelled down at me from above. "Mike!" he yelled again.

Good, Jack's still up on the ridge. My silent conversation with myself continued. *I remember, he was leading my rope, then Rick, then Keith. Keith was just in front of me. I was on the end.* It was almost like recovering from an anesthetic. The details came back slowly: the fifteen seconds of falling, the flood of pure adrenaline, the trauma wiping my mind clean. Now it was all coming back, only not everything was in the original sequence.

Not only could I not see, I could barely breathe. The pack was crushing me.

The pack. I have to shift its weight, if only so that I can answer Jack. I lifted my right shoulder enough for the pack to roll slightly to my left, just enough so I could turn my face out of the snow and call out.

"I'm all right," I finally shouted. I could barely get the three words out with one breath; the adrenaline was still circulating strong. The pressure of each heartbeat pushed up into my neck. The back of my throat was dry and sticky. My exhaled breath reverberated off the snow in front of my face.

"I'm all right," I repeated. A nervous chuckle followed.

It was a sick joke. I was uninjured, but I was definitely not all right. I was at least thirty feet below the ridgeline, perhaps close to a precipitous drop down the most isolated face of the continent's tallest mountain. I was anything *but* all right.

Jack's next words were, "You need to get yourself back up here!"

Another sick joke. Since I couldn't see anything but the small patch of snow in front of me, I had no idea how tenuous my position was or how I was going to climb the thirty feet to get back up to the team. Get back up there? Hell, I was too scared to move at all.

"OK, just give me a minute," I responded. For the next dozen breaths, I lay in the snow regaining my composure.

Then I started at the beginning, making a mental list of the few things that I *did* know. First, I could not remain where I was. Second, Jack was right, it was up to me to get myself back up there. Third, there was no time like the present to get started.

Adrenaline still pulsated through my arteries, leaving my arm muscles feeling weak and tremulous. Yet I needed them to lift my body and the crushing weight of my pack upright. I understood what needed to be done but not exactly how I was going to accomplish it.

"Kick your feet in," yelled Jack.

He was right. Stable footing would give me something secure, more than just the ice ax, something to trust my weight with.

I kicked my crampons into the snow and felt the reassurance of compact snow pushing back against the toes of my boots. Only after getting a solid purchase for each foot did I relax my grip on the ax.

I shifted my torso again, this time to position it more directly under the pack's center of gravity, and used my quivering arms to push against the snow, lifting my chest a few precious inches away from it. Looking up toward the rest of the team, I examined the distance I had to travel to reach the ridgetop again.

Wow, that is steep! I aimed for Keith's figure on the opposite end of the rope. He was lying prone on top of his buried ice ax, his entire weight pressing down on its end. What I didn't think to take note of was whether the rope between us was taut.

I began climbing back up the incline at a snail's pace. Each time I lifted my ax out of the ice, I replanted it just a few inches above its original position. In this ridiculously conservative style, I crept upward, kicking in steps to provide stable footing while holding the ax firmly with both hands. Then it was the ax's turn to advance.

By the end of the ten minutes it took to climb back up the incline, I had convinced myself that this operation was not unlike climbing the West Buttress headwall, and like then, I never looked back. I maneuvered up the forty-five-degree incline until I was back in reach of my friends. Jack grabbed my left arm and Mike and Bruce each grabbed part of the right one, and they pulled me up.

I stood more or less upright again, my hands pressing against my knees, lungs still working hard.

"What happened?" Mike asked.

"I hit a patch of blue ice" was all I could manage in response.

Had Keith's arrest on the rope stopped my slide? If that was the case, then he had saved my life as well as his own. If he hadn't held his position, the force of my fall might have pulled him, Rick, and Jack down as well. The four of us could have found ourselves a long way down the mountain.

Judging from the wide-eyed look on Keith's face, he understood this already.

"Thanks, Keith," I managed in a weak voice.

He nodded. Even his breath was trembling.

Jack, not wanting to dwell on what-ifs, quickly returned his attention to the business at hand. Dark glasses hid his eyes, but I knew there was no sympathy in them. His hard expression showed no evidence of shock, nor any sign of relief. His mouth was open and expressionless, just pulling in oxygen.

"We need to get going," he said.

Now even more mindful of each footstep, I followed Jack, Rick, and Keith onto the slightly broader section of Karstens Ridge.

An hour later, just as I was starting to regain my confidence, we came to another obstruction. The top of the ridge was broken and impassable, meaning we had to drop down again, this time a good twenty yards from the cap, in order to get through. We lowered ourselves down a steep incline on the Harper side, through thigh-deep snow, until Jack found what he was looking for. I was puzzled. There might be a path here but I sure couldn't see it. Jack hugged the nearly vertical wall of snow and moved slowly across the seventy-degree face sideways. There was nothing at his feet that could even remotely be called a ledge, so he created one. He pounded his left foot into the snow wall until he had knocked out a step, and then did the same with his ax until he had a hold for his left hand. The right side of his body followed. He continued this way until he was back on more or less horizontal ground, about thirty feet away from Rick.

Rick and then Keith followed.

When I was halfway across, my confidence began to waver. I looked back at Mike, hoping for some sort of encouragement. A silent glare told me to ignore what I was feeling and just get across.

For the next two hours after that, we enjoyed a bit of relief. It was easier going. Never flat or completely safe, just easier. It allowed me time to regain my poise. But all the time I knew instinctively that the next difficult area couldn't be far away. In fact, Jack was facing the next hurdle at this very moment. It was something vertical again, a descent through a deep trough of polished ice that led down to a steep cliff. Fortunately, an unburied piece of rope was fixed to the edge of the cliff, something to rappel down with. I first slid down in thigh-deep powder that filled the snow chute of the approach. I then grasped the top of the rope and used it to lower myself down the wall. At the bottom of the rope was a narrow crevasse to step across.

That wasn't so hard, I thought. *With a little more practice, I might even start to enjoy these sorts of challenges.*

Another easier hour followed, allowing my mind to continue its pleasant thoughts but just as I finished congratulating myself for the tenth time on my expanding capabilities, my crampon caught on a minor irregularity in the ice and I fell forward. I slid on my belly again, this time down the slope toward the Harper Icefall. A rapid flashback to my earlier fall started my heart pounding. Not again!

When I stopped after twenty feet, I was in a familiar position: facedown and uncertain of my surroundings. I hadn't noticed the details of the terrain before I fell. As it turned out, although this second slope was far gentler than the first, the ground I hit was harder—so hard that when my face hit it, it knocked off my glasses and scraped the tip of my nose. I wasn't in any danger, but I didn't know that yet. I was too afraid to lift my head.

"Oh, Jesus. Get up!" Jack barked. "Get back up here and quit fooling around." Clearly he was fed up with my clumsiness, as close to losing his patience as I was to losing my nerve. I stood up, wiped off my glasses, and trudged back up the slope.

An hour later, Jack, Rick, Keith, and I were standing on a level platform waiting for Mike's second rope team to catch up. As we turned and looked back, we saw Al suddenly fall off the steep ridge. He was sliding on his stomach, feet first, toward the Harper Icefall. From my vantage it looked like Al was falling in slow motion. Somehow it didn't look real, and because it wasn't real, I didn't feel alarmed.

But someone else *was* alarmed. *"Falling! Falling!"* Jack shouted back at a still-unaware Hamill, just as Al came to a stop on top of his arresting ax. Jack stood fast for a few more seconds and then, while Al hacked his way back up the slope, he stomped back up to Mike, dragging the three of us along behind.

Before we even got there, he started shouting again. "You guys need to say 'falling' so the rest of us know what the fuck is going on. Jesus Christ! What the hell is going on here?"

Mike just stared at Jack until he was finished and then went back to see if Al was all right.

Two hundred feet farther down, what had been a comfortably broad ridge tapered to something no more than a foot wide. To complicate matters further, a six-foot-wide crevasse interrupted the path. There was no way to move forward by dropping down off the ridge—on both sides the crevasse became even wider down below. The only option was to jump across. But a jump of six feet was no trivial matter, considering the weakened condition of our legs and the ninety pounds on our backs.

I made sure the rope in front of me stayed slack as Keith's young legs took him easily across. Watching the other three members of my rope team get safely across downgraded my terror from scared shitless to merely frightened. Because my legs were shorter than theirs, I moved back an additional fifteen feet. Truthfully, my running start didn't contain any actual running. As for style, I knew that a confident long jumper keeps his head up, looking forward at his target far out in the sand, comfortably sure of his steps and his takeoff point. I, however, kept my head down, looking at my feet as I ran, then angled my gaze forward just enough to see the edge of the crevasse as it approached. My left foot pushed off and I sailed forward, surrounded only by air, like a steel cannonball shot from a cannon primed with too little powder. My right foot touched down on the far side, but just barely. Stopping was nearly as hard as jumping. When I tried to slow my momentum, my upper body leaned danger-ously forward. I was worried I would fall right past Keith and off of the ridge entirely.

"Good job, Mike!" Keith and Rick chuckled as I clumsily came to a final stop.

"I hope we don't have to do that again," I said sourly.

The ridge broadened again. The day still had a little brightness to it, and so we continued on. Despite the setbacks, I once again found a rhythm. The snow was not too deep and the way ahead was clear. For the next two hours, nothing happened except for the gradual mellowing of brightness into twilight. More subtle hints showed that the day was winding down: the afternoon whiteness took on the familiar pastel blue of evening time, and the sharp edges of the landscape became smoother. A less agreeable reminder of nightfall's approach was the painful bite of cold in my hands. I wished I had something heavier than my fleece mitts to cover them with. The feeling of intense fatigue in my thighs from the jarring of thousands of downward steps was also unpleasant. As long as I stood still, my legs felt fine. I could lock my knees, and my upper body felt secure under the two solid posts. But as soon as we started moving again, my quadriceps began quivering like jelly.

We were nearing the end of a very long day, but we faced one final obstacle: a cliff with a sheer drop of twenty feet. It was too high to simply jump off, and there was no path or fixed rope to climb down. To make matters worse, a nasty-looking crevasse wrapped around the cliff's base. Jack pointed to the flat expanse of territory just beyond the cliff.

"There's Camp Seven, boys. But first we have to find a way to get down to it."

This time it was Mike who engineered the solution. He began by chopping out a level staging area, about the size of a tent platform, about two feet below the curved edge of the ridgetop. From there he cut out four broad steps that took him a full quarter of the way down the cliff. Into the last of them he pounded an aluminum picket (the fencepost-like anchor) and attached a climbing rope to it.

Jack liked what he saw. He maneuvered down the steep, narrow steps, clipped into the anchor, and then began to rappel the remaining distance. Rick and Keith followed. Before I started to descend, I first passed the climbing rope through the slots in my belay device (a simple tool that attached the rope to my harness) and into my carabiner. I leaned back on the edge of the last step and pushed off. The rope slid a couple of feet through the belay device with every kick away from the wall. Just above the bottom, I looked down at the crevasse's rough blue walls. A jumble of jagged ice spires poked up at me. Its opening was irregular, measuring between three and six feet. My crampons and the rappel rope held me steady as I hovered over it. Then, with one final big kick, I swung over to the other side of the crevasse and landed.

It was the only fun I had all day.

With no one left to belay him, Mike had to figure out a way to get himself down. If he followed our procedure, he would have to abandon his picket. Jack said he should just pull out the picket and jump, but Mike thought better of that option. We were a long way from help if he tore up his knee or twisted an ankle now. His answer was to construct a snow bollard (the trailer-hitch anchor) and substitute that for the picket. After finishing his rappel, he simply flicked the loop of rope off of the bollard to retrieve it.

By now we were all gassed. Fortunately, camp was just a few yards away on the only level ground we had seen since morning. From here we would have spectacular views back up the ridge behind us and out to the tundra beyond but sightseeing would have to wait. It was still foggy, plus the tents needed to go up.

By the time we had eaten, it was after midnight. The night air was extremely cold, and for the first and only time I pulled on the down mitts I'd carried all this while in my pack. I had them on for thirty minutes before the warmth started returning to my hands.

As I lay in my tent, I reflected on the terrors of the day. *What the hell was I doing up here?* There was no longer any doubt. I was in well above my head. Denali's north side had turned out to be much more than I had bargained for. What was the sense in taking these sorts of chances?

With my last peek out the tent door, I saw that it had started snowing again. I thanked God for His mercy, shut the terrors out of my mind, and rolled over to go to sleep.

SATURDAY, JUNE 7

Climbing down Denali's north side reminded me of the old saying about war: long periods of boredom punctuated by brief moments of sheer terror. The return of heavy snowfall and whiteout conditions during the night meant more of the former.

Saturday was storm day number five. The seven of us slept on and off until noon and then, after the blowing calmed down, congregated outside to enjoy a late breakfast of hot cereal and tea. I finished up the last pieces of dates and figs from my personal stash.

The only physical activity required of us that day was to remove the two feet of newly fallen snow that had accumulated around our tents. Since we had plenty of time on our hands, we even shoveled a nice, broad avenue back to the latrine.

After taking a turn at the shovel, I looked up to inspect the route we had descended. Although the storm had not completely cleared, I could see all along Karstens Ridge, all the way back up to Browne Tower. Remarkably, there were no foot trails to indicate that we had ever been up there. The wind and fresh snow had already erased them.

The whiteness of the ridge blended harmoniously with the clouds above and the snow that was still falling from them. I examined what I could of the eastern face. It was very steep. Pitches of at least forty-five degrees continued down perhaps two hundred feet from the ridgecap toward a rockier zone and, beyond that, to even steeper slopes. Although my slide had not taken me as close to the edge of a precipice as I had imagined, that knowledge did little to comfort me. The entire upper ridge looked every bit as menacing as I knew it to be, and I had no reason to think that we wouldn't face more of the same on the lower portion. I looked forward to being down on the Muldrow Glacier, having the crux of this route behind us. Then I would be able to look back at Karstens Ridge with the perspective of having "been there, done that."

I took a deep breath and had another look around. It was safe to say that none of us would ever stand in this spot again. I knew Camp Seven was one of the most remote places I would ever visit, so I did my best to capture the spirit of the place, in my mind and in the photos I took.

With the storm now showing signs of receding, I guessed we would be back on the trail in the morning. And now that the work of shoveling and the pleasures of sightseeing were complete, the seven of us returned to our tents to relax. That afternoon I ate a twenty-day-old bagel, a slice of similarly aged Havarti cheese, one of the last pieces of Al's smoked salmon, and my few remaining pecans. Food was definitely starting to interest me again. So was the printed page. I sifted through Hemingway's "The Snows of Kilimanjaro" for a second time. My tent mates and I talked. Our conversation revolved around the good and bad parts of the expedition, the details of our previous lives and activities, and more junior-high-level discussions about sex.

Once the weather cleared, we would be just two long days from the road.

FALL AND REDEMPTION

—

SUNDAY, JUNE 8

The new day dawned sunny. Except for the occasional wispy cloud, there was nothing overhead but blue sky. In finer light, the ridge above us appeared less intimidating, somewhat tamer, even groomed. It made me wonder, as I did my business at the latrine, how events might have differed if we had descended it in better weather. Would we have been better off to wait another day or two up at Camp Six? Had my hastiness to get off of Denali put me at greater risk than was necessary? At the same time, the terrifying falls I'd experienced only reinforced my desire to be off the mountain as soon as possible.

We departed Camp Seven at eleven thirty and continued to descend Karstens Ridge. With the calm conditions came additional clarity, ahead as well as above us. But that clarity brought with it a measure of disappointment. I now saw we were not near the bottom of the ridge, but only a bit more than halfway down.

After leaving camp we walked free of obstacles for many hours, wading through fresh, calf-deep and even thigh-deep snow, on persistently steep slopes. By late afternoon we were at the top of a large, snow-filled couloir. Descending it would put us onto the Muldrow Glacier.

Jack sent Mike, Bruce, and Al on ahead to find a route through the crevasse network separating us from the top of the couloir. Mike's first attempt to find a passable route failed, forcing him to retreat a good part of the way back up to us before starting off again in a different direction. On his second attempt, he was successful. Jack waited for clear evidence that Mike had succeeded before proceeding. Jack's posture during this time signaled his frustration with the delay and more of his tendency to expect failure from his junior guide. But this time the joke was on Jack. By the time he was convinced Mike had found a passable route, the forward rope team was already halfway down the couloir. In fact, the four of us hadn't even entered the couloir by the time Mike stepped onto the Muldrow itself.

As soon as Al and Bruce followed Mike onto the glacier, we heard a crack. A huge block of ice peeled off from the base of the Harper Icefall. The monstrous cliff it calved from had to be twenty stories tall. The avalanche cloud was taller still. For a moment I thought it was going to overtake the lower rope team. As the cloud approached, Mike turned around to look. We all breathed a sigh of relief as it halted well short of the couloir base. The grand scale of things on Denali made it terribly difficult to accurately judge distances.

"Geez, that looked close!" Rick said.

Keith and I nodded, but Jack remained silent. Not only did he appear unconcerned for their safety, he was agitated that between his own delaying and the delay caused by watching the avalanche, we were now far behind Mike's team. He'd fix that. Throwing caution to the wind, he took us careening down the slope at a pace that was twice as fast as Mike's had been and half again as quick as I was comfortable with. The already-strained muscles in my upper thighs took a further beating as we shot through Mike's fresh switchbacks. By the time we hit level ground thirty minutes later, my thigh muscles were visibly shaking.

But I breathed a sigh of relief as I took those final steps off of Karstens Ridge. The tough part was behind us. We'd spent three incredible days on it and almost five days already on the north side. Based on Ranger Joe's talk in Talkeetna, I had imagined we would travel from High Camp to this point in a single day.

Now that the seven of us were reunited, we sat on our packs and took a long break. I further reviewed the events of the past days in my head: multiple minor crevasse plunges on the Harper, fifty-mile-an-hour winds and subzero temperatures in Camp Six, three falls and who knows how many near misses on the ridge, ice cliff descents and snow-chute slides, crevasses to leap across, and a near-vertical wall that I'd crawled across by my fingertips. Then a late-night rappel down to Camp Seven followed by a second storm day. My thighs, shoulders, and toes were sore, and my mind was weary. All that I could do was think, *Wow!*

Summit day seemed so long ago and by now had lost much of its significance. I thought back to our early days, those days on the middle mountain on the south side when our trek had been easier and safer, and our spirits fresher. My ambition had kept me from fully appreciating it then, but now that we were back on the middle mountain again, I was looking forward to reliving those carefree times.

We had reached the Muldrow, the north side's geographic equivalent of the Kahiltna, a second major mountaineering inroad to the upper bulk of Denali. It was the final barrier separating us from the safety of solid ground. I was ecstatic to be standing on something flat. The glacier's surface appeared as smooth as a bed sheet, totally unmenacing. I felt safe for the first time in five days.

The Muldrow, like the Kahiltna, originates in a calm, sheltered valley. As I stood with my back to the Harper Icefall, I noted that Mount Carpe to my right, Pioneer Ridge and the northern extent of the Wickersham Wall to my left, and the icefall behind formed the walls of this particular three-sided amphitheater. Although I had never been to this place, it seemed oddly familiar.

Jack reclaimed the lead position from Mike and pushed us forward. The Muldrow didn't stay smooth and unmenacing for long. Crevasses, seracs, and other obstacles were everywhere.

Judging distances from ground level was at least as problematic as it had been up on the ridge, and it took far longer to complete each section than I had imagined. Routefinding added to our slow progress. If Jack remained uncertain of the best way to proceed after referring to the GPS data and studying the landscape (the rule rather than the exception), he relied on trial and error. Even in the rare instance that he was certain where to go, we never followed a straight line for very long and the resultant contorted path never represented the shortest distance between two points.

This constant probing and zigzagging back and forth across the mile-wide glacier went on for four more hours, absorbing what remained of the afternoon and then taking us into evening. Jack would move ahead for a few steps, resurvey, move left or right as the situation dictated, and then proceed again. When he stopped, the rest of us stopped, staying spread out in our usual positions along the ropes. We waited patiently until he was prepared to move again.

After we left the couloir, the ground ahead started falling away, almost imperceptibly at first and then more acutely, as we approached the Muldrow's first major obstacle, the Great Icefall. Back at the Harper Icefall, the ground underneath the glacier dropped away precipitously at a rocky cliff. Here at the Muldrow's Great Icefall, a series of slightly less severe undulations caused the ice to buckle and fracture in multiple planes.

Because there was no other way to proceed, Jack had to find us a way through this one.

We gathered together for a break at the top while Jack consulted his GPS. There was a way through. He knew this with certainty because he had been here once before. And expeditions had been passing this way ever since 1913, when Walter Harper, Harry Karstens, Hudson Stuck, and Robert Tatum first climbed Denali's south summit.

Jack took our two rope teams into the icefall well over to the glacier's left-hand side. We wandered along a serpentine path until we were completely surrounded by house-sized seracs tipped up unsteadily on their edges.

I was skeptical that Jack could find a way through on his first attempt. Mike had needed two tries to get through the crevasse field at the end of Karstens Ridge, and this icefall was exponentially more complex. At least our pace was slow enough that I could look up often and admire our incredible surroundings. Mounds of fresh snow topped many of the ice blocks, making them look like scoops of vanilla ice cream smothered in runny marshmallow sauce.

Beautiful, yes, but everything smelled of danger. On the main bodies of the Harper and Muldrow, and even on Karstens Ridge, we relaxed in between obstacles. Not so here. One hazard immediately followed another. The irregular ground often dropped away sharply in multiple directions. Even the most solid areas felt unstable. A sudden shift in the glacier would bring the entire icefall tumbling down on us. And what if we made a wrong turn? Over the next mile stretch, there were a thousand turns and tens of thousands of permutations. Yet I assumed there were only a handful of safe paths.

Halfway through, I looked back and spotted Bruce, on Mike's rope, walking along the top of a ledge thirty feet above me. The ice cliff dwarfed his figure.

Jack, it seemed, was sure of the route. He was intent on keeping us on it all the way to the bottom. On several occasions

I was sure we'd have to turn around at an impossibly wide crevasse or an unscalable ice wall. Yet he saw something other than a dead end, options the rest of us didn't appreciate. Usually this meant dropping down to a new level, circumventing the obstruction, and then moving on. It was almost as if he were changing the rules of the game in midstream. His gift was the ability to think through the problem in *three* dimensions.

His steely determination never made him behave recklessly, however. We maintained a safe distance from the most unstable-looking features—the transparently thin ice of crevasse edges and the bases of the most severely tilting seracs. But now, nearly two hours into the icefall and more than ten hours into the day, the strain of being always at the ready had risen to an almost intolerable level. Rather than being short with each other, we were unusually silent.

Just as it seemed I couldn't take it for another minute, the way ahead showed signs of opening up. The vistas broadened. Our rate of descent leveled off. Unbelievably, flat ground was spreading out in front of Jack. When he turned to look back at the rest of us, he looked satisfied.

The sun had long since fallen behind Pioneer Ridge to our left, and the late-evening air had taken on an uncomfortable chill. I zipped up my jacket's armpit vents and then followed Jack and then Rick down, looking forward to reaching the level ground in just a few minutes' time. Camp Eight had to be close. The end of the day seemed near.

With one more step beyond the last of the ice boulders, I was in the clear. Freedom at last. Mike was right on my tail, towing Al and Bruce along behind him. For the next quarter of an hour, Jack's pace picked up. Relief rushed through me as I relished taking more than two normal strides in succession.

It was then that Jack dropped suddenly out of sight.

Rick's shouting alerted me: "Jack fell in! Jack fell in a crevasse!"

I followed Rick's lead, hit the ground, and drove my ice ax into the snow. All the stress of the past five days regathered in my chest and then exploded all at once. *What the hell!?* Jack had steered us clear of every danger in the icefall. Then, just as the heavy artillery guns had fallen silent, the biggest shell of all had landed right at our feet: he was gone. What was going on?

A minute later our only remaining guide crept past me, walking with an uncertain gait. He looked flustered, barely containing his sense of panic. His appearance was hardly reassuring. My attention fixed on the back of Rick's orange jacket ahead. His elbows flared out from the line of his body, fashioning an arrow in the snow that pointed to a thin line of rope, and beyond that, the edge of a broad crevasse.

"Jack— *Jack!* Are you all right?" Mike shouted, still a safe distance away from the edge, near Rick.

There was no reply.

"Fuck!"

I lay flat on the ground with my arms quivering as my gloved hands clutched my ice ax hard. The sweat on my face was cold and my heart was pounding even faster than when I'd fallen—if that was even possible. Jack was supposed to get all of us out of here. Now what?

I looked around at Al and the other clients for any sort of reassurance, but their expressions clearly showed that their tired minds were churning out the same sort of dreadful images that mine was. The silence must mean that Jack was injured, unconscious, or worse. How could we begin to care for a broken limb or a concussion? We were, by now, a minimum of two days' walk from help.

Mike looked down and mumbled to himself, apparently thinking through his options and working to regain some sort of operational composure. He needed to devise a rescue plan, and quick.

"Rick," he said at last, "I want you to loop the loose end of the rope around your ax. That will help stabilize your anchor. Just stay where you are and maintain that anchor, OK?"

"Gotcha, Mike," Rick replied.

"Keith, you and Fenner continue to belay Rick. Al, you and Bruce belay me. Now keep the rope tight, OK? I'm going to make my way up to the lip to see what's going on down there."

As Mike inched closer to the edge of the unknown, I eyed the crevasse. Incredibly, a twenty-foot-wide hole—stretching three-quarters of a mile from one side of the glacier to the other—had replaced the totally smooth surface. The entire sheet had collapsed the instant Jack stepped on it.

"Jack," Mike shouted from near the edge, his tall frame leaning slightly forward. He dropped into a full squat. More mumbling. Was he talking with Jack or just talking to himself again? Several more painful minutes passed.

Then Mike turned and relayed bits and pieces of what he saw in the hole. What we heard was both distressing and reassuring. The rope went a long way down—thirty feet—into a horribly deep crevasse, but dangling at the rope's end, floating free in space, was an uninjured Jack.

"He said he lost a snowshoe but was otherwise OK," Mike said. "He hadn't answered my calls earlier because he couldn't hear me. Only when I shouted straight down into the hole could I communicate with him."

Turning back to the crevasse, Mike said confidently, in a voice loud enough for us all to hear, "We're going to get you out, Jack." But that confidence clearly waned again when he looked back to take inventory of his support staff.

A few more minutes passed, and then Mike relayed calmly, "Jack says 'no worries.' He's already got his ascender set, and he's in the process of fixing a prusik for his foot. He says he'll be out in no time."

Remarkably, using his ascender for a handhold and a single prusik for his foot, Jack shimmied up the rope entirely under his own power. During that time we heard parts of Mike's side of the conversation, but until we knew how this would play out, we didn't dare relax fully. By now the adrenaline from the initial shock had worn off, but we all started shaking again—this time from the cold. It was late evening, and we had been lying or crouching in the snow for almost an hour maintaining our anchors. The longer we waited for Jack to appear, the colder we got. "Out in no time" came and passed. I switched from worrying about Jack to fretting about myself. *What was taking him so long? Hurry up, damn it!*

An hour and a half after the fall, Jack's head finally popped out. He was smiling.

"That was wild!" we heard him say. He brought his arms out and rested his chest on the crevasse edge. The rest of what he said was for Mike's ears only. After the junior guide grabbed his boss's shoulder and pulled him the rest of the way out, Jack recounted the experience for all of us.

"The ground just disappeared," he said. "The snow looked no different than any other I had walked on since leaving the icefall, but shit, it just disappeared! I mean, can you guys believe that? Wild, just wild! So I'm hanging at the end of the rope and calling up for Hamill, but I get nothing. I've got no idea what's going on up here and what's taking him so long. Anyway, I figure I've got to get myself out."

Typical Jack. What did he think we were doing up here, cooking dinner? As I listened, I felt much more relieved for myself than I did for him. What I didn't understand was how he could possibly be smiling. Wouldn't crying and screaming be more appropriate? I shook my head while the rest of me shuddered, this time in another burst of fear. This descent had become a nightmare. Five days into it with no end in sight. Everyone else looked the same as I felt.

It was eleven thirty at night, but Jack insisted that we needed to press on. I shook my head silently.

Mike assumed the lead since he still possessed two snowshoes. Jack limped along at the head of our second rope, his "bare" leg plunging into the snow to his upper calf with each step.

Mike probed every meter of snow in front of him numerous times before trusting it with his weight. As he moved ahead, his velocity seemed only a bit faster than the forward creeping of the glacier itself.

Just a few yards ahead of Jack's crevasse, we came upon a second one. Mike walked up to a sturdy-looking snow bridge that spanned it. He looked back at Jack, questioningly. Jack just stared back at him. Obviously still not easy with his decision, Mike moved forward tentatively onto the bridge. I could see its thickness in cross-section. It looked substantial enough to support him. But in the next instant, the entire bridge evaporated into a cloud of white powder. Mike disappeared with it.

The war was back on again.

Jack, instead of showing shock or concern, looked only annoyed.

The chief then turned in a circle to look at what he had to work with. He shook his head as if to say, *Not much.* He then strutted up to the very edge of the crevasse, standing fully upright.

"We'll set up a pulley and yank you out. Just give us a few minutes. I've got to show these guys what to do," he called down to Mike. His voice was resolute.

The six of us on the surface ran the third rope (the one that Ryan and Armando had been on) twice through a set of pulleys—to improve our mechanical advantage—and then anchored its far end to a picket. We lowered the loose end down to Mike, and he clipped into the new rope so the five of us clients could pull him up. The entire process took just under an hour.

Before Mike's head was entirely out of the hole, Jack knelt down and confronted him face-to-face. "Couldn't you tell that was a shitty snow bridge?" he said, loud enough that we could all hear. "Unbelievable! Come on. Get up here. It's late. We've got to get moving."

As Hamill pulled himself the rest of the way out, he was not smiling. He did not comment on what a wild ride it had been, nor did he say anything in response to Jack's scolding. Physically he appeared fine. He walked back from the edge of the precipice with no signs of a limp or other injuries. Both of his snowshoes were still on his feet. His pack was undamaged. But I could tell that he was not in his usual state of mind. His square-jawed, confident expression was absent. His eyes focused down. He opened his mouth as if to say something but then closed it, as if thinking better of it. A moment later he did the same thing again. Shell shocked. I was surprised to hear him say later that despite all of the time he had spent in the mountains, this was his first crevasse fall.

"Let's get going," Jack barked.

We five clients looked at each other and then at our feet, silently wondering, *Who's next?*

Jack reworked the rope teams, then commandeered one of Mike's snowshoes and took back the lead. He found a nearly identical bridge a hundred yards away and went across. Rick, Bruce, and Al followed. Keith and I came last on Mike's rope.

We had crossed at least a dozen snow bridges by now, but this was the first one since Mike's collapse. As I started across, I ventured a peek down. The crevasse was terrifyingly beautiful. Surprisingly, it wasn't the hazard itself that rattled me; it was the reflection that stared back at me—how it made me see myself. The dangerous crevasse forced me to look inward and face my inadequacies. I knew there was no way I could get myself and my heavy pack out without assistance like Jack had. Nor could I hope to approach Mike's level of composure when he emerged. Silently, I worried how I might react if I dropped into one. But I attempted to show no sign of weakness and instead maintained as stoic a face as I could manage.

On the far side of this second crevasse, four hours after Jack had stepped onto the "safe ground" at the base of the icefall—a distance that should have taken us only twenty minutes to cover—we established Camp Eight. We ate an abbreviated dinner and collapsed in our tents. It was four o'clock in the morning. I went to sleep thinking we were only two more days from the road. Always, only two more days.

MONDAY, JUNE 9

The nights and days were starting to get mixed up. Indifferent to our normal circadian rhythms, we walked or slept in half-day periods. We might eat dinner at breakfast time or breakfast in the middle of the day. This "morning," we ate our oatmeal at two o'clock in the afternoon. We marched out of camp at teatime two hours later. Jack reasoned that the glacier was cooler and the snow more stable when the sun wasn't directly overhead. In theory it made sense, but my experience thus far indicated that the snow of the Muldrow was never completely safe.

Before we departed camp, I wanted to fashion a ditch loop for my pack. If, at some point, I found myself down in a hole, the loop would let me transfer the weight of my pack onto either the climbing rope (helping me to stay upright while I awaited extrication) or a second rope (like the one we had dropped down to Mike when we pulled him out yesterday).

If I fell into a crevasse, the rope tied into my waist harness would support my entire weight. But because the tie-in was only a single point of fixation, my body would tend to swivel back on that fulcrum due to the force of my heavy pack. I would be at risk of flipping upside down. In broad crevasses like the ones Mike and Jack fell into, there was a lot of maneuvering room, and this might not be cause for alarm. Given time, I could probably eventually right myself. But if the crevasse was very narrow, that rotation might cause me to become wedged in tight.

I was embarrassed that I didn't already have a ditch loop or know how to fix one. Considering what had happened yesterday, I thought it best to swallow my pride and ask for help.

"So, Mike," I stammered, "I was wondering if you'd . . . I think I need to have a ditch loop on my pack, but I don't . . . do you take a prusik and put it around . . . does it go through the carabiner here on my strap, or . . . oh, hell! Mike, can you just fix a ditch loop for me?"

He fixed it before we were under way.

The farther beyond the icefall we got, the more regularly and predictably the glacier behaved. After thirty minutes of exceptionally smooth progress, we were all back in "safe" mode again, enjoying what was left of the warm afternoon.

The stacked blocks of the Great Icefall were still visible behind us, but the crevasses that the guides had fallen into were not. The ground ahead was finely manicured, without even a ripple to suggest hidden dangers.

Jack took another step forward. It was identical to the hundreds of steps he had taken since leaving camp. Only this time, a huge crevasse opened up six inches beyond the end of his boot. The opening extended for another thirty feet in front of that. A hundred tons of snow dropped away in a second, leaving nothing in its wake but a rising puff of vapor and the open jaws of seven flummoxed climbers.

We instinctively stared down at our own feet, wondering what other horrors were hidden under the snow, and then forward at the gaping hole. The crevasse was one and a half times as broad as the one that had swallowed him and extended fully from one side of the nearly mile-wide glacier to the other. Not a single snow bridge was left for us to cross on.

"Did you see that?" Jack exclaimed.

We all nodded silently. The memory of the snow falling and the nearly inaudible, low-pitched sound it had produced were imprinted in my mind—*thuuumph!* How was it possible for such a large defect to be so perfectly concealed at one moment and then completely exposed in the next? The covering of this monster had obviously been building up over a period of months, if not years. And yet the slightest vibration from Jack's footstep had brought the entire thing tumbling down in a flash. The more I thought about it, the more I realized that had the snow waited to collapse until Jack was out in the middle, Rick might have been pulled in, too. Hell, the entire rope team could have been lost!

Jack took us left, on a line parallel to the crevasse, to find passage where the Muldrow met the walls of the mountain. The "minor" unnamed icefall on the right side looked so hazardous that even my novice eyes knew we should avoid it. Unfortunately, we found no passage to the left, only a sheer wall of rock. After thoroughly exploring the dead end, we retreated. We had no choice but to push our way through the icefall.

Getting through the jumbled mess required more of Jack's expert three-dimensional puzzle solving, and this time he didn't have any old GPS data to consult. In this mini icefall, we found heaps of fractured ice the size of buses and multistory cliffs separated by deadly crevasses. Jack sent Mike's rope ahead on the next section, where he worked his way down a series of ramps that ran beside tilting ice blocks.

An inward-leaning sheer wall of turquoise ice, which had somehow remained attached to Mount Carpe's vertical rock face, was equally impressive. It rose as a single unbroken span for hundreds of feet. Had it been a building, it easily would have been the tallest in Alaska. I breathed a sigh of relief when I noted the lack of an avalanche cone at its base.

After successfully traversing the icefall, Jack reexamined his GPS readings, which indicated that our desired route was all the way back over to the left. So across we went again. Because crevasses run perpendicular to the glacier's long axis and we were now walking parallel to a visible one, we walked quickly and confidently. I expected that we would cover the mile-wide expanse in twenty minutes or less. But two minutes into the walk, I heard another low-bass sound, slightly different from the one made by the crevasse cover falling.

Whuuump!

I pictured a percussionist striking a huge bass drum with a cushioned mallet, then immediately muffling it.

Mike explained. "When a large volume of fresh, uncompacted snow collapses under its own weight, the air trapped inside of it is forced out all at once. The sudden rush of air creates the sound."

As the settling of the snowfield did not open up any new crevasses, we pressed forward on the same course. Fifteen minutes later, Jack found what he was looking for on the left side of the glacier. There we made a right turn and resumed our forward progress.

The Muldrow's second major icefall is aptly named the Lower Icefall to differentiate it from the upper, or Great Icefall. As Jack approached it, he first led us across a half-dozen snow bridges, each spanning a modest crevasse. By now we had safely crossed enough of them, ranging in length from ten to twenty feet, to make it seem commonplace again. Jack was a good judge of bridges, and I found it entertaining to watch him solve another one of this great glacier's giant puzzles. I also appreciated that our two rope teams seemed finely tuned and successful today. The worst was finally behind us, it seemed.

We traveled at a luxurious pace, so there was time enough for me to look up from the path. We were below eight thousand feet. The terrain was less severe than any we had seen for a very long time, the air was as rich as that first day at base camp, and my legs had fallen into a regular, confident cadence, something they hadn't done since the south side of Denali Pass. I looked ahead to see Jack, followed by Rick, crossing over another stout snow bridge. As Al walked across, he suddenly dropped out of sight.

"Not again!" I said out loud, to no one in particular. My confidence disappeared as quickly as Al. His drop did not cause the same sense of dread as Jack's or Mike's had, for me or any of the other clients. But the cumulative effect of these recurrent catastrophes on the whole team was plain.

Something snapped in my mind like a twig that was part of a bigger bundle. The more twigs that broke—each an irreversible event—the more unstable the bundle became. With this particular snap, a barrage of thoughts ran through my head. *I hope Al's OK. He should be, Jack and Mike were fine. But how long will it be until someone is hurt in one of these falls? That bridge already held two climbers. Why did it break when Al went across? What if that had been me?*

"Back to survival mode," I mumbled to myself. I recalled the time back at Camp Three, during the first storm day, when Jack had told us that he was putting us in survival mode. I almost laughed aloud. That had been nothing.

Since this time both guides could coordinate Al's rescue, we had him back up in no time. None of us was surprised that Al came out looking rather cheerful. It was almost as if he was relieved that he hadn't been robbed of the experience. Tempering his enthusiasm somewhat was his sore left shoulder. Nothing was broken, but he said he banged it pretty hard against the wall on the way down.

I kicked the snow at my feet. *Twelve miles we've got to walk on this Muldrow, and at least half of that still to go—a hell of a long way when not a single step can be trusted!*

"Back to business," I said quietly, mimicking Jack. We had already been on the trail for four hours. It was eight o'clock.

For the time being, I decided to suspend my little periods of wonderment, of taking pleasure in the beauty surrounding me. Doing so was a luxury I could no longer afford. I needed the time in between falls to get myself back to baseline. It was a shame, too. The landscape here was every bit as enthralling as it had been when I first stepped off of the plane at base camp.

During the next hour, I imagined that we were playing a deadly game of chance. I looked down at the eleven-millimeter purple string that tethered me to Keith. How many times could it stop a 250- to 300-pound weight (climber plus pack) before it failed? I found myself being extra careful to never to step on *that* rope.

My daydream continued: *Funny, Keith doesn't look too far away. I'll count paces. Mark. One, two, three . . . Yep, fifteen paces, three feet per pace. That's how far I'd be down in a hole, forty-five feet. Maybe more, the rope stretches under tension. Sooner or later, this rope's going to be holding me. My time's coming.*

Rick's fall yanked me out of my daydream. The group let out a loud moan. I wondered how long it would take before we felt not just exasperated, but apathetic.

Jack and Mike went to work. Bruce and Al were quick to volunteer to help. Keith and I belayed Mike. Jack looked down from the edge of the twenty-foot-wide crevasse. Rick was hanging free thirty feet down, seventy feet above the dark shadows at the bottom. The extraction routine was by now well practiced. The third rope, which Mike carried wrapped around his shoulder, dropped down to Rick in a matter of minutes.

I looked around at our surroundings. I had been simply following Keith's footsteps. We hadn't been moving quickly; in fact, we had been crawling. I noticed that we had walked into what looked like a minefield—one in which all the mines had already exploded. This part of the glacier was very heavily crevassed, not a full rope's length between openings. And the snow was different: softer, wetter, and less cohesive. We weren't even at the Lower Icefall yet, and the glacier was already showing signs of being less predictable.

My tent mate's head popped out of the Muldrow forty-five minutes later. He was smiling nervously. It was an expression not of joy but of relief. He, Al, and I talked after he came out.

"The ground simply disappeared from under my feet," Rick said in a raspy voice. "I was falling before I even knew what had happened. It was a pretty bumpy ride. Got jostled around quite a bit, but I don't think I hurt anything. I'm telling you, this Muldrow is a death trap! Can't wait to be gone from here."

For the most part, though, Rick took the fall in stride. He had even taken photos as he dangled from the rope. "My camera was handy, just had to unzip my waist pack and take it out. Plus, there was nothing better for me to do while I waited for you guys to pull me up," he added with a weak laugh. In spite of his outward calm, his hands shook as he struggled to put the camera back in its case.

As Jack moved us out, I promised myself that I would start paying better attention to where I was. There would be no more getting lulled to sleep. *Still a long way to go. Gotta be careful.*

We worked around the side of Rick's crevasse until we found a suitable snow bridge. There weren't any of the huge, open, side-to-side crevasses down here. Instead, the whole area was broken up, crisscrossing lines of snow winding around the open pits. The trick was to know which patches of snow were safe enough to walk on.

Despite my recent promise, I couldn't keep my mind from wandering. Partly to blame were Jack's stop-and-go movements. Start forward and then stop. Probe and study. Never did his momentum carry us forward for more than a few paces at a time.

Why did we even come to the north side? What was Jack thinking by bringing us on the traverse? Didn't he know that conditions would be like this?

I knew the answer, of course. The truth was, he *didn't* know it would be this bad. No one put the question to him directly—that sort of brashness wasn't acceptable under any circumstance— but from what we had pieced together from his comments, everything about his previous traverse had gone without a hitch. They were down and out in three long days. Why would he have expected it to be any different this time around?

And then, just like that, Keith was gone.

I hit the ground to arrest Keith's fall.

Silently, right there in front of me, he had simply vanished from sight. The snow that Mike had walked on just a minute ago disappeared with him. The space between me and Keith was empty except for the nasty-looking black hole that hadn't been there a moment ago.

The group was stunned. The day had begun with such promise, but this was the third crevasse drop, all in the past three hours. I looked around. The glacier was a mess but there was nothing safer to be found anywhere on the whole fucking thing. Jack had had no other choice but to take us through here. At this rate we'd never make it down to McGonagall Pass, much less the road!

Although crevasse falls had become commonplace, they certainly had not become trivial. This latest fall was especially difficult for me: it had happened close to home. *Only a matter of time,* I thought for the hundredth time.

As it turned out, two things kept Keith from dropping in very far. Like when Al fell, he was in the middle of the rope, so Mike and I both supported him. Also, he happened to land on top of a huge subterranean stalagmite ten feet down. The crevasse was extraordinarily complex and treacherous looking; it was fortunate that he did not fall farther.

When he came out a half hour later, he had the shakes. His voice, while never strong, now crackled and wavered when he spoke. While he told us about the fall, his gaze remained lowered and his hands fidgeted with his pole handles. He wasn't the only one who looked haunted. With the exception of Jack, we were all displaying signs of stress-induced paranoia. Shallow expressions and angular stances had completely replaced the confident, joyful faces and erect postures we had on day one. It didn't help that our faces were sunburned, scabbed, bearded, and gaunt.

My questions were the same with every fall: What were we doing here, who was next, and how long would it be until somebody got hurt? There had to be some purpose in all this, but what I could no longer say. Denali had long since stopped being an adventure. I had never expected the north side to be a picnic in the park, but this?

The day's light was fading, but we needed to press on. There was no alternative. We couldn't camp here, and we sure couldn't turn around and go back up.

Camp Eight, just beyond the Great Icefall (up at 8,500 feet) was three miles behind us. Al's, Rick's, and Keith's crevasse falls had all occurred in the last mile. Now, seven hours into the day, as we began the passage through the Lower Icefall (elevation 7,000 feet), I noted how it was a completely different animal than the upper one. This one was more spread out and dropped in elevation less severely. But I saw that in every way it was just as treacherous. Crevasses riddled the entire thing, and the snow was rotten. For two hours, our route followed a seemingly random path between cracks and ice blocks that resembled squares of white wedding cake dipped in thick, creamy icing. I made an exception to my new wonderment rule and allowed myself to enjoy the sight. It was heavenly, especially now in the twilight's soft light.

Nothing happened in the icefall, a relief after all the buildup on the approach and the knowledge of how dangerous it was. Calmness returned to me once we exited, that and a sense of liberation. The Lower Icefall represented the last of the known major hazards on the Muldrow. The route ahead would be easier.

At a rest break, Bruce and I noted that we were the only two who hadn't taken a crevasse fall. Still, we dared not let our guards down entirely. I didn't very much like the look of the next part of the glacier, and I remembered that Jack had taken his fall just a little way beyond the Great Icefall, when all of us thought it was safe to breathe again.

After pressing on for another hour, we congregated together while the two guides worked out a plan. Jack concluded that we needed to drastically change our strategy. The mangled section of ice just ahead was impassable. We would exit the glacier entirely and proceed on the rocky moraine for a time to get around it. But the whole area between us and the moraine was a maze of potholes—highly volatile. Jack sent Hamill ahead to find a way through.

"Crevasse bait!" Al chuckled to Mike. As Mike passed us, I noticed a queer sensation, as if I were standing on a concrete bridge deck just as a heavy truck traveled across it. I felt the slight vibration for only a moment, and when it was gone, I didn't give it another thought.

Keith and I stood ready to follow Mike on his rope once he found the way through. Jack, remembering how he had been left behind at the couloir, quickly became impatient. After only ten minutes, he pressed forward into an area that Mike hadn't yet tried. It looked even more hazardous. Rick, still riding shotgun, followed behind Jack. The two made good initial progress, meaning that before long Al, too, was forced into the maze. But as Jack hit an impasse, Bruce, the fourth man on Jack's rope, was told to hold his position next to Keith and me.

Just then we heard a shout. Rick broke through a patch of thin ice less than thirty feet away from Jack. Although he was only in up to his waist, he had nothing to push his feet off of, so he was finding it difficult to bring his lower half above the beveled lip of fractured ice. An exasperated Jack suspended his search while he went back to help Rick. Al remained out in no-man's-land, halfway between them and us. Bruce, Keith, and I—sixty feet away from the action—could only watch and wait.

With Rick still not out of the hole, Jack called over for Mike. He was to circle around and continue exploring Jack's promising area. The low level of light was making both their jobs difficult. It was now past midnight. Even the normally radiant surface of the icefall had taken on a dull shade of gray. And up close to the black shale of the moraine, the snow was dark and dirty with sediment. From where I was standing, it was impossible to see much in the way of detail.

Bruce, Keith, and I had to back out of Mike's way a second time to allow him to backtrack. Potholes were all around us, and there was only a little room to maneuver. The area where we three clients stood was the broadest, most benign-appearing island of ice available, but still, it was no larger than the floor space of a small bedroom. As Mike passed us, I felt the weird sensation for a second time.

After Rick got out, the two guides kept up their search for a safe path over to the rocks. Al was still stationed in between. The three of us back on the island stared longingly at the ever-darkening rocks only forty yards away, wishing we were already standing on them.

"Sure would be nice to be over there," I said, nodding toward the moraine, shivering as I spoke. We hadn't moved for thirty minutes, and the air had turned noticeably colder.

"No doubt," said Bruce.

"What's the time, Mike?" Keith asked.

I checked my watch. "Quarter of one."

"Long day," Bruce added as he swung his foot at a fist-sized chunk of ice. "Another long day."

"Yeah, and it's not over yet. I don't see any place nearby to set up camp," I said, still shivering.

"Hey, Bruce," Keith began. "Do you—"

Both Bruce and Keith vanished. Only they hadn't gone anywhere. I had. The ice had disappeared from under my feet, and I was falling rapidly.

Wham! My shoulder hit the wall of a slender crevasse. Then again and again. Clusters of ice crystals showered my face. My head struck the wall forcefully, and my right cheek scraped along the abrasive ice, nearly knocking my glasses off. Under my feet was nothing but air. Down, down, down I went, into an icy crypt.

Oooh . . . God! What was that? Feels like something hit me. What hit me was a violent tug on my pelvis. The rope had gone taut.

It pulled hard against the waist tie-in of my harness, and the leg loops pressed tightly into my upper thighs. The abrupt stop knocked all of the air out of my chest—but at least I was stopped.

I looked down and my heart jumped again. I struggled to see, there was so little light, but I could make out a few dark shapes: rocks and shattered fragments of gray ice, the tops of which came very close to reaching me.

I then remembered Keith and Bruce. We had just been talking. I tried to look up, to see where they were now but I was disoriented.

Which way is up? I couldn't tell. I noticed that my hands were empty. My ski poles had been knocked loose in the fall. I tried to find them, but they were lost in the shadows.

I felt around. The cramped crevasse was nothing like the broad, voluminous ones that my fellow climbers had fallen into. In fact, when I looked from side to side, I found that the distance between the walls was only a few inches wider than my pack—only about three feet.

Wow, this is tight! I tried twisting around the pivot of the rope. After only an eighth of a turn in each direction, my pack hit the wall. I wasn't wedged in, but there wasn't much room to maneuver.

Bumping into the walls wasn't a big deal, but the intense backward force trying to flip me upside down was. I soon discovered that the crevasse was slightly wider front to back, five feet or so, and the weight of the pack was steadily pulling me backward. My head was only slightly above the level of my hips. I had to pull as hard as I could against the rope just to keep myself from going completely head down.

I can't let myself flip over. Gotta pull harder.

I knew that if I flipped, I wouldn't be able to get right-side up again in this tight space. Then I probably *would* get wedged in between the walls. All the blood rushing to my head, I would continue struggling until I passed out a few minutes later.

I wouldn't be awake to assist my teammates as they tried to pull me out.

I could die in this hole.

Using all my strength, I worked my hands up inch by inch on the taut rope until I was nearly fully upright. It took a tremendous effort to hold that position, but at least I had some time to think.

Like in the early seconds of my fall on Karstens Ridge, I had felt only surprise when I broke through the ice. Now the details were coming back.

So that's what that funny sensation up there was, I thought. *The ice underneath me was hollow.* And just like after the fall, now that the initial surprise had passed, I was faced with finding a way out of a totally foreign situation with no idea how to even begin. At least this time I was calmer.

Within a few minutes, a new problem became obvious. I was shivering, but not from nerves. It had gotten very cold. I knew that the longer I hung from this rope, the colder I would become. I was dressed in only a lightweight fleece jacket and thin liner gloves. They would hardly be sufficient to keep me warm down in a crevasse. And I could not reach anything in my pack: parka, gloves, glasses. At least after the icefall I had exchanged my dark sunglasses for clear lenses. Otherwise I wouldn't have been able to see a thing.

Five more minutes passed—then ten and fifteen. I hadn't heard any noise from above since the rope stopped me. I listened. Nothing. Nothing but the sound of my choppy breathing. A bolt of panic struck.

Where's Jack? Why hasn't he called down!?

But then the voice of reason chimed in. *Jesus, get a hold of yourself. He was over by the moraine, looking for a way onto the rocks. It will take him a few minutes to retrace his steps. And as he gets closer, Keith and Bruce will warn him how unsafe the ice is. He'll have to move in slowly.*

My grip on the rope was noticeably weakening. My hands were getting colder and my fingers were cramping. Quickly, I wrapped one of my arms around the rope. *There. The strength in one arm will hold me up for several minutes, and when that arm grows tired, I'll switch to the other. Now, be patient, damn you. Patience, patience.*

Suddenly, my heart jumped up into my throat again. Ice was falling on my head and face.

The hole's collapsing!

I didn't dare look up to see, because just then another heavy chunk hit the top of my head—hard.

A minute later the shower of ice stopped, and I heard what sounded like a voice. And this one wasn't coming from inside of my head, although it sounded just as muffled.

It's Jack. He's calling down to me. Can't understand what he's saying.

"I'm OK," I shouted up.

He said something else—to sit tight?

The ice started falling again and didn't stop for several more minutes. When it did, Jack shouted down again. Now I could hear him.

"The entrance to the hole is still too small to get you out," he was saying. "I'm going to use my ax to make it bigger. Watch your head." He sent more plate-sized chunks of ice showering down on me. The projectiles had plenty of time to accelerate during their thirty-foot drop.

"Ow, that hurt!" I cried as a particularly large chunk hit my forehead before smashing into hundreds of fragments.

"Are you OK?" he shouted.

"Yeah," I said. "I'm OK. It's the pack. Not sure how long I can hold myself upright. It's pulling me backward."

"You need to get the pack off as soon as possible. You've got a ditch loop, right?"

"Yeah, I've got one." I had forgotten all about it. I glanced over at the blue loop tied around my right shoulder strap, the one with Hamill's signature on it.

"Take the 'biner from the ditch loop and clip it into the rope. Then the pack can pull you back only so far."

I reached around with my left hand—*Ow, my shoulder hurts!*—and fastened the loop. I was still supporting all of the pack's weight, but at least the backward force was diminished. "Thanks, Mike," I whispered under my breath.

"I'm going to lower a second rope to you," Jack said. "We're going to have to bring your pack up first. It's still a really small hole up here, and I can't get you and the pack through it at one time. I'm afraid the whole top will collapse if I try to make it too big."

I was not encouraged—in fact, my heart was ready to burst out of my chest. As if fighting the ongoing battle with the pack and worrying about the hole collapsing weren't enough, I now had to hear that he was going to have a hard time pulling me out? What else didn't I know?

The ditch loop bought me some additional time, but as soon as I stopped struggling to stay upright, it became even more difficult to stay warm.

It's so cold. Icebox cold. But there was absolutely nothing I could do about it.

I noticed how this crevasse was so unlike the practice one on Rainier. These walls were dark, in part because so little light was reaching down from above and in part because of the large amount of dirt mixed in with the snow. There was nothing beautiful or fascinating about this crevasse, I decided. I stopped breathing for ten seconds and listened. It was deathly quiet and still, almost like a tomb.

Another wave of panic mixed with anger struck. If only I could be out of here—not just this hole but the mountain! Pictures of home flashed through my thoughts: warm flowers blooming beside green grass, Will chasing tiny Calvin, a sympathetic look filling my wife's face.

Right now I'd rather be anywhere but here, I thought, as several more twigs snapped.

But after a few deep breaths, I was calm again.

I studied the space below me once more. The details were slightly clearer now that my eyes had adjusted to the low light. The space continued to narrow until the chasm ended at a pile of irregular rocks only three or four feet below my snowshoe-covered boots. Had Keith been standing only a body's length closer to me, then I would have smashed my legs on them. As it was, I felt fortunate to be dangling free.

Speaking of my legs, the pain in my groin was worsening. My number-one safety item, the harness, had done its job well. But its design wasn't without compromises. Its circular leg straps had been digging deeply into my groin and the backs of my thighs since I'd stopped, putting constant pressure against my femoral vessels and sciatic nerves. Within ten minutes, both legs were numb and hanging useless. Now, after more than thirty minutes, they burned with agonizing fire.

I returned my attention to my tender left shoulder. I had probably bruised it when I broke through the ice or hit the wall on the way down, as Al had when he fell. (I learned later that it was more serious than that. Part of my triceps had been traumatically torn from the shoulder joint.)

Thinking of Al reminded me of our conversation up at Camp Six. I said that things would be more dangerous the farther down the north side we went. Well, no shit. Ditto about the feeling of being backed up against a wall.

Hanging like a beef carcass in this freezer for thirty minutes had started to affect my thinking. Ideas oozed into my brain and passed through haphazardly. It was difficult to stay on any one topic for long or to follow a thought through to its logical conclusion. The length of my extrication frustrated me immensely, but I could do little about that either, only wait.

In between the short bursts of time when I needed to manage something of immediate concern—like the pack pulling me backward or ice falling on my head—there were longer periods of quiet when my thoughts turned to broader subjects. Many of those thoughts started with the word "why." *Why had I come to the north side? Why had I been so ambitious? Why was I so naïve?*

I realized that in my forty-two years of life, this was the first time that I didn't feel sure I would live another day. As I dangled from that rope, the answer to whether or not there would be a tomorrow was much less clear. I began imagining the worst.

As a smoker, especially early on, I rarely took seriously the fact that my habit was slowly damaging my health or might eventually kill me. I laughed away the risk, saying things like "Well, a person's gotta die from something," or "Why shouldn't I smoke? There's a better chance I could be killed in a car accident tomorrow."

And then, when I was involved in a serious accident a few years before the climb, T-boned in my driver's-side door by a Chevy Suburban while we were both traveling at highway speed, my car's safety features allowed me to walk away from the accident without a scratch. The terrible sounds of metal bending and glass shattering, along with diabolical flashes of fire and smoke as the airbags inflated, were upsetting as they occurred. But since the entire event was over in a matter of only seconds, the accident stopped short of being a truly terrifying experience.

But the crevasse—the whole goddamn fucking glacier, for that matter—was a different story. This "wreck" was dragging on and on, and I truly didn't know how it was going to end. Would I again be fortunate enough to walk away without a scratch? *Not if it keeps going like this I won't.* I banged the wall with the back of my fist, sending a fresh shower of crystals down on my feet. *Just look at this mess!*

In more ways than one I sure missed my "warm jacket". . .

I felt the cold starting to harden my heart. *Maybe if I could stop feeling entirely. Somehow make it so that I was no longer affected by Denali, by either its beauty or its horrors. That would be better, wouldn't it? Gotta give up this crap about feeling spiritually connected. Look where that's gotten me. Hard and cold, that will be the new reality.*

Only impassivity would prevent me from going completely crazy in this claustrophobic hole. And then, if and when I did get back up top, it would smooth out the wide variations of emotions that I'd been feeling of late.

But just when I thought I had a solution to master my emotions, other issues started creeping in, like the things that had brought me to Alaska in the first place. I had never considered the individual parts of my path to Alaska—or the journey itself—to be anything less than virtuous. I stopped smoking so I could live a more active life. I ran because of the simple pleasure of being active. And I discovered a divine connection to these physical activities while trekking. Stepping up the stakes once again, I found on Rainier a way to not only exert myself but commune with mountain landscapes. If I had any regrets as I came down from Rainier, it was that the experience was too short. Denali was the answer to that.

Always reaching out, trying to be better, trying to be something more than just a workaholic family man leading a mundane life in the heartland. I chased my dreams and found I *was* able to do these wonderful kinds of things.

I pounded the wall again. *But this is nuts.*

Then a tiny ray of hope crept into my thoughts. I remembered Jack saying something several days ago about calling RMI when we got off the glacier to tell them we were on our way out.

How is he going to call? I bet that bastard has a satellite phone after all! I thought. There's no way a cell phone's going to work out on the tundra. Maybe I've got a ticket out of here after all. When he pulls me up, I'm going to tell him that I've had it, that he's got to get me out of here. I'm done putting on a tough face. I'll say or do whatever it takes!

"The second rope is coming down," Jack yelled. It had been twenty minutes since I had heard from him.

When the rope reached me, Jack gave me instructions. "Attach the end loop of this rope to your ditch loop using another carabiner from your belt. Then disconnect the ditch loop from the climbing rope. When that's done, unbuckle your waist strap. Oh, and make sure your pack is rotated in the right direction, so it will fit through the narrow channel."

I tried my best to follow Jack's instructions, but persistent bouts of uncontrolled shivering interfered. It took fifteen minutes to manage the simple task.

Hands are cold, so cold.

As my pack started climbing, it banged and scraped against the walls, causing more large chunks of ice to crash down. Just as Jack feared, it wouldn't fit through the small opening up top. I heard muffled curses as they dropped it down a few feet and then tried a second and a third time. Finally, a huge shower of ice hit me as the six of them gave it one last big yank.

"Sit tight. We're going to lower the rope down again in a few minutes," he called down through the somewhat larger entrance. "Once it gets there, clip it into your harness."

By now over an hour had passed since the fall. Mike would have needed that time to set up the pulley system on the other end of the rescue rope. The pack had almost been too much for them to manhandle, and I weighed more than twice as much. There was no way they could lift me without the pulleys.

A few minutes later, the rope returned and I clipped my harness into it. I pictured the guys pulling arms' lengths of rope through the gears as I inched past the same walls that had raced by in seconds during the fall. All the way up, I failed to find anything admirable about this most unpleasant of places. Even the air was foul. Moist, musty, with a stiff texture of death.

Near the end of the extrication, I heard Jack complaining to Mike about his pulley setup. "Who taught you to do it that way?" he bitched.

I couldn't believe my ears. "Jesus Christ, Jack," I mumbled, "can't you just shut up for once and get me the hell out of here?"

After fifteen minutes of hoisting, I was staring at the crevasse lip. Damn, the ice was only four inches thick. No wonder I broke through. Using my ax as a handgrip, I pulled the rest of my body up and onto the top. I stayed propped up on my elbows and knees, not moving, for several minutes. I breathed heavily and waited for the feeling to come back into my burning legs, the legs that had been nearly strangled by the harness over the past ninety minutes. Although I was thankful to be out of the crevasse—to say nothing of being alive and uninjured—my spirit was completely shattered. I wanted so desperately to be gone from this place.

Finally, in a dry, thin voice, I thanked Jack and the guys for saving my life and pulling me out. A few breaths later, I turned to look up at Jack, who was patiently squatting down next to me. I wasn't able to bring my eyes up to his. As much to the ice as to him, I said, "I'm finished. For me, this climb is over."

I had rehearsed those words even before I emerged from the crevasse, thinking that if I appeared pathetic enough, he would pity me and somehow find a way to call for a helicopter. I no longer gave a damn about completing the traverse or walking out across the tundra. I just wanted to go home.

"That's fine, but we still have to walk out." Seeming totally unaffected by my fall—or by any of the events of the past six days, for that matter—he looked directly at me, unblinking. His lips creased slightly upward, his mouth held open in its characteristic patronizing grin. He waited for a response, but I had none.

I remained silent.

So he repeated his last six words, just in case I didn't understand him the first time. "We still have to walk out." They carried no compassion, relayed not an ounce of sympathy, and suggested no alternative.

God, I hated that son of a bitch right then.

Reality hit me as hard as the crevasse wall had. I had known what his answer was going to be even before he said a word. We really didn't have a satellite phone. The cell phones weren't working. We hadn't seen a single plane fly over since we hit the north side. We had no way to call for a rescue, and there was no one to send a signal to.

There was nothing else Jack could have said. And in his unsubtle way, he had told me something more. The tone of his voice made it clear that if I had lost my nerve, then I better find it again, and right now.

I silently nodded my head.

I became uncomfortably aware of the five other members of my audience as I continued to wait for cool reason to assume control of my senses. When I stood up to acknowledge my comrades, I was met with pained looks. They clearly intended to relay empathy and encouragement, but weak smiles couldn't begin to conceal that they were as devastated as I was. Coming down the north side had been like playing a weeklong game of Russian roulette. Al would later put numbers to it: fourteen crevasse falls—six requiring a full, formal extrication. Yes, the raw numbers were impressive but I was now connected to them in a personal way. I knew from the moment I saw how close I was to the bottom of my hole that things could have turned out much differently.

My teammates' continuing support did little to comfort me. Their pity only made me hate myself more than I did Jack. The reflection I had glimpsed of myself as I walked over the snow bridge was clearer than ever. And I despised what I saw. If it would have made any difference I would have sobbed and groveled at Jack's feet, begging him to find me a way home. I would have done anything if he just would have said, *"Alright, Mike, you've been through enough. I'll find a way to get you out of here."*

With the words "I'm finished," I'd played my last hopeless card. And I'd lost my self-esteem as my stoic teammates stood watching. I felt ashamed. Pathetic.

I expected Jack to tell me it was time to get going, but this time he surprised me. "Take as much time as you need," he said.

One of my friends dug into my pack and pulled out my parka, and I put it on. It felt good to be warm again and no longer alone.

I turned to Keith, who had once again been at the end of my rope. "Thanks, Keith," I said.

"No problem," he answered with typical humility.

It was three o'clock in the morning. Time to press on. I stowed the parka and Jack took aim again at the rocks. Now armed with the knowledge of which way *not* to go, we soon found ourselves standing on them.

After thirty minutes on the rocks, we understood why we hadn't left the glacier any sooner. It was tough going, moving across an endless pile of snow-covered and bare shale that was loosely heaped onto the thirty-degree slope. But walk we did, for three more hours, clambering up one intersecting ridge and then sliding back down the other side, time and again. The effect on my already battered legs was pain beyond description. Yet as difficult as it was, it was still better than walking on the Muldrow.

Now that we were on safe ground again, my mind reentered its contemplative state. My head stayed down, not only to keep an eye on where my feet were going, but also as an act of penitence. I'd always believed that I would act honorably if I ever faced true adversity. I imagined that I had it within me to be a hero. Like Neil Armstrong's landing on the moon—a difficult job well executed—Denali was to be my finest hour. But now I knew none of that was true.

While tackling one scree slope after another, I desperately searched again for a way out—this time not from the mountain but from myself. Twenty-three days ago, when I had looked into my eyes in the hotel bathroom in Chicago, I put the question to myself: Could I do this? Was I a mountaineer? I thought I knew what I was getting myself into. Serious mountaineering meant taking risks—risks of falls and injuries, and the risk of personal failure. I'd thought I'd accepted all that.

But I found that it was one thing to say that I accepted the risks of what I was doing (in comfortable places like the Chicago hotel room and the Talkeetna ranger station) and quite another to gracefully accept the consequences of that risky behavior when the chips were down. In the end, my ultimate lack of grace at the crevasse lip seemed to bring everything else down with it. The next time I looked into a mirror, I would have to face the truth: I had, in fact, failed to measure up to my own expectations.

My head was still down as I watched my foot slip for the thousandth time on the wretched heap of slag. What I hadn't bothered to notice was that the rock I was walking on was no longer colored black in the twilit night. It was six o'clock, and the moraine had lightened to a mix of brown and gray.

Bruce, who was on the rope ahead of me, called back. "Hey, Mike!"

"What now?" I looked up, annoyed that he had the nerve to interrupt my silent pity party. The rope leaders had stopped for a breather at the top of an especially tall pile of rubble, and Bruce was standing up there with them. The Marine was posed like a statue, pointing the tip of his ski pole toward something on the opposite valley wall. "Look, Mike. Alpenglow."

Winded by the climb, I first took several deep breaths of crisp, refreshing air, then stood up tall and looked across the glacier at what Bruce was pointing to. He had said all along that he wanted to experience the sight of alpenglow while here on Denali, and now there it was. For the next few minutes, oblivious to what the other members of the group were doing, the two of us watched the entire valley of ice turn from pale gray to the color of fire.

My stiff, frozen heart started to thaw. Tears welled up in my eyes. By God's grace, I had survived my ordeal and was able to stand on two strong legs to witness an unbelievable event.

This event was much more than an especially beautiful sunrise. It was the beginning of a new day—the dawn of renewal.

All of the darkness from the north side of Denali washed away in the time that it took the fiery crimson to fade.

I could think of nothing to say.

"I wish I could have taken that fall for you, Mike," Bruce said quietly.

What had I done to deserve his kindness?

As we watched the quiet valley come to life, I thought of my early mantra, "Lord, give me strength and endurance to climb this mountain." Without my realizing it, my prayer had been answered. I had crossed over Denali, and in the process had learned more about myself than I wanted to know, certainly more than I could have known if we had gone back down the south side. Along with an understanding of my failings, I learned that even in the darkest night, there is room for hope. My redemption had nothing to do with who I am or how I see myself. This was pure grace—mine *despite* who I am.

The sun was rising, and with the morning came acceptance and peace.

—

After we walked another hour on the rocks, Jack led us into a sheltered cove on the edge of the glacier, onto a little patch of flat, welcoming snow. On that snow, we built Camp Nine. It was midmorning. Our days and nights were completely reversed.

He said that we'd hit the tundra later that afternoon, but first we would eat something and get a little sleep. Breakfast was ramen noodles doused with recently thawed-out Tabasco sauce.

As I lay on top of my sleeping bag inside the safe, warm confines of the tent, my last thought was—what else?—that we were only two days from the road.

GREEN GROWING THINGS

—

TUESDAY AND WEDNESDAY, JUNE 10 AND 11

Camp Nine was the only camp that we didn't spend at least a part of one actual night at. We established it on Tuesday morning and dismantled it at ten o'clock in the evening that same day. Rick, Al, and I awoke in the evening to a comfortable tent that had been warmed all day by the sun. Lifting our spirits further was the knowledge that at some point within the next twenty-four hours, we would step off the ice for the last time.

We ate a leisurely breakfast and milled around unroped on the snow. From the safety of camp and with a few insulating hours of sleep, the Muldrow didn't seem as threatening. In fact, the Lower Icefall, the ice tower on Mount Carpe, and even the potholed area where the glacier had devoured me looked beautiful. We took turns having our photographs taken with the Muldrow in the background if for no other reason than to document that we had survived its horrors. The photograph of me shows the tanned skin of my face stretched directly on top of the bones with minimal softening from underlying fat. The tip of my scabbed nose (from the second Karstens fall) and my slim figure (now inside an obviously overloose jacket) suggest someone twenty years older. But on my face is a smile! It really hadn't been so bad up there, had it?

I started wondering how I was going to put all of this into context when I explained to family and friends what transpired up here. These weren't just ordinary vacation experiences. For my teammates and me, they had been life changing. But the folks back home would be the same as when I left; they wouldn't have changed. They had been going to work, driving their cars, sleeping in comfortable beds, enjoying summer by grilling burgers on the patio. Their predictable rhythms hadn't been interrupted. They had not spent the last month battling and soul-searching like I had.

And what would hearing about it make them think of me? That I was crazy, probably. I'd be proud to tell them that we had spent a total of three-and-a-half weeks on Denali, reached the summit, and successfully traversed the mountain from south to north. But although they might show interest, the experience was so far removed from their everyday lives that it would be difficult for them to relate.

For most of the people back home, I decided it would be best to stick with the superficial facts, a few vacation highlights that were easy to communicate. But I wanted to be able to explain to those closest to me how it felt to be dangling alone at the end of a rope or how three people in a tent can endure a violent two-day blizzard separated from the wind by only a millimeter of nylon? I wanted to be able to explain how it felt to live for nearly a month in the wilderness, how the mountain reduced life to its simplest terms—muscles working hard, bodies toughening beneath heavy loads, the world feeling fresh all over, finding wonder in it again. How would I explain that on Denali I learned to live in the moment, in each and every moment? Or how Denali made me feel the full spectrum of emotions—from exhilaration to despondency and from courageousness to cowardliness—sometimes all within a few hours' time?

These thoughts were not easily packaged into snippets for casual conversation. In the end, I'd have to write a book to explain it all.

Then I wondered how successfully I'd adapt to my normal life with all its complexities and responsibilities: cooking, changing diapers, waking up in the middle of the night to do appendectomies—all the things required to be a husband, father, and surgeon.

But it was time to shoulder the pack and get going. The adventure was not yet finished. As Jack had so succinctly put it, we still had to walk out. And though I didn't know it yet, the mountain was still very much in control of me and it hadn't played its final cards.

So the march went on. At ten o'clock, we cinched up the hip belts on our packs and started walking. The sun that had warmed our bodies inside our tents had also warmed the surface of the glacier, making the snow sloppy. Even the cooler air of evening was above freezing at this lower altitude. We tramped through wet snow and, in places, even heard the sound of running water under the surface.

We stopped briefly when Mike, who was leading, fell up to his waist in a crevasse. He pulled himself out before I had a chance to react.

Even the lateral portion of the glacier was riddled with crevasses, so we stayed far to the side, or went back for a time onto the moraine, walking alternately on slush and rock for the next five hours. It was far from safe or easy, but it was the most uneventful day of travel we had enjoyed in a week. The rest of the minor crevasses we happened to break into or knowingly step across were minor nuisances instead of menaces. That sound of running water never stopped being unsettling, though. The thought of falling through the ice and being swept away by a subterranean river was too terrible to even consider.

Finally, there was only rock.

It was three o'clock in the morning when we stepped off of the Muldrow for the last time. As had been the case last night, the dimness of the light was more pronounced once we stepped away from the glacier's reflective surface. Had it been any darker, we would have needed headlamps to climb up to McGonagall Pass.

I looked down to watch a black spot that was circling around my legs in a random pattern, just above the rocks. It was a bee! A bee. My eyes squinted to focus on other extraordinary things, green growing things. Sparsely scattered among the ubiquitous gray rocks were tiny plants—flowers, stems, leaves, and all.

We took a break before beginning the climb up to the prominent saddle. It was an important transition point for the team, in terms of not only geography but also psychology. We had not stood on truly solid ground since exiting the tarmac in Talkeetna. And, for twenty-three days after that, whenever we moved we were tied together at the waist into rope teams. Now, the stability of the rock allowed us to walk about unclipped. How different it felt to function as individuals again.

Someone got us started, and then we all started shouting, "So long, Muldrow! Goodbye, you fucking Muldrow!"

It was just the sort of foolish, giddy reaction that our fragile moods needed. We laughed and hugged and congratulated each other. In some respects it was a more significant moment than standing on the summit. My favorite photo from that morning shows Rick lying back on the rocks, pack off, coat unzipped. His face wears a marvelously gleeful smile.

As we approached the top of the saddle, I saw that a permanent snowfield covered the upper stretch. It was one of the many sources for the meltwater that filled the streams we would soon cross. We started climbing down again, wading through snow that came up to our knees, our feet slopping through the running water that ran underneath the surface. Then, halfway down the other side, we stepped onto the cushiony carpet of the tundra itself. Plants and soil, rather than ice and snow, covered the surface our boots touched.

We were still at four thousand feet, well above tree line for this latitude, and the plants were only a few inches tall. In and around them hovered our latest nemesis: mosquitoes. There were millions of them, each sporting a two-inch wingspan. Bug repellent and head nets prevented them from landing on our skin and clothing, but that didn't keep them away entirely. We eventually accepted the constant, nearly maddening buzzing around our ears as a part of this newest reality. There was so much life here. And we had been so unprepared for it. Overwhelming, yes, but also sensual.

Coming down from the pass, we lost elevation rapidly at first and then more gradually. We followed a trickle of water through a series of small cascades that became an ever-widening stream. The farther down we dropped, the taller the vegetation grew. Soon enough we became familiar with yet another troubling pest, the alder. These water-loving, fast-growing, thicket-forming trees did everything they could to impede our progress. None of us had considered that a hatchet might be essential equipment for climbing Denali, but one certainly would have come in handy. Still, we made better time on land than we had on the snow, and by early afternoon we were five miles out from the bottom of the pass. There we set up Camp Ten. It was Camp Finale on Denali. After first dusting away the larger rocks and pebbles, we set the tents up on bare ground. It felt wonderful to run the warm dirt through my hands.

And then, after we had fetched water from the nearby stream and completed all the other group chores, I sat down to remove my boots and socks. I was going to get a proper look at my aching feet, the first in several days. Including the second half of summit day, we had been traveling downhill for nine days, descending over eighteen thousand feet. With each of those steps down, my toes had slid forward a bit, sometimes forcefully jamming into the inflexible toe box of the plastic boots.

Custom molded liners had helped minimize the sliding, but they hadn't completely prevented the formation of blisters. I saw some small ones now on the balls of my feet. I also saw that the nails of both my big toes were black from hemorrhage underneath. I had some hot spots on my heels and the tops of my toes, but thankfully, there was no evidence of frostbite. I leaned back and let the sun and comfortable breeze dry them. They appreciated the feeling of warmth that afternoon more than any other part of me.

I had forgotten how enchanting a warm breeze could be. The wind carried fresh scents—the smell of sunbaked dirt and perfumed vegetation. As I napped that afternoon on top of an unzipped sleeping bag, lying between my two fine friends with the tent windows open, I had pleasant dreams. The underlying tension of the past few days was quickly fading. My mind and my tight, tired muscles started to unwind. That night I slept for even longer stretches, the rest putting even more distance between the nightmares and me.

THURSDAY, JUNE 12

We had thirteen miles yet to go.

As planned, Jack woke us at two o'clock in the morning so we could cross the streams early in the day, before their water levels rose due to afternoon snowmelt. But he said there was no rush to get started, so the morning's pace was leisurely.

Once on the trail, we found more thickets of alders to squeeze between and then the knee-deep icy waters of Cache and Clearwater creeks to wade through. The bottoms of the two streambeds were irregular and slippery, covered in loose, moss-covered rocks and silt. Since I had lost both of my ski poles in the crevasse fall, I was at a disadvantage as far as balancing myself. During the first crossing, Bruce came to my rescue and lent me one of his.

The trail started climbing again, out of the second stream's valley. We ascended several hundred feet to the top of a ridge, where we took in an outstanding view of Denali's entire north side. I peered through the low saddle of McGonagall Pass to the Muldrow beyond; the long, winding course of Pioneer Ridge; the bulk of the Wickersham Wall; Mount Carpe and Karstens Ridge. The Harper Glacier and twin summits topped it all. As we came together for a group picture, the first since summit day, and put our arms around each other's shoulders, I realized just how badly we smelled. The only disadvantage of the warm air, it turned out, was that it speeded up the release of twenty-four days' worth of stench.

Facing north again, the mountain once again at our backs, we looked ahead to the last few miles. The trail was not indistinct, but neither did it show signs of heavy use. In a small wooded glade just off the trail, we heard the clanging sounds of pots being scrubbed. It wasn't a bear but rather a party of Norwegians, the first outsiders we had seen since leaving High Camp. They were making hauls up to the Muldrow in an attempt to summit from this side. Jack shared his concerns with them regarding what he called "poor snow conditions" on the glacier. Furthermore, he couldn't promise that our trail through the crevasse fields and icefalls would still be visible.

Traversing Denali from the north side, hauling three weeks' worth of supplies over eighteen miles of tundra and then doing double carries up the Muldrow and Karstens Ridge represented a much more difficult task than ours. And although the earliest climbers of Denali approached it from this side, only a few hardy souls like these Norwegians still follow their path to the top today.

After wishing them luck, we started out again. Looming far out in the distance, but getting progressively closer by the hour, was a dark-green ridge that rose on the other side of McKinley Bar. I knew that somewhere on top of that ridge, we would find the road.

The next section of trail took us first through a particularly dense thicket of alders, and then down a dusty slope, and finally into a prime example of an Alaskan muskeg. The pools of water in it were inky black, their bottoms thick with boot-sucking mud. To keep our boots from being pulled off, we walked on the intervening patches of dry ground, on top of grass-covered mounds called hummocks. Whatever else these hummocks functioned as for the muskeg, they worked as conveniently spaced stepping-stones for us.

Our arrival at the river bar was anticlimactic—there was no water. We'd have to walk another mile across an uneven layer of flat, smooth, palm-sized rocks to see water.

And then, when we did reach the mighty McKinley River, it disappointed us again. *This can't be right,* I thought. *It's nothing but another small stream.* But this also was a deception. Large rivers in Alaska are braided. That is, rather than following a single channel, the water flows in interlocking streams of varying widths and depths. To cross a river like the McKinley, we needed to wade through several of these individual streams.

As I stood looking at the first of these braids, it seemed logical to cross at its narrowest point. But as Jack said, "That would be the absolute worst thing to do. The narrows contained the deepest, fastest-moving water." His experience told him to look instead for the broadest sections, where the water was shallower and slower.

After we passed through several of these easy channels, only the main channel stood between us and the base of the green ridge. It was the final obstacle. Rick darted across the forty-foot divide before anyone even knew he was in the water. We could have easily thrown a rope to him once he was across, giving the rest of us something to hold onto during our crossings, something to stabilize us . . . but we didn't.

After tying my socks and boot liners to the top of my pack, and unbuckling the hip belt so I could quickly jettison it if necessary,

I waded out into the rushing water. My bare feet slid around inside the voluminous outer boots as they struggled to find a solid purchase on the shifting, slippery rocks. Even close to the bank, the current was surprisingly strong and markedly greater than in any of the previous streams. When the water rose above my knees, I found it extremely difficult to resist the constant force that was trying to push me downstream and to maintain my course straight across, toward Rick. The water was numbing cold and made my already weak legs feel even less trustworthy. If only the guides had shared one valuable little trick with me . . . but they didn't.

My next step was too much. I went down. The frigid water yanked at me. It would have been easier to just let go, to let the water pull me along. Fighting it was taking every ounce of energy that remained.

Jack acted fast, before I had to resort to ditching the pack. Just before the current took complete hold of me, I felt his hand grab my shoulder. Somehow he was able to wrestle me and my waterlogged pack out of the current and back to the shoreline.

Along with my last sliver of pride, I lost two valuable things in the dousing: Bruce's loaner ski pole and my eyeglasses.

"Goddamn it!" Jack yelled. "Why didn't you have your glasses hooked to a lanyard?"

Thanks for your concern, Jack, and by the way I can still see and I'm OK, too. I just looked up at him and shrugged my shoulders.

The trick that I should have known was to avoid fighting the current. I should have allowed it to take me slightly downstream along a diagonal path, instead of trying to maintain a straight-across tack.

"Go with it, go with the current," Mike shouted over the roar of the river as he led me back in for a second attempt. The two of us crossed together, me nervously clutching the rear of his pack for security. Because I had none, he used his poles to balance the two of us.

I'll never forget what he did once we reached the far side. He could have just shaken his head in disgust and washed his hands of me once and for all, but instead he looked at me like a loving parent would, one who was practically at wit's end, tired of dealing with his wayward child—me. At the same time, his look showed that he accepted part of the blame himself, for somehow failing to protect me from harm.

"Mike," he said to me as he clutched my shoulder with one of his strong hands, his face close to mine so that I could hear him over the deafening roar of the nearby water, "you'll never have to climb big mountains again."

In other words, what I'd endured was enough. I didn't have to prove myself by climbing Cho Oyu or anything bigger than this. I could retire if I wanted to.

Right then I started mentally preparing a testimonial to submit to RMI. It would say of Mike Hamill, "I'd climb anything with that guy!"

In the end, these two big, strapping guides had fulfilled the promise of the office lady who answered RMI's phone—they *had* carried me off the mountain, alive and in one piece. I couldn't have done it without them. At that moment I didn't feel especially proud of my accomplishments, but I wasn't so worried about my shortcomings, either.

—

As I checked the condition of my pack, I was thankful for one more thing. I had thought to put my camera and film into a ziplock bag. They were dry and undamaged. But everything else was soaking wet. Even after I emptied out the standing water and wrung out all of my clothes, I was still carrying an extra ten pounds of river.

A crude pair of dirt steps led from the sandy riverbank up to the exit trail proper. The first step was six inches higher than my exhausted leg muscles could manage.

"I'll get you up there," Al said, and he literally pushed me up from behind.

As Jack searched around in the tall grass for the main branch of the McKinley Bar Trail, we ran into a group of twenty-year-olds coming the other way from the road. They were on a National Outdoor Leadership School (NOLS) expedition attempting the summit from the north side, just like the Norwegians. Their fresh faces and enthusiastic movements gave them away as Denali initiates. I could only imagine what they thought when they looked our way.

Jack talked to their young but capable-appearing leader. "Just to let you know, we ran into some pretty poor snow conditions up there," he started.

With the beginning of that reprise, I turned off the audio. I knew the rest of the litany already. Remaining at a distance, I admired the group members' strong physiques and eager smiles. They reminded me of our group twenty-five days ago. I had a sudden urge to say something to them, but I didn't know whether it was better to wish them well or start shouting like a madman, begging them to turn around and go back home to their families.

I settled for mumbling under my breath, "I don't think you quite understand what you're getting yourselves into."

Jack and the rest of us then returned our attention to the business of getting ourselves home.

Thanks to the NOLS leader, we soon found the main trail and marched through some impressively deep Alaskan muck. We were inside a dense spruce forest up until the very last moment. There were no clues to suggest that we were even close to the road, but then one final turn in the trail pointed us to a small clearing. A brown van bearing the markings of the Kantishna Roadhouse was parked in a small gravel parking lot. At last! I threw down my pack, bent down, and kissed the ground. I was simultaneously delighted and disappointed by this abrupt return to the ordinary.

While we sat on our packs and waited for the public shuttle bus, a park ranger pulled up in a big white Chevy Suburban. He got out to investigate, no doubt curious to know what such a motley crew was doing loitering on his beat. Instead of listening to Jack's third recitation on snow conditions, I chose to walk up to a higher point on the road with an unobstructed view of the Alaska Range. The range's shining star dominated the scene. It was a fine, beautiful day.

Tourists spend a hell of a lot of time and money, I thought, *to get here.* They cruise for several days up the Inside Passage and then spend another day riding up from Anchorage on the train. Then they endure a bumpy, eight-hour bus ride along this unpaved, dusty Park Road—all in the hope of standing here and seeing the mountain.

The clear weather today made me feel like a lucky tourist. The clouds stayed away and I enjoyed, for a little while longer, my personal connection to one of the most breathtakingly beautiful mountains in the world. I walked fifty miles for the privilege of this view.

By now I was fully recovered from my dousing in the frigid river. My whole body felt warm for the first time in weeks. Sure, I'd worked up a sweat multiple times while toting my gear up Denali's slopes, but the warmth I felt today was different. Everything—my bones, my feet, even the hair on my head—was pleasantly toasty.

I took a deep breath, held it for a few seconds, and then blew it out. It wasn't another example of Brother Mike's pressure-breathing technique. It wasn't to gather up enough gumption to face Denali's next obstacle. Nor was it to recover my nerve one last time after yet another terrifying event.

This time, the deep sigh was nothing more than an affirmation, to accept that my quest was finished. With that breath I finally knew true satisfaction. I wasn't wanting for more, wondering if this was all there was.

"We knocked the bastard off," Edmund Hillary famously said after he and Tenzing Norgay conquered Everest. I guessed I would find a better way to sum up my personal feelings about Denali later on, but his way suited me just fine for now.

GOING HOME

—

Angie's tone of voice suggested that she hadn't been overly concerned about me. She *did* sound very happy that I was down and that she could finally talk to me again.

"Where are you calling from?" the voice from almost three thousand miles away said.

"A pay phone at the campground. We just got out today." I found the lack of concern in her voice to be oddly disappointing, but how could she know? As she talked my mind wandered: What should I say, where should I start? I concluded it was better to save that for another time.

"I think we'll probably start toward Anchorage sometime tomorrow or the next day, so it will probably be at least three more days before I'm home."

"Well, the kids and I can't wait to see you," she said. She also sounded distracted, but in her case it was because one of our rascals was doing something naughty that was occupying the other half of her attention.

"I missed all of you, too. See you soon. I love you," I said.

Yes, the rest could wait.

Within an hour of our arrival at the McKinley Bar trailhead, a green school bus pulled up. It was one of the last of the shuttles that ran throughout the day, ferrying passengers the eighty-five miles between the Denali park entrance, where our campground for tonight was, and Wonder Lake. Since the majority of the road was off-limits to private cars, these buses provided the only motorized access to the park's interior.

We shoved our packs in through the emergency door and claimed seven empty seats in the rear. Only a handful of other people—retirees, mostly—were on the bus. All of them appeared relieved that we had chosen to segregate ourselves in the back. I felt mildly self-conscious about my rough looks, but an occasional sideways stare from one of the normal-looking people on the bus didn't prevent me from removing my boots and socks and kicking my sweaty feet up on the seat. Across the aisle from me was Mike. He was picking at a wide tear in the knee of his favorite pair of Helly Hansen climbing pants, bemoaning their ruin.

We ate the few scraps of food that remained in our packs. But after it was gone, we were still ravenous. A true meal was still several hours away, in one of the restaurants in Denali Park.

The bus driver, recognizing our state, shared what was left of his lunch with us. It didn't amount to much: two small sandwich baggies, one containing carrots and celery and the other some cherries. My share amounted to just two vegetable sticks and two pieces of fruit. They gave me a better appreciation of the comfort charity can bring.

An hour later, Denali disappeared from view for the last time after the bus took a sharp left-hand turn in the road.

At the Denali Park village, Jack steered us away from the hotel district. We each had cash and a credit card in our packs and could have purchased a comfortable room for the night, but as we carried no fresh clothes, paying good money for a shower and clean sheets at this juncture made little sense. Instead we took up residence in the local campground. There, we assembled our tents one final time. The conditions were luxurious compared to the Alaskan bush. The facilities included clean running water, electric lights, and the all-important telephone.

Once the tent was set up, I inspected the campground's bathroom. I took advantage of the conventional toilet and tried to have a look in the mirror on the wall. It was darkly stained and streaked. The careful inspection of myself would have to wait just a little longer, like the shower.

Being suddenly thrown back into civilization was shocking, even in a place as rough and simple as this frontier town. Speeding cars, smooth asphalt, the smell of fried food. So many people making so many noises. I dug the bag of money out of my pack and started spending it. I loaded up on Doritos, Diet Coke, and orange juice from the campground commissary. Then, at dinner that night I parted with a few more dollars for fried halibut, French fries, and two Alaskan Ambers.

Although dinner had a note of finality about it, I wasn't sad that the expedition had come to an end. I was ready to go home. Every one of us at the table looked like he felt likewise. Each of these men was somewhat less strong and confident today than when he had started out twenty-five days ago. They, like me, were dazed and spent. There was nothing left to do, nothing else of consequence to say to each other. We had already done it all and said it all.

Rick, Al, Keith, and I were leaving early the following day. The standard transportation RMI arranged would have had us waiting for the 4:00 p.m. train to Talkeetna. That meant spending not only another full day here but also an overnight in Talkeetna before traveling to Anchorage the next morning. By departing for Talkeetna first thing in the morning we moved everything up a day.

Bruce decided to stay in Denali Park with the guides. The three of them would take the train down as scheduled.

FRIDAY, JUNE 13

At six thirty in the morning, our group formally split. While we disassembled our tent and prepared to meet the van, Al told Rick and me a story from last night. Bruce, who had come home with Keith and the guides in the middle of the night, apparently felt like sleeping outside in the open. Al awoke at three o'clock after hearing some commotion. When he peered out of our tent door, he saw Bruce lying on his bag, propped up on his left side, puking his dinner on the ground. A fox was standing right next to his head, lapping up the warm vomit as it came out. We squirmed and laughed, adding this latest unique Alaskan tale to the long list of memories.

Talkeetna hadn't changed much since we saw it last. For our few hours there, we had two priorities: showers and a Roadhouse breakfast. Showers were available at the general store at a cost of four dollars for ten minutes. Rick and I went into the store to pay, both of us smelling like a pig pen.

Rick smiled at the young lady at the cash register. "You probably can't guess what we're here for, can ya?"

Rick bought twelve dollars' worth. One of my two four-dollar plastic tokens broke in the machine before my sunbaked brain figured out how to use the blasted thing. The ten minutes of hot water that I did get was a good start to washing away a month of filth, though.

After showering, brushing my teeth, and throwing my month-old underwear in the trash can, I spent a few moments staring at my naked profile with the help of a brightly polished, full-length mirror in the dressing room. I examined the dime-sized scab on the end of my nose; my peeling, sunburned earlobes; and the hollows that had formed under my cheekbones.

Looking lower, I noted excess handfuls of loose skin hanging down like empty leather water bags from my armpits and waist due to the loss of twenty pounds.

I found it difficult to look straight into my eyes, for in them was an uncomfortable knowledge. But in the end, I did. I asked the person looking back at me, *Is this the face of a successful mountaineer? Will they believe that I am when I get off the plane in Springfield?*

I stood at the mirror a little longer. There was no rush. Rick was still popping tokens into the shower. The reflection couldn't convince even *me* that I was looking at a victorious mountain warrior. My figure looked maimed and diseased. What had I done to myself? If I hadn't been so hungry and anxious to get to the Roadhouse before they stopped serving breakfast, I would have started crying.

"Come on, Rick. Let's go get some food," I finally said to him through the curtain.

"Sounds good. Be right out," he answered.

My tent mates and I did get to the Roadhouse on time. My full-portion breakfast contained four eggs, two slices of Texas toast, six strips of bacon, a heap of fried potatoes, a tall glass of orange juice, and several cups of steaming coffee. For dessert there was a slice of apple pie à la mode. Our "Alaskan" waitress spoke with a heavy eastern European accent. The Bulgarian beauty continued to bring additional courses of food to our table long after the stomachs of those around us had been satisfied.

The morning meal served as a celebration—not so much to reward ourselves, but to celebrate life in general. The noonday sun felt deliciously warm on the patio as Rick, Al, and I enjoyed each other's company this one final time. Yet, while we talked of splitting up, I knew that we'd never really be apart. Even separated by distance, we couldn't help but carry a piece of each other with us. These pieces would remain solidly integrated in our souls, deep inside where no one else could get to them. Even the forgetfulness that comes with the passage of time couldn't change that.

In the van on the way to the Anchorage airport, I sat alone on the rear bench while Rick, Keith, and Al sat in the seats in front of me. I looked forward and smiled contently, gazing at the relaxed figures of my dear friends.

I instinctively fondled the gold ring that hung around my neck, still hanging by its purple cord. The knot holding the cord together was a double fisherman's knot. A successful mountaineer had tied that knot.

SATURDAY, JUNE 14

I wrote my final journal entry on the flight home, in the darkness of night:

Well, what did I learn from this? Every day was hard. There were no easy parts. The physical demands were impressive. I burned up so much subcutaneous fat I'm sure I was burning muscle at the end, which contributed to leg weakness and fatigue. Overall, I handled going up better than going down and the first half better than the second. A truly exhausting experience.

Walking without the weight of the pack, eating and being satisfied, feeling safe, reaching the conclusion of the climb were all pleasurable, simple experiences. There is little in the way of true satisfaction regarding the climb, even when strangers ask us about the experience and congratulate us. We [clients] do shake each other's hands, hug, and smile. We're more relieved that we're alive, that we survived. Yes, there is a feeling of accomplishment, but for now it is muted. Time will smooth out the edges and make the bad seem more tolerable.

Those minutes in the crevasse will be my defining moments. The risks outweighed the accomplishments. The hazards were real, too real for what I and the other climbers felt were tolerable. Had we just gone up and down the West Buttress, I would have felt totally different. I would be looking for a bigger mountain. Now I want to scale back. Maybe do Florida or Colorado instead of Montana (Glacier National Park camping vacation planned with the kids for the fall). Doing a three-week family trip instead of on my own. Keeping the familiar closer. Enjoying the day-to-day, simple pleasures more. Less attention to the extreme and still preserve the adventure. I thank God for being safe, for cool breezes and rest. Maybe things will feel different in two weeks. There will be physical and mental adjustments, time for healing. Would I do it again?

—

After landing in Springfield, I went to the baggage carousel, where I immediately saw Angie and all four kids. The person they were searching for was *not* there, however. Their husband and father had changed; he was now considerably thinner, newly bearded, and not wearing his glasses.

I went over to them and said hello. My wife, startled by this stranger's talking and staring at her, stepped away. She tilted back her head, looked up, and saw that it was me. Her next movement was forward. Her arms wrapped around my neck in a loving embrace.

EPILOGUE

McKinley is no longer a reality. It has reverted back to being a dream. Most of the subjects in my photographs are no longer tangible. Keith, Bruce, Armando, Jack, and Ryan are static images in my memory. I have not seen them since. Al and I still keep in touch. Mike, Rick, and I went on to climb Aconcagua in the Andes together, and Rick and I still see each other from time to time. All of us have moved on to become different people than the nine who tackled Denali together. The intervening days and nights have seen to it.

On rare occasions I can reenter that world, though. Tonight is one of them. My family is away, and I am alone in the house. Lying in bed, in a waking dream, I imagine myself back in the world of Denali. Only, it is not so much a place as a feeling. The feeling exists as a room without walls, a volume without dimensions, its only boundaries the distant peaks surrounding a glacial valley. The air is the same as it was then: cold, clean, and clear. The key that opened the door for me tonight was an olfactory memory: the aroma of sunscreen evaporating off of my face and the rancid saline scent that rose off of my hiking shirt all those days while I was climbing on the mountain.

In that waking dream, I sense again the peculiar pairing of cool solitude and warm companionship. I know that a part of me will never leave Denali. An impression of me remains somewhere there on the mountain, perhaps in a fissure on a rock or within a crevice in the ice.

Everything that Denali is continues inside of me as well. Sometimes it is haunting and terrifying, but more often it is welcoming—enticing and familiar. It is a very strange thing to have these conflicting emotions inside, but what would I be without them?

Would I do it again? Yes. There is no other credible answer. Who I am today is the result of all I have done in all of my yesterdays.

I do not wish to be anyone else.

ACKNOWLEDGMENTS

Living the life of adventure on Denali meant the realization of a dream for me, but I didn't scale that mountain alone. Neither did the story of that adventure come to these pages without considerable help from others. Since returning from the climb, I felt that the story in *Crossing Denali* was a good one that needed to be told. The problem was that I was not a writer. As *Star Trek*'s Dr. McCoy may have said of my ordeal, "Damn it, Jim. I'm a doctor not a mountain-climbing author!"

I am deeply grateful to Ingrid Emerick, Kristin Mehus-Roe, and Kathryn Wagner at Girl Friday Productions for their editorial skills and advice during the many rewrites. At Mountaineers Books I extend heartfelt thanks to editor in chief Kate Rogers for accepting the manuscript, Laura Shauger and her team for bringing it to publication, and to Kirsten Colton for always believing in it.

To my guides and climbing mates on Denali, I say thank you for your friendship and for the unforgettable experience.

To my loving wife, Angie, I say thanks for putting up with me and for being one of the things (along with Mozart and coffee) that makes life worth living. To my impressively talented children, Grace, Will, Emma, and Calvin, I say thanks for keeping me humble and for giving me the privilege of witnessing your own adventures.